Societies and Political Orders in Transition

This book series presents scientific and scholarly studies focusing on societies and political orders in transition, for example in Central and Eastern Europe but also elsewhere in the world. By comparing established societies, characterized by well-established market economies and well-functioning democracies, with post-socialist societies, often characterized by emerging markets and fragile political systems, the series identifies and analyzes factors influencing change and continuity in societies and political orders. These factors include state capacity to establish formal and informal rules, democratic institutions, forms of social structuration, political regimes, levels of corruption, specificity of political cultures, as well as types and orientation of political and economic elites.

This series welcomes monographs and edited volumes from a variety of disciplines and approaches, such as political and social sciences and economics, which are accessible to both academics and interested general readers.

Topics may include, but are not limited to, democratization, regime change, changing social norms, migration, etc.

More information about this series at http://www.springer.com/series/15626

Reiner Osbild • Will Bartlett
Editors

Western Balkan Economies in Transition

Recent Economic and Social Developments

Springer

Editors
Reiner Osbild
University of Applied Sciences
Emden, Germany

Will Bartlett
European Institute
London School of Economics (LSE)
London, United Kingdom

ISSN 2511-2201 ISSN 2511-221X (electronic)
Societies and Political Orders in Transition
ISBN 978-3-030-06702-1 ISBN 978-3-319-93665-9 (eBook)
https://doi.org/10.1007/978-3-319-93665-9

This Springer imprint is published by the registered company Springer Nature Switzerland AG
The registered company address is: Gewerbestrasse 11, 6330 Cham, Switzerland

Preface

The Western Balkan states face a dilemma. They attract worldwide attention above all if there is some trouble. The wars and conflicts of the 1990s following the breakup of the former socialist republic of Yugoslavia were such an example, while another has been the wave of migrants heading for Central and Northern Europe in 2015, especially to Germany, Austria and Sweden.

Less attention has been paid to the determined efforts of these countries to catch up with the social, political and economic standards of the European Union. It is the aim of the six Western Balkan states to become full members of the EU, although it is widely acknowledged that there is still a long way to go. Nevertheless, they are already well integrated with Europe, as most of their trade is with EU countries, their banking systems are mostly under the ownership of EU financial institutions and many of their people work in the EU and send substantial flows of remittances back to their families at home. Furthermore, the Euro is widely used for savings and credit, while two countries (Kosovo and Montenegro) have adopted the Euro as their own official currency.

In this situation, the University of Applied Sciences Emden-Leer held a conference in April 2016 in order to shed light on selected topics regarding the current economic situation in this region. From this conference, it was a small step to plan this book, which presents some of the papers from the conference along with other specially commissioned chapters to provide a comprehensive view of the main economic and social issues facing the region. In the meantime, the Western Balkan summit held in Trieste in July 2017 as part of the "Berlin Process" has proposed a new action plan for further regional integration on the road to EU membership.[1] It was followed by a fourth summit held in London in July 2018. The pace of activities

[1] See https://www.esteri.it/mae/en/sala_stampa/archivionotizie/approfondimenti/trieste-western-balkan-summit-declaration.html

has been quickened by the new Enlargement Strategy[2] issued by the European Commission in February 2018 and a major EU summit on the Western Balkans held in Sofia in May 2017 under the auspices of the Bulgarian presidency of the EU.[3] This has reaffirmed the EU membership perspective for the region, with a target date for EU membership of at least some of the countries of the region in 2025. All this indicates that the Western Balkan region is again back at the top of the European agenda, but this time for all the right reasons. In this context, we hope that this book will provide both academic researchers and policymakers with a useful resource for a better understanding of a group of countries, which are now well on the road to future EU membership.

Emden, Germany — Reiner Osbild
London, UK — Will Bartlett

[2]See https://ec.europa.eu/commission/sites/beta-political/files/communication-credible-enlargement-perspective-western-balkans_en.pdf

[3]See http://www.consilium.europa.eu/en/meetings/international-summit/2018/05/17/

Contents

List of Figures

List of Tables

Public and Private Debt: Recent Developments in Bosnia and Herzegovina

Trade and Industrial Development in Kosovo

Social Policy During a Decade of Centre-Right Governance in Macedonia

The Global Financial Crisis and Fiscal Policy in Montenegro

The Western Balkans on the Road to the EU: An Introduction

Reiner Osbild and Will Bartlett

Introduction

The Western Balkans is a divided region.[1] This does not only apply to the various ethnics, cultural groups, languages and religions, which gave rise to several wars even in the recent history, but also with respect to the level of economic development.

Much attention was paid to the successor states of former Yugoslavia during the wars of Yugoslav succession that began with a short conflict for Slovenian independence in 1991 and quickly progressed to major armed conflicts in Croatia and Bosnia and Herzegovina (1991–1995), which claimed thousands of lives and destroyed millions of livelihoods (Ramet 2006). Later, internal conflict over the status of Kosovo, an autonomous province within Serbia, led to armed intervention by NATO and the imposition of international administration on Kosovo by the UN Interim Administration Mission in Kosovo (UNMIK). Kosovo issued a unilateral declaration of independence in 2008, but this has not resolved the status issue (Ker-Lindsay 2009). A conflict between the Macedonian government and armed Albanian rebels in 2001 was only brought to an end through the Ohrid Agreement brokered by the EU. Less noticed was the civil conflict in Albania in 1997 following the collapse of some pyramid banks, which wiped out the savings of a large proportion of the population (Vaughan-Whitehead 1999). Following the decade of

[1]The Western Balkans comprise six European transition countries that are not yet EU member states: Albania, Bosnia and Herzegovina, Kosovo, the former Yugoslav Republic of Macedonia (which we refer to as Macedonia in this book), Montenegro and Serbia.

R. Osbild (✉)
University of Applied Sciences, Emden, Germany
e-mail: reiner.osbild@hs-emden-leer.de

W. Bartlett
LSEE, European Institute, London School of Economics and Political Science, London, UK
e-mail: w.j.bartlett@lse.ac.uk

R. Osbild, W. Bartlett (eds.), *Western Balkan Economies in Transition*, Societies and Political Orders in Transition, https://doi.org/10.1007/978-3-319-93665-9_1

bitter conflicts, in 2003, the European Union promised to work towards the accession of these countries as EU member states, provided that a stringent set of political and economic conditions were met.[2] More recently, especially in autumn 2015, international attention has returned to the region due to the wave of mass migration that passed through the Western Balkan states, inter alia, to Germany, Austria and Sweden which directed the attention of the German and EU media to this region again. In this situation, the German Hochschule Emden-Leer (University of Applied Sciences) held a conference in April 2016 in order to shed light on selected topics regarding the current economic situation in this region.

Economically, one would exaggerate to take the Western Balkan region as terra incognita, but in politics, sciences, and media, it was the crisis of the southern European Eurozone members, especially Greece, that ranked at the top of the agenda. The reason was the huge financial involvement of EU, European Central Bank, International Monetary Fund (IMF) and the European Financial Stability Fund amounting to over €1 trillion.

It is worth noting that the Western Balkan countries started from very different points in the 1990s after the breakdown of the socialist systems. While Albania was fully isolated, having maintained a weak relationship only with China up to 1978, ex-Yugoslavia had experienced many freedoms (Sjöberg and Wyzan 1991). Citizens were allowed to travel and work abroad, and there were trade relations with both the east and the west. A Yugoslav passport permitted visa-free travel to many more countries than the passports of west European citizens.

The path to the market economy in the Western Balkans involved many disruptions, such as the end of safe lifetime employment that had been harmful to productivity, innovation and economic progress. Many mostly state-owned and socially owned companies that had been privatised failed to survive the competitive pressure from abroad.[3] But these companies often employed many workers, and it was risky for governments to privatise them or close them down, dismissing the staff. For this reason, a mixed economy has emerged in Bosnia and Herzegovina, Montenegro and Serbia with substantial public sectors. These economies have many state-owned companies which are subsidised and kept alive in order to avoid even more unemployment and political instability, but they also have many new private enterprises that account for much of the GDP growth that has taken place in the post-socialist era. Elsewhere in the region, in Albania and Macedonia, the public sector is smaller, and the formerly state-owned or socially owned sector has been almost completely privatised, leaving a much lesser role for the state and facilitating the emergence of more liberal market economies. Kosovo, although it has a small public sector, maintains numerous public enterprises which are potential targets for

[2]These conditions were known as the "Copenhagen criteria".

[3]"Social ownership" in the former Yugoslavia was a form of non-state, non-private ownership akin to "trust" status in the UK in which assets are held in trust for the wider society. This meant that enterprises in former Yugoslavia had a much greater autonomy to operate on the market than did state-owned enterprises in Albania, which were subject to central state planning.

privatisation (see chapter “Trade and Industrial Development in Kosovo”). It is noticeable that these three economies experienced a lesser adverse impact of the recent economic crisis (Bartlett and Prica 2011). Over the crisis period from 2008 to 2013, the average growth rate of GDP per capita in the three mixed economy countries was just 1.3%, whereas in the three more liberal market countries, it was 3.1%.

Still, the standard of living throughout the Western Balkan region is well below the EU average (EU 28). Using purchasing power parity, Montenegro looks best with 40% of the EU 28 level of GDP per capita, followed by Serbia (35%), Albania (29%) and Bosnia and Herzegovina at just 28% (European Commission 2015: 42).

The Path to the EU

The ex-Yugoslav states moved at different paces into the EU. While some of those states are already members of the EU, like Croatia (which became a member state in 2013) and Slovenia (2004), the latter even being member of the Eurozone, the Western Balkans of countries still strives for EU membership. The regular annual reports of the European Commission assess that these countries have not yet met the required standards as to economic, political, administrative, legal and human rights policies. That is why the EU has made agreements with future potential members, called Stabilization and Association Agreements (SAAs).

Stabilisation and Association Agreements

The bulk of SAAs have been made since 2004. The early bird was Macedonia, followed by Albania (2009), Montenegro (2010), Serbia (2013), Bosnia and Herzegovina (2015) and Kosovo (2016). While being aware of the complicated political situation of Kosovo, we will not focus so much on political issues here.

Let us have a look to the objectives and contents of the SAAs. “The EU involvement in the Western Balkans is a long-term process. The engagement is on a number of levels: strategic and political, holding out the prospect of EU membership to all the countries of the region, through the Stabilisation and Association process; institutional, to build up the capacity of the countries in the region enabling them to adopt European and international standards and eventually to apply the body of EU law (acquis); economic, with budgetary assistance and the opening of EU markets to the region; and financial, with some of the highest per capita assistance in the world, for the period 2000–2006”.[4]

---

[4]http://europa.eu.int:80/comm/enlargement/enlargement.htm, accessed 2017-11-02.

Example The SAA Between the EU and Albania
SAAs aims are the following:

- to support the efforts of Albania to strengthen democracy and the rule of law;
- to contribute to political, economic and institutional stability in Albania, as well as to the stabilisation of the region;
- to provide an appropriate framework for political dialogue, allowing the development of close political relations between the Parties;
- to support the efforts of Albania to develop its economic and international cooperation, also through the approximation of its legislation to that of the Community;
- to support the efforts of Albania to complete the transition into a functioning market economy, to promote harmonious economic relations and develop gradually a free trade area between the Community and Albania;
- to foster regional cooperation in all the fields covered by this Agreement.[5]

The SAAs should pave the way for some ex ante harmonisation. It is orientated on the European acquis communautaire ("acquis"), which is a multi-chapter collection of legal status quo which underpins the European Union. For the negotiation process with the Western Balkans, there are 35 chapters comprising, inter alia, free trade issues; human and social rights; environmental, health and consumer protection; public finance; and corporate law, institutions and some special regional or sectoral policies like agriculture, energy and telecommunications.

In the framework of SAAs, the EU has allocated substantial resources to the partners in order to help prepare them for eventual EU membership. For example, the EU supports the Bosnian alignment programme with financial assistance of €165.8 million (2014–2017), while the European Bank for Reconstruction and Development (EBRD), an international development bank that focuses on transition countries, has made cumulated investments of €1.8 billion in 130 projects in Bosnia and Herzegovina.[6]

Nevertheless, the progress so far has been less than expected. Although EU membership for any of the Western Balkan countries cannot be expected in the next few years, the prospects for the accession leaders to join the Union by 2025 are feasible given the requisite political will for reform. According to EU statements:

> The Western Balkan countries now have a historic window of opportunity to firmly and unequivocally bind their future to the European Union. They will have to act with determination. Accession is and will remain a merit-based process fully dependent on the objective progress achieved by each country. The countries may catch up or overtake each other depending on progress made… Accession negotiations are already well underway with

[5]http://ec.europa.eu/enlargement/pdf/albania/st08164.06_en.pdf, accessed 2016-05-05.
[6]http://www.ebrd.com/ebrd-in-bosnia-and-herzegovina.html, download 2016-05-05.

> Montenegro and Serbia. With strong political will, the delivery of real and sustained reforms, and definitive solutions to disputes with neighbours, they could potentially be ready for membership in a 2025 perspective. (European Commission 2018: 2)

Economic Transition and Growth

In later chapters we will see an in-depth description of various aspects of the West Balkan countries. Here it is sufficient to focus on some main aspects of recent economic developments:

- *Transition*: Balkan countries followed different paths to create a market economy. While Albania had a long period of isolation until the beginning of the 1990s and has begun to integrate into the world market, the republics of the former Yugoslavia still suffer from post-war disruption. Yugoslavia was remarkably free given the standards of the socialist world in the post-World War II era, allowing for emigration to and trade with Western countries. The post-war political order created six (and later seven) new countries and a loss of the comparatively big Yugoslavian market.
- *Bureaucracy*: Another feature has been the related increase in the number of government entities. For example, in the special case of Bosnia and Herzegovina, there are 14 governments covering for 3.7 million inhabitants. Elsewhere, in ex-Yugoslavia former local republic governments have had to take on the mantle of national responsibilities. Of course, according to the theory of bureaucracy, governments often aim to protect their power, giving less attention to privatisation and political reform. Without adequate governance standards, corruption may grow. This has been the ubiquitous consequence of state break-up, vicious armed conflicts and UN sanctions which generated mafia-like smuggling and organised crime networks throughout the Western Balkans. After all, to take Bosnia and Herzegovina as an example again, the abundant need for government financing is obligated by IMF loans nominally under conditionality requirements for structural reforms, but which corrupt governments have managed to mainly avoid for 20 years since the signing of the Dayton Agreement in 1995.[7]
- *Unemployment*: Despite low wage levels—the average wage in the Western Balkans is little above 400€—many factors hamper domestic and foreign investment, including bureaucracy, bribery, lack of transparency regarding taxes, weak provision of human capital and insufficient investment in modern machinery, accompanied by destroyed and obsolete infrastructure. Hence, unemployment is relatively high with an average rate of almost 25% in the Western Balkans (EEAG 2016: 107). Among

[7] A recent report has observed that the two reform programmes that were attempted between 2009 and 2014 "did not achieve significant structural reforms" (p. 4) and that while a new "Reform Agenda" was initiated in 2015, since "BiH enters another general election cycle in 2018, it will unfortunately become increasingly difficult to pursue their implementation" (p. 32) (Toperich et al. 2017).

the employed population, perhaps a fifth are working in the informal economy in which employers pay lower wages than normal and evade the payment of social contributions for their workers, undermining the long-term welfare of their employees and causing high levels of in-work poverty.

- *Trade and foreign direct investment*: Despite of low wages, the Western Balkan economies often fail to attract FDI and record high import-to-export quotas, which point to the lack of competitiveness of the domestic economy. European FDI often goes to Romania, Hungary and other EU members with similar low wage levels, but a better compliance with EU standards.
- *Remittances*: Most families rely on remittances granted by their relatives working in more advanced countries. In former Yugoslavia, these remittances amounted to US$6.2 billion in 1989, 19% of all world remittances at that time (EEAG 2016: 99). According to recent news, nothing has changed: the Western Balkan countries still depend on income transfers from abroad.[8] The level of such remittances could erode in the years to come as, more and more, the whole family moves to the "West" (mainly, the USA, Germany, Austria), leaving behind fewer and fewer relatives, with corresponding lower transfer payments home. This could lead to a vicious circle of low demand, low investment, more unemployment, more emigration, etc.
- Due to high remittances and low confidence to the domestic currencies, four of the countries allow for a double currency regime, i.e., with loans and deposits partly denominated in domestic currency, partly in Euro. On average, some 60% of private deposits and private loans are denominated in Euro (EEAG 2016: 117). Practically, in these countries the governments are forced to fix the exchange rates of their domestic currency to the Euro to maintain people's confidence, while at the same time, fixed rates prevent devaluations which may be necessary to improve international competiveness. Two countries, Montenegro and Kosovo, have gone even further and have adopted euro as their domestic currency.
- High levels of poverty, related to high unemployment rates, stimulate emigration and depopulation of various countries. In total, Western Balkan countries lost two million people or 4% of the total population between 1991 and 2014. The most affected was Albania (EEAG 2016: 105).

Growth in the period from 2000 to 2007 was fuelled by an inflow of cheap money from abroad (see more below). Following the 2007–2009 crisis, the region experienced a slowdown in growth or even outright recession (apart from Albania and Kosovo) in 2009 and again in 2012. Since 2013, economic growth has picked up again, but so has private and public debt, mainly in the form of risky external debt. We will see later that, whatever yardstick is used, the debts of Albania, Montenegro and Serbia have reached outstanding levels (see Bartlett and Prica 2018). The IMF, which agreed emergency loan facilities for Bosnia and Herzegovina and Serbia, has

[8]n-tv: Balkanlaender haengen am Tropf, http://www.n-tv.de/wirtschaft/Balkanlaender-haengen-am-Tropf-article17685891.html download 2016-05-18.

made its loans conditional on the implementation of structural reforms.[9] In the IMF context, structural reforms often mean supply-side policies, i.e., all the things that make investment and production more profitable. Of course, this may also include sharp austerity, and here the overstaffed public sector—government, bureaucracies and public companies—needs to be resized.

Demand-Side Versus Supply-Side Policies

In our conference, Will Bartlett warned that this policy, often referred to as *austerity*, could produce a demand shock which in turn could make life more difficult for the emerging private sector. Yet, there are various arguments against this point of view, as Reiner Osbild argued from a supply-side point of view. This view holds that excessive demand damaged the Western Balkan countries over the last two decades rather than promoting their economies. In the years 2000–2008, there was already a high, probably excessive demand. Due to falling interest rates in the anchor currency *Euro*, domestic demand for consumer and mortgage loans soared. At the same time, the current account deficits rose and reached, expressed as a percentage of GDP, up to double-digit values.[10] This shows that a great bulk of the demand was spent abroad. Obviously, the consumer demand was better met by foreign than by Western Balkan firms.

Even more, like in the case of Greece (Sinn 2012, 2014; Osbild 2014a, b), the credit-financed demand created an artificial boom, or even bubble, in the Western Balkan economies with prices and wages rising beyond productivity gains. With de facto fixed interest rates, the domestic currencies appreciated, and local industries lost competitiveness. Moreover, given the poor investment climate in many of the Western Balkan states, and delayed privatisations in some, the private sector could not develop that well.

In such a situation, the stimulation of overall demand by further loans would not support domestic businesses, but rather the industries in the core of the Eurozone. The already high debt levels rose even further, turning country credit ratings down, thus raising the cost of investment. The result was often higher public debt, higher current account deficits (external debt), lower business activity and higher unemployment.

---

[9] Bosnia reached a 3-year €800 million Stand-By Arrangement (SBA) with the IMF in 2009 and a further €400 million in 2012; further lending from the Extended Fund Facility (EEF) of €553 million was made in 2016. Serbia reached a 15-month €400 million SBA with the IMF in 2009, an additional 3-year €1.25 billion SBA with the IMF in 2015. Kosovo began a €107 million SBA in 2012. Albania was a latecomer to this process with a 3-year €330 million EEF in 2014.

[10] For example, this ratio was circa 15% in BiH on the average of the years 2000–2008, and well above 10% in the same period in Serbia and Montenegro, and oscillating around 10% for Albania for the whole 2000–2015 period (EEAG 2016, p. 102).

When Keynes put forward his theory of demand-driven business cycles, he took into account strong and fully developed countries like the USA and the UK. These countries already had broad industrial and manufacturing sectors which just needed some impetus from additional state expenditure financed through additional borrowing or additional investments by lower interest rates. Today, in the Western Balkan environment, governments have adopted "flat tax" strategies, so financing additional government expenditure from raising taxes is not an option. When borrowing is used, a great deal of the stimulus from this additional debt-financed demand simply leaked abroad in the form of demand for additional imported goods and services rather than stimulating domestic industries and services.[11]

Yet, the supply-side case presented in the previous paragraphs may be overstated, or at least premature, since in the Western Balkans, the debt ratio did not increase before the crisis, but afterwards. The ratio of public debt to GDP actually fell in the boom years (from about 72% in Serbia in 2002 to about 26% in 2008, with similar reductions in other countries). Keynesian management of the demand side is a short-term antirecession weapon, and in most of the Western Balkan economies, this policy was implemented after the 2009 crisis by default as countries initially failed (or refused) to cut back on public expenditure as they had been advised to do by the IMF and other advisors of austerity measures.[12] To some extent this prevented a worse recession that actually took hold. Governments were unwilling to impose real austerity from fear of political instability, and also because it would remove the powerful political weapon of clientelism, which enables ruling parties to award jobs in the public sector to their political supporters (Bartlett and Prica 2018).

Thus, in the period following the onset of the crisis, the public debt ratio increased from relatively low levels, reaching a high of 76% of GDP in Serbia in 2015, and similar levels in Albania and Montenegro.[13] It was only at this point that the concerns raised by supply-side theorists have come into the horizon. Debt levels have now risen to such high levels that it turns out to be difficult to raise new money. These high debt levels and the low confidence of investors due to the questionable use of credit in the past—too much was flowing into consumption, not enough into productive investments—make more such lending risky. Even more, as Jelena Poljašević and Jelena Trivić show in chapter "Public and Private Debt: Recent Developments in Bosnia and Herzegovina", in the case of Bosnia and Herzegovina, the country has no access to international bond markets and is supported by IMF loans which have been extended and rolled over again and again in the past. But even the IMF now starts to ask for real reforms.

[11]Rahmann (2014) and Osbild (2014a, b).

[12]As Koczan (2016) has observed: "In the aftermath of the crisis, the Western Balkans experienced difficulties in regaining control of their public finances. . .In particular, public sector wage-bills and pensions. . .proved to be very rigid" (p. 473).

[13]In 2015, the ratio of public debt to GDP was 72.5% in Albania, 63.3% in Montenegro, 41.9% in Bosnia and Herzegovina and 38% in Macedonia (Eurostat online data—variable code: cpc_ecgov). External debt was even higher reaching almost 90% of GDP in Serbia in 2015 (Bartlett and Prica, 2018).

Essentially, demand-side policies stabilise the political scenery for a while. For governments, trying to remain in power, it is impossible to impose hard austerity policies upon the citizens. For example, neighbouring Greece has seen a lot of strikes and violence because of various expenditure-cutting and tax increase programmes. In Bosnia and Herzegovina, with 14 governments on different levels, there are frequent elections, and no government would do anything which is, or seems to be, unpopular. Hence, demand-side policies designed to stabilise the political system may work in the short-run, but the potential adverse long-term consequences have mostly been neglected.

In most Western Balkan economies, real reforms will now have to be implemented, as the option of further borrowing is not available. This means that real austerity measures will have to be implemented for the first time. In order to prepare for the likely political backlash, governments in the region have taken steps to take greater control over the instruments of democratic accountability such as the media and the judicial system. Progress in democratisation has ground to a halt in most countries of the region, and democratic backsliding and the re-emergence of competitive authoritarianism[14] are real dangers to eventual EU membership of the Western Balkan accession states. It is not surprising that the EU has made Chapters 23 and 24 of the acquis, on the rule of law, the first chapters to be opened and the last chapters to be closed in the ongoing accession negotiations in the region.

The Chapters in This Book

The chapters in this book begin with four overviews of the Western Balkan countries covering the key issues of the creation of a regional economic area, regional trade integration focusing on the topical issue of trade in services, labour markets and migration and the performance of higher education systems in contributing to productivity of the graduate labour force. Following these four overview chapters, the remaining chapters provide country case studies presented in alphabetic order of country name and focusing on key issues related to economic and social development in each case. The issues chosen for each chapter are chosen by the authors to reflect the most topical problems facing each country.

In chapter "The Western Balkans Regional Economic Area: From Economic Cooperation to Economic Integration", Peter Sanfey and Jakov Milatovic examine the main objectives and assess the likely impact of the recently proposed Regional Economic Area for the Western Balkans initiated at the Trieste summit of the Berlin Process in July 2017.[15] The aim is to develop a regional space in which goods, services, investments and skilled workers can move without obstacles (European

[14]On the notion of "competitive authoritarianism", see Günay and Dzihic (2016).

[15]See: https://www.rcc.int/docs/383/multi-annual-action-plan-for-a-regional-economic-area-in-the-western-balkans-six

Commission, 2017). This programme is set out in a multi-annual action plan (MAP) consisting of four components of trade, investment, mobility of professionals and research workers and digital integration following the EU's digital single market agenda.[16] In chapter "Trade in Services in the Western Balkans", Ivana Prica picks up the trade issue with an analysis of the liberalisation of trade in services in the region, a key part of the first component of the MAP. She argues that while tourism currently accounts for the largest share of trade in services in the region, the greatest potential for future growth lies in the development of trade in business services. Currently, the CEFTA free trade agreement for the region is moving towards a further liberalisation of trade in services; this will be one part of the needed adjustment. But more broadly, the region will have to engage more thoroughly with the EU and global markets for services if economic prosperity is to be achieved in the future. In chapter "Trade and Industrial Development in Kosovo", Petrit Gashi investigates the role of international trade policy in Kosovo. He argues that trade liberalisation is a necessary but not a sufficient condition to boost exports and that greater emphasis should be placed on domestic efforts to improve competitiveness and production capacity. Similar considerations apply to Albania which, as Engjëll Pere and Will Bartlett demonstrate in chapter "On the Way to Europe: Economic and Social Developments in Albania", lacks a diversified export profile and needs additional policy measures to raise the international competitiveness of the economy. In chapter "Higher Education and the Graduate Labour Market in the Western Balkans", Will Bartlett and Milica Uvalić turn to the role of human capital as an important policy field supporting improved competitiveness. The quality of the higher education systems in the Western Balkans and the entry of university graduates to the labour market are far from being optimal, and the higher education sector needs deep reforms to become a factor in stimulating improved competitiveness and stronger growth in the region in the future.

Several of the country chapters explore the issues of macroeconomic policy and governance in greater depth, especially in the wake of the severe economic crisis that affected most of the region since 2009. As suggested above, one of the most negative consequences of the crisis has been the build-up of both public debt and external debt, as governments have sought to protect their voters from the worst effects of the crisis by maintaining social welfare spending and public sector employment. In chapter "On the Way to Europe: Economic and Social Developments in Albania", Engjëll Pere and Will Bartlett show that Albania has allowed public debt to soar to excessive levels during the post-crisis period, a factor that may partly explain why the country was able to avoid the worst effects of the crisis at least for a time by drawing on fiscal buffers. In the recent years, however, economic growth has begun to slow down, and unemployment has increased. As the country most reliant on remittances of income from emigrant workers abroad, the loss of Albanian emigrants' jobs in Greece and Italy during the crisis period has led to a reduction in this important source of foreign exchange. In chapter "Public and Private Debt: Recent

[16]See: https://ec.europa.eu/digital-single-market/en

Developments in Bosnia and Herzegovina", Jelena Poljašević and Jelena Trivić demonstrate that public debt has also increased sharply in Bosnia and Herzegovina, even during the period under IMF conditionality since 2009. They argue that although all debt indicators have worsened since the onset of the crisis, the increase in public debt is the most problematic issue since the country does not have access to international capital markets and is reliant on the goodwill of donors and international organisations such as the IMF. The complex bureaucracy with many layers of government only adds to the problem, as mentioned above. Private debt indictors are less worrying, but this only reflects the low level of economic activity and should not be taken as an indicator of economic progress. The case of Montenegro is covered by Nikola Fabris in chapter "The Global Financial Crisis and Fiscal Policy in Montenegro", who argues that fiscal sources available at the onset of the crisis have now been exhausted, despite some successful attempts at fiscal consolidation, mainly due to decisions taken to relax the fiscal breaks in the 2000s and due to an expensive highway project funded through large-scale external borrowing. Since public debt has now passed the legal debt ceiling of 60% of GDP, real and credible fiscal consolidation will be needed in the upcoming period. In chapter "Economic Reforms in Serbia and Prospects for Economic Recovery and Growth", Will Bartlett investigates the role of economic policy in the economic recovery of the Serbian economy in the post-crisis period. He argues that economic reforms have been relaunched under the SNS-led government that came to power in 2014, with priorities on fiscal consolidation, financial sector resilience and structural reforms designed to boost productivity, employment and growth. The chapter questions the conventional explanation for poor investment and growth performance that focuses on an oversized public sector, a high level of employment in state bodies and overregulated labour markets. He argues that banking sector deleveraging, capital flight and tax avoidance may provide more plausible explanations of the low investment rate observed in the Serbian economy. The chapter concludes that a boost to public investment is needed to support private sector growth, rather than policies that aim to shift the costs of adjustment onto low-paid public sector workers and pensioners.

Several chapters in the book focus on the social consequences of the recent economic crisis period and the relatively slow growth that has characterised the recovery period. In chapter "The Labour Market, Social Inequality, and the Role of Emigration: The Case of the Western Balkan Economies", Mehmed Ganić argues that although it has been more than two decades since the beginning of the transition in the Western Balkan region, there has been little improvement in the quality of life. The process of privatisation, deindustrialisation and associated job cuts led to widespread unemployment rate and a reduction in living standards. The chapter focuses on the social issues of unemployment, migration trends and income inequality. Ganić argues that although the region has made some progress in creating functioning market economies, the high unemployment rates and the huge outflow of educated and skilled workers have led to widespread poverty and inequality. These themes are taken up in chapter "On the Way to Europe: Economic and Social Developments in Albania" by Engjëll Pere and Will Bartlett who note the existence of widespread poverty in Albania, and that although the extent of poverty was cut in half by rapid economic growth in the 2000s, it has begun to creep up again following the onset of the economic crisis. In chapter "Social Policy During a Decade of Centre-Right Governance in Macedonia", Maja Gerovska Mitev investigates the response of social policy to the economic crisis in Macedonia during a decade of centre-right political governance. The focus of the chapter is on the reforms adopted in the fields of social protection, employment, child protection and social insurance. She argues that a new approach to social policy has been introduced that represents a break with the past. Social welfare benefits are no longer targeted at the most vulnerable, but based on categorical principles, which has opened the door to preferential treatments and arbitrary amounts of entitlements. This has enabled a deepening of the practices of clientelism and the "electoral tuning of welfare spending according to political preferences".

As these chapters demonstrate, most countries in the region have built up large public and private debts through extensive external borrowing. In most countries, these debts have reached critical proportions, and the easy options of foreign borrowing in response to the crisis conditions and the associated slowdown in demand for goods and services has reached its limits. Instead, the countries of the Western Balkans will now have to turn their attention to real economic reforms and real improvements in competitiveness and export growth. In chapter "Trade in Services in the Western Balkans", Ivana Prica argues that the growth in service exports will be an important area in which high-value exports can be generated in the future. Currently, the technological level of goods exports is very low, and there is little prospect of the region upgrading its production capacity to provide competitive high value-added high-technology production in the near future. This is why service exports, whether in the form of tourism, transport, ICT or construction services, will be important in the future, especially high value-added services in the business service sector. Currently the CEFTA free trade agreement in the region is moving towards a further liberalisation of service trade. This will be one part of the needed adjustment. But more broadly, the region will have to engage more thoroughly with the EU and global markets for services if economic prosperity is to be achieved in the future.

References

Bartlett, W., & Prica, I. (2011). The variable impact of the global economic crisis in South East Europe. *Economic Annals, LVI*(191), 7–34.

Bartlett, W. & Prica, I. (2018). Debt in the super-periphery: the case of the Western Balkans. Third World Thematics. https://doi.org/10.1080/23802014.2017.1438850

EEAG. (2016). Western Balkans: Coming together. *The EEAG Report on the European Economy, 15*, 99–123.

European Commission. (2015). *EU enlargement strategy*. Communication from the Commission to the European Parliament, the Council, The European Economic and Social Committee and the

Committee of the regions. Brussels, 10.11.2015. http://ec.europa.eu/enlargement/pdf/key_documents/2015/20151110_strategy_paper_en.pdf

European Commission. (2018, February 6). *A credible enlargement perspective for an enhanced EU engagement with the Western Balkans*. COM(2018) 65 final. Strasbourg.

Günay, C., & Dzihic, V. (2016). Decoding the authoritarian code: Exercising 'legitimate' power politics through the ruling parties in Turkey, Macedonia and Serbia. *Southeast Europe and Black Sea Studies, 16*(4), 529–549.

Ker-Lindsay, J. (2009). *Kosovo: The path to contested statehood in the Balkans*. London: I. B. Taurus & Co.

Koczan, Z. (2016). Fiscal policy, business cycles and discretion: Evidence from the Western Balkans. *Post-Communist Economies, 28*(4), 468–486.

Osbild, R. (2014a). *Finanzkrise – Geld, Gier und Gerechtigkeit*. Holzgerlingen: SCM Hänssler.

Osbild, R. (2014b, September 17). Warum die keynesianische Politik Schaden anrichtet (Why Keynesian Policy is Harmful). *Wirtschafts Woche*.

Rahmann, T. (2014, October 22). Europa hat nicht zu viel gespart, sondern zu wenig (Europe has not saved too much, but not enough). *Wirtschafts Woche*.

Ramet, S. P. (2006). *The three Yugoslavias: State-building and legitimation, 1918–2005*. Bloomington: Indiana University Press.

Sinn, H. (2012, März). *Die Target-Kredite der Deutschen Bundesbank* (Ifo Schnelldienst Sonderausgabe).

Sinn, H. (2014). *The Euro trap: On bursting bubbles, budgets and beliefs*. Oxford: Oxford University Press.

Sjöberg, O., & Wyzan, M. L. (Eds.). (1991). *Economic change in the Balkan States: Albania, Bulgaria, Romania and Yugoslavia*. London: Pinter.

Toperich, S., Obermayer, H., & Ivanovic, T. (2017). *Vision 2020: Bosnia and Herzegovina towards its European future*. Washington DC: Centre for Transatlantic Relations, The John Hopkins University.

Vaughan-Whitehead, D. (1999). *Albania in crisis: The predictable fall of the shining star*. Cheltenham: Edward Elgar Publishing.

[illegible]

The Western Balkans Regional Economic Area: From Economic Cooperation to Economic Integration

Peter Sanfey and Jakov Milatović

Introduction

Doing business, trading and investing and working across borders in the six countries of the Western Balkans—Albania, Bosnia and Herzegovina, FYR Macedonia, Kosovo, Montenegro and Serbia—are complicated and often difficult activities. The violent break-up of the former Yugoslavia in the early 1990s ultimately led to the creation of seven new states in place of one country. Albania entered the 1990s as a closed society, opening up for the first time after more than 40 years of isolation characterised by minimal or non-existent cooperation with its neighbours. These developments in the region inevitably gave rise to a host of obstacles associated with barriers on the border: low levels of international trust and associated political instability, weak institutions, limited and relatively more expensive access to finance, flight of human capital abroad, complicated and time-consuming trading processes and poor-quality infrastructure.

Various initiatives over the years have been proposed to address these problems. The European Union has been at the forefront of promoting regional cooperation and opening its markets to Western Balkan countries through the Stabilisation and Association Process. International financial institutions such as the European Bank

The views expressed in this chapter are those of the authors only and not necessarily those of the EBRD.

P. Sanfey (✉)
Department of Economics, Policy and Governance, European Bank for Reconstruction and Development (EBRD), London, England
e-mail: sanfeyp@ebrd.com

J. Milatović
Department of Economics, Policy and Governance, European Bank for Reconstruction and Development (EBRD), Podgorica, Montenegro
e-mail: milatovj@ebrd.com

R. Osbild, W. Bartlett (eds.), *Western Balkan Economies in Transition*, Societies and Political Orders in Transition, https://doi.org/10.1007/978-3-319-93665-9_2

for Reconstruction and Development (EBRD), European Investment Bank (EIB) and World Bank have invested, and continue to invest, in major cross-border infrastructure projects, as well as promoting trade and investment through other instruments. A free trade agreement, supported by the international community, is in place for more than a decade among the six countries, along with Moldova.

Partly as a result of these initiatives, there has been a significant increase in regional cooperation and EU approximation in the past two decades, and a positive impact on overall economic activity in the Western Balkans. Tensions following the conflicts in the 1990s have been reduced, allowing more attention to be focused on common economic challenges. Regional cooperation has emerged as a conscious choice of the region itself, rather than something forced from the outside, and has brought various practical benefits, including enhanced trade and competitiveness and a more attractive investment destination. But despite these efforts, the levels of trade and investment in the region remain well below those of comparable regions. The time is ripe, therefore, for a new impetus to strengthen regional economic cooperation.

Regional cooperation in the Western Balkans has received strong political support from the EU through the establishment of the Berlin Process. This is a series of annual meetings of the six Western Balkan prime ministers with the heads of states of those EU members with a particular interest in the region, launched in August 2014 in Berlin, and serving to discuss important regional topics related to future EU membership of all countries in the region.[1] The complementary biennial Western Balkans summits at the EBRD have a strong focus on investment promotion.[2] One of the main early results of this formal regional cooperation was coordination of major regional transport and energy connectivity projects, as well as the extension of the trans-European infrastructure network to the region. At the meeting between the European Commission and Western Balkan prime ministers in Brussels in April 2015, the EU announced an allocation of €1 billion over 7 years for funding key infrastructure projects in the region.

At the same time, the full potential of this improved physical interconnection cannot be achieved without a parallel promotion of "soft connectivity". A key element of the soft connectivity agenda is moving the region from economic cooperation towards stronger and more formal stages of economic integration. This includes harmonising legislation, removing non-tariff barriers, improving capital markets integration, strengthening the business environment and facilitating trade and investment across borders.

A consolidated multi-annual action plan, intended as the basis for an EU-compliant regional economic area in the Western Balkans six, was adopted by

[1]The 2014 summit in Berlin was followed by summits in Vienna in 2015, Paris in 2016, Trieste in 2017 and London in July 2018.

[2]The EBRD Western Balkans summits are held in February every 2 years, with the first one in 2014, the second in 2016 and the third in 2018.

all parties at the fourth Western Balkans summit, in Trieste in July 2017.[3] The broad aim of the plan is to advance cross-country economic cooperation in the context of the Berlin process. All six Western Balkan countries are now committing to deepening further their collaboration within the current regional free trade agreement (CEFTA) to the point where goods, services, investments and skilled people can move freely within the region without tariffs, quotas or other unnecessary non-tariff, and other, barriers.

This chapter outlines the main objectives of this important agreement and assesses its likely impact on the region. We argue that the plan correctly identifies some of the main areas where the region lags behind EU comparators, such as free movement of goods, services, investments, labour and information. It outlines a number of sensible and practical actions to address the problems, so that the region can move from economic cooperation towards a stronger, and more formal, economic integration, ahead of the ultimate goal for all six countries of EU membership. At the same time, the plan is relatively silent about some of the long-standing and pervasive problems that hold back the region's economies, such as weak governance in public administration, limited access to finance for SMEs and widespread corruption and informality. Our view is that, unless these problems are also addressed in parallel, the prospects for success of the action plan are limited.

Overview of the Plan

There are four components of the Regional Economic Area to be addressed by the action plan: (1) trade, (2) investment, (3) mobility and (4) digital integration.

1. *Trade*. Western Balkan countries have committed to deepen further their collaboration on areas such as trade facilitation of goods and services, electronic commerce and trade dispute settlements. The CEFTA Secretariat will continue to monitor non-tariff measures in the region and prepare an annual report on the main impediments to trade.
2. *Investment*. The plan foresees the harmonisation of investment policies through the development of a Regional Investment Reform Agenda. To this end, they have inaugurated the idea of the Regional Chamber Investment Forum and launched an Online Investment Platform for the Western Balkans.
3. *Mobility*. The plan envisages better integration of students, academics and high-skilled professionals in the region into professional and research networks. The Mobility Agenda aims at removing obstacles to the mobility of (1) professionals, through regional mutual recognition agreements of professional qualifications (doctors, dentists, architects, etc.) as well as automatic recognition of academic

[3]A copy of the regional economic area action plan is available on the website of the Regional Cooperation Council: https://www.rcc.int/docs/383/multi-annual-action-plan-for-a-regional-economic-area-in-the-western-balkans-six

qualifications and (2) students, researchers and academics, through joint academic mobility and cooperation programmes.
4. *Digital integration*. Measures will be taken to further the integration of the region into the pan-European digital market, through synchronised digitisation strategies, updated regulatory frameworks, improved broadband infrastructure and digital literacy. A roaming-free region is also part of the action plan.

Important advances on the plan have occurred since its adoption in July 2017, and some measures had already begun to be implemented. A needs assessment for the region is being undertaken, under the direction of the Sarajevo-based Regional Cooperation Council (RCC), which is in charge of the support and implementation of the action plan in the areas of investment, mobility and digital integration. The CEFTA Secretariat will continue to coordinate work in the area of trade integration. The EU is expected to play a major role in supporting the implementation of the agreement, particularly through its Instrument of Pre-Accession (IPA) national and multi-country programmes, as per the words of the EU's new enlargement strategy, adopted in February 2018[4]:

> [T]he Regional Economic Area is an essential step for furthering economic integration between the EU and the Western Balkans and boosting the attractiveness of the regional market. The Commission will continue supporting the development of intraregional economic integration, including by mobilising its expertise to assist with the implementation of Regional Economic Area action plan, in particular in areas covered by the EU acquis.

International Financial Institutions are expected to play an important role through targeted support of actions. In addition, work is under way to ensure that each country's economic reform programme is aligned with the objectives identified in the action plan.

The Four Pillars: An Assessment

The multi-annual action plan is designed to help address a fundamental and overarching problem for the Western Balkan region, namely, that all six countries fall a considerable way short of being considered well-functioning and sustainable market economies. But does the action plan focus on the key areas? To answer this question, it is worth considering first what we mean by a "sustainable market economy" and where the main gaps lie in this regard.

To do this, we use the recently adopted EBRD methodology for assessing transition, as outlined in the most recent EBRD Transition Report (EBRD 2018). According to this new approach, every economy can be assessed in terms of six desirable qualities of a sustainable market economy, namely, competitive, well

---

[4]The EU's new enlargement strategy is available at https://ec.europa.eu/commission/sites/beta-political/files/communication-credible-enlargement-perspective-western-balkans_en.pdf

	Competitive	Well-governed	Green	Inclusive	Resilient	Integrated	Average
Montenegro	4.9	5.1	5.2	5.6	5.9	5.6	5.4
Serbia	4.9	4.4	5.8	5.2	5.6	6.4	5.4
FYR Macedonia	5.4	5.2	4.9	4.7	5.3	6.0	5.3
Albania	4.4	4.3	4.9	5.1	4.9	5.8	4.9
Bosnia and Herz.	4.7	3.7	4.8	4.8	5.3	5.5	4.8
Kosovo	3.4	3.7	3.8	4.7	5.1	4.9	4.3
WB-6	4.6	4.4	4.9	5.0	5.3	5.7	5.0
EU-11	6.5	5.7	6.3	6.3	7.3	7.5	6.6
EBRD	4.9	4.8	5.4	5.4	5.7	6.0	5.4

Fig. 1 Transition scores for six qualities of a sustainable market economy. Source: European Bank for Reconstruction and Development (EBRD)

governed, green, inclusive, resilient and integrated. The EBRD has adopted a data-driven approach to measuring these qualities for all countries in which it currently operates—37 at present—converting the data to a numerical score on a scale of 1–10, where 1 represents the lowest possible score and 10 the (theoretical) highest. The results for 6 Western Balkan (WB6) countries (and regional average), as well as averages for the 11 countries of central and eastern Europe that joined the EU in 2004 or since then (the EU11) and the whole EBRD region, are shown in Fig. 1.

The results vividly illustrate that the Western Balkan region fall short of being considered a well-functioning sustainable market economy, in all six qualities.[5] Particularly problematic areas are competitiveness and good governance, which have the lowest average scores. In addition, the results also show large gaps between the WB6 and the EU11.[6] The gaps range between 1.3 and 2.0 points on the 1–10 scale. Furthermore, the WB6 countries also lag behind the EBRD average on all six dimensions, a worrying finding given the relatively low level of development and weak commitment to market-oriented reforms in parts of the EBRD region.

A measure of success of any regional action plan would be the extent to which it tackles the obstacles and constraints that drive down the quality scores in the region. The following sections discuss further the degree to which the plan is expected to improve the scores.

---

[5]For further analysis, see Sanfey and Milatović (2018).

[6]The EU11 refers to the 11 former socialist countries from central Europe, the Baltic states and South-Eastern Europe that joined the EU in 2004 or since then, namely, Bulgaria, Croatia, the Czech Republic, Estonia, Hungary, Latvia, Lithuania, Poland, Romania, the Slovak Republic and Slovenia.

Trade

The focus on trade in the action plan is welcome, as the region is performing below potential. Average trade openness, defined as the sum of exports and imports as a percentage of GDP,[7] of the WB6 stands at just 65% of the EU11. The main reasons why trade in the Western Balkans is still low compared to its EU11 peers include not only the crumbling transport infrastructure and inadequate business environment but also the failure of the region to develop value chains with western European markets, or even within the region.

Intra-regional trade in the Western Balkans is far less important at present that trade outside the region. On average only 20% of Western Balkan exports go to neighbouring countries. This figure covers a range from a 46% share in Kosovo to a mere 9% in Albania. Although exports from the WB6 countries grew by about 60% on average over the past 10 years, most of this growth was driven by the rise of exports to EU countries, rather than from higher intra-regional trade. One reason for this might be in the similarity of the Western Balkan countries' main export products, though there are important differences among the six countries in terms of revealed comparative advantage.[8] At the same time, the EU is by far the region's most important trading partner. Two-thirds of the region's exports are with the EU (see Chart 1). The share ranges from 80% in FYR Macedonia to just 23% in Kosovo. All WB6 countries have a Stabilisation and Association Agreement with the EU, which gives the countries preferential access to EU markets for most goods (Fig. 2).

Poor quality of transport infrastructure is still a major obstacle for trade enhancement, including with the neighbouring countries. The assessment of the quality of infrastructure by the World Economic Forum's Global Competitiveness Index highlights the extent of the challenge facing the region. However, some progress has been made recently in this area. Cross-border infrastructure is being gradually improved as major investments in roads, railways and ports gather pace. These projects are helping to address the pervasive problem of low-quality infrastructure and, over time, will help speed up journeys and allow commerce to flow more freely.

In addition, efforts are being made to make the passage of goods across borders a less painful process. Recent major reforms include (1) implementation of an electronic risk-based inspection system, which reduced the time for border compliance in Albania in 2016; (2) rationalisation of the customs fee schedule and permit structure, improvement in the risk-based inspection system, simplified customs procedures and the elimination of a document previously required in FYR Macedonia; and (3) the recent streamlining of the customs clearance process and implementation of the Albania–Kosovo Transit Corridor.

---

[7]These statistics are based on 5-year averages.

[8]This issue is analysed further in A. Kresic, J. Milatovic and P. Sanfey, "Firm performance and obstacles to doing business in the Western Balkans: evidence from the BEEPS", EBRD Working paper No. 200, January 2017; http://www.ebrd.com/publications/working-papers/firm-performance

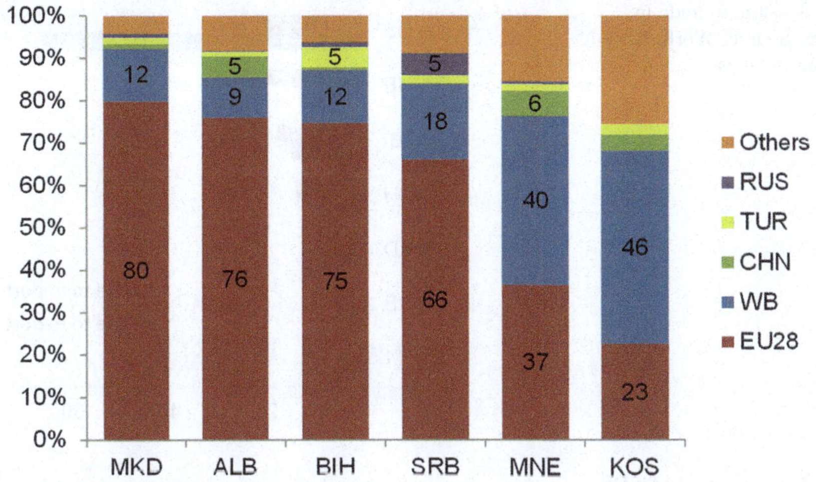

Fig. 2 Exports by destination as per cent of total exports. Source: UNCTAD and the Central Bank of Kosovo, authors' calculations

In the World Bank's *Doing Business* report, trading across borders is less problematic than other obstacles. The region's "distance to frontier" (i.e. remaining gap to best practice) in the area of cross-border trade is typically the lowest among a range of business obstacles such as resolving insolvency, getting electricity or enforcing contracts. However, the problems that businesses face in trading across borders should not be underestimated, as significant trade barriers still exist in the region. The bureaucracy associated with exporting or importing is often onerous. The time and costs to trade are much higher compared to the EU11 average. For instance, World Bank estimates place the average cost to export in the EU11 at US$ 34 per unit compared with US$ 65 in Albania or US$ 232 in Kosovo. At the same time, average time to export in EU11 is 5 h per unit, compared with 6 h in Serbia or up to 66 h in Kosovo (Figs. 3 and 4).

In addition, evidence from the EBRD–World Bank Business Environment and Enterprise Performance Survey (BEEPS), last carried out in 2013, shows that customs and trade regulations were often perceived as problematic. Almost 5% of firms in this region saw it as the biggest business environment obstacle (out of 15 options), and on average, every tenth firm in the region viewed customs and trade regulations as a major or very severe obstacle for doing business.

The regional action plan envisages that Western Balkan countries will deepen further their collaboration on areas such as trade liberalisation, electronic commerce and trade dispute settlements. More specifically this includes (1) facilitation of free trade in goods, including through trade dispute settlements, joint border controls, closer cooperation between the individual market surveillance authorities, etc.; (2) facilitation of free trade in services, including through adoption of the Additional Protocol 6, dialogue on regulatory issues in electronic commerce and other measures; (3) harmonisation of CEFTA markets with the EU; and (4) creating a

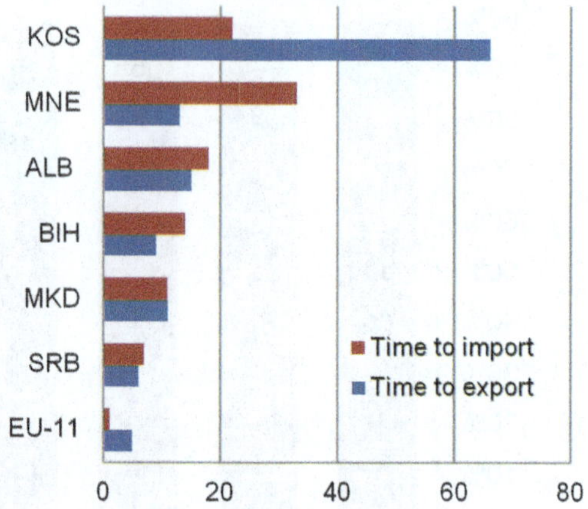

Fig. 3 Time to trade in hours. Source: World Bank Doing Business Report 2018

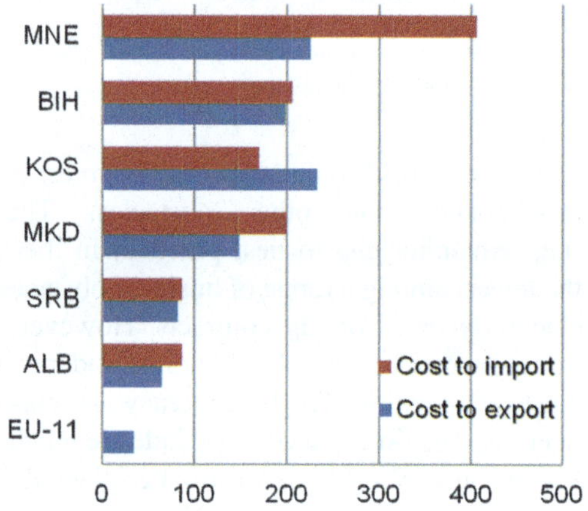

Fig. 4 Cost to trade, USD$. Source: World Bank Doing Business Report 2018

non-tariff measures (NTMs)-free region, including through information exchange between competition and state aid authorities. The CEFTA Secretariat will continue to monitor implementation of this action plan in the region and prepare an annual report on the main impediments to trade. Taken together, these steps should help the region to become more integrated.

Investment

To date, the region has had limited attraction for foreign investors, highlighting the failure of the region to be competitive. The competitiveness quality is one in which the WB6 countries score particularly poorly relative to the EU11, as shown in the table earlier. These results broadly chime with the World Economic Forum's annual perceptions-based *Global Competitiveness Index* (WEF 2018). The overall average

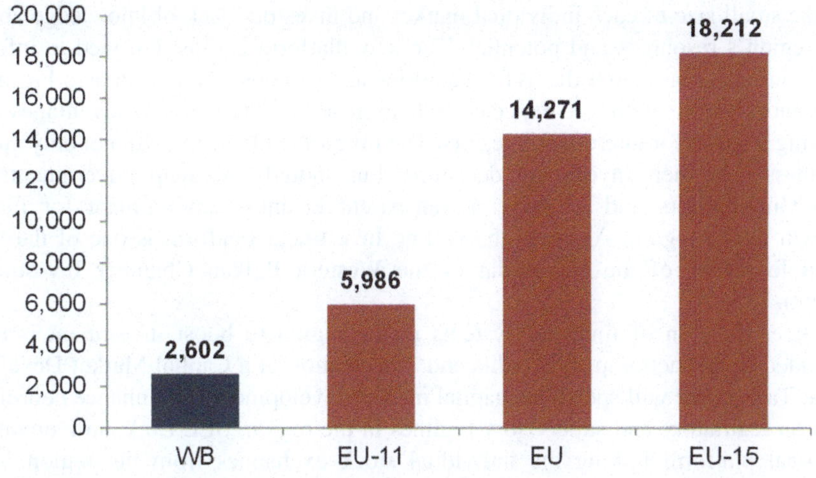

Fig. 5 FDI stock per capita (€). Source: Authors' calculations based on UNCTAD database

ranking for the region (excluding Kosovo, which is not included in the index) is 80th out of 137 countries, versus 50th for the EU11. The scores are particularly poor in several areas of concern to foreign investors, such as market size, labour market efficiency, business sophistication, innovation capacity and the state of institutions.

It is not surprising, therefore, that Western Balkan countries lag significantly behind the EU11 in terms of FDI stock per capita received. The average FDI stock per capita in the Western Balkans is around €2600, compared with almost €6000 in the EU11 (see Fig. 5). In addition, much of the existing FDI did not target the tradeable sectors, and hence the export capacity of the region, but rather came through privatisations of sectors intended primarily for domestic consumption. Although Western Balkan countries have significant advantages in terms of stable economies, the prospect of eventual EU membership, low labour costs, favourable tax regimes for investors and a strategic geographical location, none of these has been sufficient to overcome the obstacles highlighted above.

The action plan foresees the development of a single investment space and the harmonisation of investment policies through a number of measures, most importantly through the development of a Regional Investment Reform Agenda. The six countries have agreed to promote the WB6 region as a unique investment destination. To this end, they have inaugurated the idea of the Regional Chamber Investment Forum (CIF) and an Online Investment Platform for the Western Balkans. Although it grew out of the Berlin process, CIF is very much a locally owned forum for cooperation and collaboration between the regional Chambers of Commerce.

The new Western Balkans online Investment Platform, launched at the EBRD Western Balkans Investment Summit in February 2018 and managed by the Secretariat of the EBRD-funded Chamber Investment Forum, serves as a one-stop window for investors looking to invest in the Western Balkan region. It may therefore help improve FDI inflows to the region. Up to now, investment has been hampered by the small size of each individual market and investors' lack of knowledge about the region's resources and potential. The new platform is thus designed to inform potential investors about the WB6 countries and promote the region as a business destination and is therefore expected to help in selling the region's advantages and making it easier for interested investors. The Investment Platform will not only guide businesses in their investment decisions, but should also help governments in removing barriers and fostering a transparent business environment for future growth in the region. As such, the Online Investment Platform is one of the first tangible results of the Secretariat of the Western Balkan Chamber Investment Forum.

Diversification of financial systems in the region to boost investment is also included in this action plan. To this end, the creation of a Capital Market Development Task Force will spearhead capital market development and enhance coordination on regulatory and supervisory regimes in the region. SEE Link, an innovative regional platform linking the individual stock exchanges from the region, was launched in February 2016 (at the second EBRD-hosted Western Balkans Investment Summit). Today, SEE Link covers a combined equity market capitalisation of over US$ 50 billion allowing order routing of almost 1200 securities listed on the seven exchanges: Bulgaria (BSE), Bosnia and Herzegovina (BLSE and SASE), Croatia (ZSE), Macedonia (MSE), Serbia (BELEX) and Slovenia (LJSE). The system aims to increase liquidity and improve access for investors and local brokers and is an excellent example of improving the depth and horizontal links of individual capital markets in the region.[9]

Mobility

The action plan envisages better integration of high-skilled professionals and academics in the region into regional professional and research networks. The Mobility Agenda aims at removing obstacles to the mobility of (1) professionals, through regional mutual recognition agreements of professional qualifications (doctors, dentists, architects, etc.), as well as through automatic recognition of academic qualifications, and (2) students, researchers and academics, through joint academic mobility and cooperation programmes.

Lack of skills is often a problem in the region and is one of the reasons why the EBRD scores on the inclusive quality are well below those in the EU11, as shown earlier in Fig. 1. In the Business Environment and Enterprise Performance Survey (BEEPS), last carried out in 2013, more than one-third of all firms cited an inadequately educated workforce as an obstacle to current operations. At the same time, vocational education and training (VET) institutions struggle to adapt their programmes and teaching methods

[9]More information on SEE Link is available at http://www.see-link.net/

to market needs. Entrepreneurship and self-employment, particularly among the youth, are also held back by the limited supply of access to training and finance.

Lack of skills and appropriate education is a significant problem that cannot be easily fixed. The action plan's proposals to enhance the intra-regional mobility of skilled individuals are welcome as far as they go, but will not fully address the major skills gap across the region. Studies show that the region lacks both hard and soft skills. Results from the OECD's PISA assessments point to a significant deficit in the three tested areas (science, reading and mathematics) of 15-year olds in the Western Balkans vis-à-vis the EU average. For example, 78% of students in Kosovo, 70% in FYR Macedonia, 53% in Albania and 52% in Montenegro do not possess basic mathematical skills, compared with 30% on average in OECD countries. At the same time, the policy framework and incentive systems are underdeveloped and do not encourage public–private partnerships in developing and delivering lasting improvements in skills.

Digital Integration

The action plan envisages that measures will be taken to further the integration of the region into the pan-European digital market, through synchronised digitisation strategies, updated regulatory frameworks, improved broadband infrastructure, digital literacy and supply of digital skills, uptake of smart technologies and enhancement of cyber security. A roaming-free region is also part of the action plan. This is another feature of making the Western Balkans more competitive and integrated.

The region currently lags far behind EU standards in terms of digital transformation. The plan's focus in this area is much needed, particularly in light of the fast-developing EU-level framework for ICT networks and services. At present, most Western Balkan economies have established a supportive strategic framework for digital growth. It is encouraging that they have prioritised telecom and broadband-related structural measures within the 2017–2019 Economic Reform Programmes (ERPs). With the legislative framework mostly in place, the latest European Commission Enlargement progress reports stressed the needs to strengthen the capacities and the independence of the regulatory agencies for electronic communications. Pressing challenges also include finalising the delayed digital broadcasting switchover process (where not already completed), allowing the use of the digital dividend spectrum for broadband services, and increasing the use of e-commerce.

The region needs to accelerate high-speed broadband roll-out so as not to be left out of the pan-European digital infrastructure map. A regional approach in this context is crucial. The success of this approach in advancing the digital agenda is clearly demonstrated through the recent regional initiative to reduce roaming costs. The Regional Roaming Agreement has led to tangible impacts in terms of reduced roaming prices and increased roaming traffic. This demonstrates how such a regional "home-grown" initiative, driven and supported by all parties, can be instrumental in achieving positive outcomes for consumers within the Western Balkan region.

Nevertheless, the region is still far from the "Roam like at Home" EU model, and there is still ample room for implementing further legal and regulatory measures to match EU standards.

Conclusion

The regional action plan is a welcome step forward. Combined with the EU's new enlargement strategy issued in February 2018, it helps to focus attention on the region, at a time when the EU is consumed by other problems and there is much talk of "enlargement fatigue". The ideas laid out in the draft plan are broadly sensible and can lead to concrete improvements in key areas related to trade, investment, mobility and digitisation. This in turn can contribute to further convergence in living standards between the Western Balkans and the EU.

Small market size has been seen as the largest deterrent to competitiveness according to Global Competitiveness Index. Further economic integration of the Western Balkan region towards a single economic space will raise the competitiveness of the individually small Western Balkan markets by moving them beyond the existing free trade agreement and unlocking untapped investment potential, bringing multiple benefits, including enhanced trade and investment, leveraging each other's comparative advantage and strengthening economic and political institutions.

At the same time, the plan has little to say about other important obstacles. Returning to the EBRD's framework for sustainable market economies, the one quality in which the region scores worst is governance. Problems with governance are pervasive throughout the region, whether it concerns public institutions or corporate governance in the private sector. Weak institutions are a breeding ground for corruption, which is acknowledged to be a serious problem in all Western Balkan countries. Businesses on the ground also complain about unfair competition from the informal sector, which arises when taxes (including labour taxes) are high, tax administration is cumbersome and bribes to inspectors and other officials are commonplace. The problem is aggravated by the heavy presence of the state in the economy, holding back the private sector. Many state-owned enterprises are loss-making, while those that report profits are often highly inefficient; however, resistance to privatisation remains strong. All of these obstacles are likely to be highly off-putting for potential investors.

Enterprises in several countries, notably Albania and Kosovo, also worry about unreliable electricity supply, which would be another worry for investors. Energy market integration has stalled, despite the fact that the countries' infrastructure in the electricity sector is relatively well interconnected. Given the small size of national energy markets, the Western Balkan countries will not be able to develop liquid markets in isolation. Cross-border cooperation is therefore essential for achieving important cost savings for energy consumers through increased competition and more effective use of existing generation and transmission infrastructure in the region. However, with the exception of a common platform for coordinated allocation of electricity cross-border capacities (SEE CAO), there has been little progress in cross-border cooperation. For example, according to the Energy Community, with the exception of Serbia, the Western Balkan countries are yet to establish functioning power exchanges. Cross-border electricity trade is therefore below the region's potential, reflecting the high level of market fragmentation.

And, while the region has proved relatively resilient over the years to economic shocks, low access to finance is another common problem, especially for SMEs. A quarter of all BEEPS surveyed firms in the region described themselves as credit-constrained, meaning that they need a loan but are either rejected when they apply or feel discouraged from applying. Many banks in the region are still burdened by relatively high levels of non-performing loans and are therefore cautious about extending new credit, particularly to clients with whom they are unfamiliar.

In summary, the success or otherwise of the action plan will be judged by the extent to which, after some years, we have seen a marked improvement in trade and investment flows, a noticeable increase in the mobility of certain groups of individuals and a digital agenda that is firmly embedded across the region. But countries in the region should not lose sight of the bigger picture and the ultimate challenge of speeding up convergence towards average EU living standards. To achieve that, a more comprehensive growth agenda is needed and one that focuses firmly on improving competitiveness and governance, enhancing integration in areas of potential such as energy and strengthening the resilience and reach of the financial sector.

References

EBRD. (2018). *Transition report 2017/18: Sustaining growth*. London: European Bank for Reconstruction and Development.

Sanfey, P., & Milatović, J. (2018). *The Western Balkans in transition: Diagnosing the constraints on the path to a sustainable market economy*. European Bank for Reconstruction and Development. http://www.ebrd.com/news/2018/towards-higher-productivity-in-the-western-balkans.html

WEF. (2018). *Global competitiveness report 2017–2018*. World Economic Forum. https://www.weforum.org/reports/the-global-competitiveness-report-2017-2018

Trade in Services in the Western Balkan Countries

Ivana Prica

Introduction

During the 1990s while former Yugoslavia was in the throes of break-up and conflict, the rest of the world experienced a boom in telecommunications sector development, a surge in international trade and the formation of the World Trade Organization (WTO). Due to technological developments, services have become more 'tradable', and for the first time, international trade in services has been included in the global services trading regime, and services trading rules have been defined in the WTO's General Agreement on Trade in Services (GATS). The WTO is the legal successor to the General Agreement on Tariffs and Trade (GATT), and all countries that were GATT members became WTO members (so-called original members). Even though Yugoslavia was a GATT member, out of all the successor states of the former Yugoslavia, only Slovenia managed to claim 'original member' status, while all the others have had to negotiate their entry to WTO. Some are still negotiating.

All the Western Balkan countries have European Union (EU) membership as their primary development goal and are in various stages of the EU accession process. This process impacts directly on the services sectors in the Western Balkan countries as they are harmonising their laws with the EU *acquis communautaire* and opening their economies, including their services sectors, to the EU market. Finally, all the Western Balkan countries are members of the Central European Free Trade Agreement (CEFTA) where they are negotiating further liberalisation of their services sectors within the region.

This chapter reviews the development of the services sectors in the Western Balkans both from the point of view of their international integration (EU and

I. Prica (✉)
Faculty of Economics, University of Belgrade, Belgrade, Serbia

R. Osbild, W. Bartlett (eds.), *Western Balkan Economies in Transition*, Societies and Political Orders in Transition, https://doi.org/10.1007/978-3-319-93665-9_3

Table 1 Progress achieved in international integration processes (in December 2016)

Country	EU accession			WTO membership
	SAA	Membership status	Accession negotiations	
Albania	Came into force in April 2009	Candidate country as of June 2014	Not started	Member since 2000
BiH	Came into force in June 2015	Potential candidate country	–	Accession negotiations ongoing
Kosovo	Came into force in April 2016	Potential candidate country	–	To apply for membership
Macedonia	Came into force in April 2004	Candidate country as of December 2005	Not started	Member since 2003
Montenegro	Came into force in May 2010	Candidate country as of December 2010	Started in June 2012	Member since 2012
Serbia	Came into force in September 2013	Candidate country as of March 2012	Started in January 2014	Accession negotiations ongoing

Source: EU and WTO sites

WTO membership and accession processes) and from the point of view of their domestic development levels and perspectives.

Liberalisation of Trade in Services

Due to the strong resistance of domestic stakeholders, the process of liberalisation of services sectors in the Western Balkan countries has been mainly externally driven. When market reforms began, the services sectors were dominated by state-owned public monopoly service providers (including postal services, telecommunications, all utilities, some distribution sectors, education and health services) or strong domestic incumbents that have significant market shares. The workers employed by these state-owned companies naturally have a strong interest in maintaining their secure job positions. Even the regulatory bodies have been resistant to change, since they were unwilling to accept that there is a need to change the old ways, while the decision makers feared losing political support due to the job losses that could result from dismantling large state-owned enterprises. Therefore, there was little public support for such reforms. However, the regulatory reform of the services sectors, which inevitably involved their liberalisation bearing in mind their starting position, was required by their need to integrate with international markets. In particular, in the context of this chapter, this includes WTO accession, EU accession and the Central European Free Trade Agreement (CEFTA).

All Western Balkan countries are now either WTO members or are in the process of becoming WTO members (see Table 1), all have EU integration as their goal, and all are members of CEFTA, a regional free trade agreement. As explained above, these processes also shape the trade in services regime in the Western Balkan countries and the liberalisation of their trading regime in services. Since more than 80% of total trade of Western Balkan countries is with EU and CEFTA,[1] I will first look at the progress that they have achieved in their EU and WTO accessions, specifically with respect to trade in services.

European Union Accession

The Western Balkan countries have clearly identified EU membership as a primary goal but are at different stages of the accession process, as Table 1 illustrates. All have signed a Stabilisation and Association Agreement (SAA) with the EU. The SAA with Macedonia came to force as long ago as 2004 and with Kosovo as recently as 2016. An SAA is the first step to approximating the regime of an accession country to that of the EU *acquis communautaire* and contains many dimensions of approximation. It establishes a free trade agreement between the EU and the signatory country, harmonises the laws of the candidate country to the EU and requires countries to engage in regional cooperation, now including full involvement with CEFTA.

Among other things, an SAA requires countries to liberalise the movement of workers, the rules of establishment, the supply of services and the movement of capital and the key elements of the liberalisation of trade in services. The SAAs also require countries to liberalise the markets on which state monopolies operate.

Movement of workers' provisions relates to the rights of Western Balkan countries' workers who are legally employed in EU countries, including the coordination of social security and pension system. Provisions regarding establishment allow for cross-border branches, i.e. allowing EU companies to establish branches in a Western Balkan country as dependent legal entities that are not a resident in that country. The same right is provided for branches of Western Balkan companies in EU countries. This means achieving full liberalisation in this mode of trade in services ('movement of legal persons' in the WTO). Provisions on establishment also allow for additional liberalisation regarding the movement of workers employed in EU companies set up in a Western Balkan country or the movement of workers employed in Western Balkan companies set up in the EU ('intra-corporate transferees') and other issues related to operating these companies.

The SAA provisions on the supply of services provide for the progressive liberalisation of services trade between the EU and each Western Balkan country. Provisions regarding liberalisation commitments mainly cover road transport (unrestricted transit, non-discrimination and progressive harmonisation of transport legislation), international maritime transport and air transport. SAA provisions on

[1] See Mojsoska-Blazevski and Petreski (2012) or Kurtović and Talović (2015).

the movement of capital allow free current and capital transactions that relate to the provision of services, to the movement of workers and to the rights of establishment. This section of the SAA also proposes further capital movement liberalisation between SAA signatories.

As this brief explanation of SAA provisions relating to services trade suggests, the key elements of market reforms and liberalisation of services sectors are already set out in trade between each Western Balkan country and the EU. The idea is that upon their EU membership, these countries should have a trading regime that is as liberal as (but not more liberal than) that of the EU.

The greatest progress in EU accession has been achieved in Montenegro. The country started its accession negotiations in June 2014 and, at the time of writing, had opened 24 negotiating chapters, and a further 11 negotiating chapters remained to be opened. Serbia started its EU accession negotiations in January 2014 and has so far (December 2016) opened only four chapters.

WTO accession is a prerequisite for EU accession and hence a necessity on the EU road for all of these countries. Before proceeding with the analysis of WTO membership terms for these countries, it is important to explain one more thing. Namely, the terms under which a prospective EU member country enters the WTO should not be more liberal than are the terms of the EU's WTO membership. If the prospective EU member had previously negotiated a more liberal trading regime with the WTO, according to WTO rules, the EU would then have to renegotiate its own terms of WTO membership with all other interested WTO members.

The logic behind this is as follows. Once a country becomes an EU member, it should apply the same regime as the rest of the EU members (EU is one member in the WTO). So, if country A had previously negotiated with WTO a more liberal trading regime than the regime the EU has agreed with WTO, it means that after acceding to the EU, the territory of country A would now apply the less liberal trading regime of the EU. This means that country A would effectively take away from the rest of the WTO members some of the concessions they had already achieved on the territory of country A. According to WTO negotiating rules, in that case the member (the EU, since country A in the meantime became its member) that wishes to change its commitments needs to negotiate with other members and offer interested members adequate concessions.

World Trade Organization Accession

As shown in Table 1, three of the Western Balkan countries (Albania, Macedonia and Montenegro) are already WTO members (they became members in 2000, 2003 and 2012, respectively). BiH has formally applied for WTO membership, and Working Party (WP) for negotiating the accession of BiH was formed in 1999.

Serbia has also formally applied for WTO membership, and its WP for negotiating accession was formed in 2005. Kosovo has not applied for WTO membership yet but is expected to do so.[2]

The WTO accession process broadly follows two tracks: multilateral and bilateral. Multilateral negotiations deal with the regulatory regime and policies in the area of trade of the acceding country and are aimed at bringing them in line with WTO regulations.

Bilateral negotiations deal more with terms under which trade is done (the level of trade liberalisation). They cover trade negotiations on market access in goods and services between the acceding country and the interested WTO members. The negotiations begin with the acceding country submitting its initial offers on goods and services as a basis for negotiations. During negotiations, interested WTO members may request further levels of liberalisation. Even though negotiations are bilateral, the results are applied to all countries equally in line with the most favoured nation (MFN) principle of the WTO, which states that members may not discriminate against one another. If one member is given a preferred, more liberal treatment, then the same treatment shall be extended to all the other WTO members.

In relation to trade in goods, the tariff rates (or equivalents) define the level of liberalisation of trade for each product. However, in services trade, the liberalisation levels are defined in terms of more or less liberal regulatory regime regarding the provision and consumption of services, whenever it involves transactions between a domestic and a foreign resident. Once the bilateral negotiations are over, the final regime (or final 'bindings' in a particular services sector and for a particular mode of supply) is adopted as the new members' Schedule of Specific Commitments in Services. The Schedule in services lists levels of liberalisation defined for a particular sector.[3] These are also called 'bindings' because they bind the lowest level of liberalisation. The member may apply in its regulatory regime measures that are at least as liberal as the ones defined in its Schedule of Specific Commitments in Services. Similarly, the results of bilateral negotiations in goods are defined as tariff rates and related bindings in the Schedule of Concessions for goods of a new member.

The process of new member accession negotiations led to WTO members requesting more and more liberal regimes from the newly acceding members, so that the later the country acceded to WTO the more liberal would be its trading regime. This can be seen in the Western Balkan countries: the Schedule of Specific Commitments in Services of Albania, which became a WTO member in 2000 (see Table 1), provides for a significantly less liberal trade regime in services than does the WTO schedule in services of Montenegro[4] which became a WTO member in

---

[2]See http://www.eutrade-ks.eu/kosovo_content_3715498.html and http://www.rtklive.com/en/?id=3&r=5950 from September 2016, which announce Kosovo's application for WTO membership in 2016.

[3]They are also defined separately for each of the four modes of supply of services, but one need not go into those details here.

[4]Schedules for all WTO members are available on the WTO site (www.wto.org).

2012. Requests for liberalisation that are now on the table for Western Balkan countries that are still negotiating their WTO accession (BiH and Serbia) suggest that an even higher level of liberalisation of their services trade regime may be expected.

Because the schedules of the existing members have not changed substantially over the years, the WTO-'bound' regime (the WTO schedules of commitments in goods and services 'bind' the least liberal regime a WTO member may apply) is in some cases above the member's applied regime, i.e. the country applies a trade regime that is more liberal than the regime they bound in their WTO schedules. This is particularly the case with the 'original members', countries that became members during the Uruguay round in 1995 when the WTO was formed (these had previously been GATT[5] members). These countries, including most developed economies, which became WTO members more than 20 years ago, have not made significant improvement to their schedules since then.

On the other hand, the new acceding members are forced to liberalise their services regime often far more than their currently applied regime (and more than they are prepared for), in order to become WTO members. Even if such additional liberalisation should in most cases prove to have positive effects on the liberalising country's economy, as supported by numerous academic studies,[6] and also well-illustrated in the Communication from Slovenia, Bulgaria, Czech Republic, Poland and Slovak Republic to the WTO Council for Trade in Services,[7] this approach has nevertheless increased the gap between the old and the newly acceding members.

It is important to understand that the WTO framework also envisages further negotiating rounds for the *existing* members, in order to achieve 'progressive' trade liberalisation (i.e. more liberal WTO bindings). These negotiations on progressive liberalisation of the existing members' trade regimes were to be based on members increasing their levels of trade liberalisation while expecting at the same time that all the other members give them in return concessions (in the form of increased liberalisation of their regimes) of similar weight. However, these negotiations were not as successful as was hoped for. This led to countries unilaterally liberalising their services trade regimes (in line with the needs of their economic development) while at the same time not binding this more liberal regime in their WTO schedules—since they could not achieve substantially equal concessions from the other WTO members through negotiations. On the other hand, now that the starting position for trade negotiations between the trade partners is not equal, especially in terms of the

[5]The General Agreement on Tariffs and Trade was the predecessor to the WTO. The WTO encompasses both GATT and trade in services via the General Agreement on Trade in Services (GATS) and, separately, rules on intellectual property rights.

[6]For more recent evidence, see, for example, Gervais (2015), Nordas and Rouzet (2016), van der Marel and Shepherd (2013), as well as region-specific papers of Kurtović and Talović (2015) and Bjelić and Dragutinović Mitrović (2012).

[7]Note on Assessment of Trade in Services in Certain Transition Economies,—communication from Slovenia, Bulgaria, Czech Republic, Poland and Slovak Republic to the WTO Council for Trade in Services, Special Session: Assessment of Trade in Services, 5 December 2000, S/CSS/W/18, WTO.

applied regime (some members already apply a far more liberal regime, while new members may have had to liberalise above their capacities in the first place in order to become a member), negotiating based on the premise that each member should give substantially equal concessions does not seem to provide fertile grounds for successful negotiations.

Currently only Bosnia and Herzegovina and Serbia are negotiating their WTO accessions. These negotiations are confidential and not much information about them is available to the public, so most of evidence provided here comes either from the interviews that BiH and Serbian officials have given to the press, as indicated in the links provided, or official information from WTO site that deals with these accessions.[8]

As explained above, WTO accession negotiations follow multilateral and bilateral tracks. The multilateral negotiations are de facto over for both Serbia and BiH.[9] At this moment, however, neither BiH nor Serbia has finished their bilateral market access negotiations on goods and on services. They submitted their initial market offers on goods and services (used as a starting point for negotiations) in 2004 (BiH) and 2006 (Serbia) but the negotiations are continuing and have not yet been concluded with the USA, Brazil, Ukraine and Russia. Negotiations with the USA and Brazil are entering their final stages, and there are only a few issues left to resolve (regarding a few agricultural lines in the USA where it has its trading interests and regarding meat products with Brazil,[10] where it has its trading interests).

However, negotiations with Ukraine and Russia do not seem to be so constructive.[11] This is because both these countries have made requests for comprehensive market access concessions in numerous goods and services sectors of BiH and Serbia. In many of these sectors, there are no clear trading interests of the requesting countries. Yet the negotiating requests are of such a scope to make the WTO accession of these two countries unappealing. Accepting such requests may hurt their own trading interests indirectly as well, since it would bar them from EU membership.

Serbia and BiH have EU integration and not WTO accession as their primary goal. While WTO accession is a prerequisite for EU membership, the terms of WTO accession (WTO commitments or 'bindings') of an aspiring EU member country may not be more liberal than are the WTO commitments of EU, as explained above. Otherwise, if a new EU member country had WTO commitments that were more

[8]At https://www.wto.org/english/thewto_e/acc_e/acc_e.htm

[9]However, if the process of accession continues to take time, members may ask Serbia and BiH to update this information that then may be re-examined.

[10]According to *B92 news* from December 9, 2015: http://www.b92.net/eng/news/politics.php?yyyy=2015&mm=12&dd=09&nav_id=96310 and *Večernji list* daily, from April 20, 2016: According to *B92 news* from December 9, 2015: http://www.b92.net/eng/news/politics.php?yyyy=2015&mm=12&dd=09&nav_id=96310

[11]These countries became WTO members in 2008 (Ukraine) and 2012 (Russia), during the process of access negotiations of BiH and Serbia, so their negotiation requests also came later in the process.

liberal, then the EU itself would have to negotiate and agree additional concessions for the resulting loss of market access with the other WTO members. This procedure may be just too impractical and costly. In short, until the situation changes, the WTO accession of BiH and Serbia cannot go forward, and they will not be able to complete their EU accession until this issue is resolved.

CEFTA

The current members of CEFTA are all the Western Balkan countries plus Moldova. This regional free trade agreement has been established with the idea of fostering the economic development of the pre-accession countries. Removing trade barriers provides a larger market for Western Balkan companies that should result in a higher competitiveness of the region. Significant progress has been made in CEFTA in liberalising trade within the region, and the work is still ongoing. One of the priorities of CEFTA is liberalisation of trade in services.

The Subcommittee on Trade in Services is the main CEFTA body that deals with trade in services. It coordinates, oversees and streamlines the work of the Negotiation Group on Services that deals with the ongoing negotiations on trade in services of the CEFTA Parties. These negotiations formally started in July 2014 with a view to develop an 'Additional Protocol on Trade in Services' together with a first annex on 'The Presence of Natural Persons' and a second annex detailing a 'Schedule of Specific Commitments in Services' which will cover 12 services sectors (business and professional services, tourism, recreational and environmental services, communication and construction services, distribution, education and health services, as well as financial, transport and audio-visual services).[12] Since this is a free trade agreement, the commitments undertaken should be deeper and wider than the commitments that CEFTA Parties have made in WTO GATS, the so-called 'GATS plus' commitments.

Parallel to these negotiations, the CEFTA Subcommittee on Trade in Services is busy on other services topics (FDI, mutual recognition agreements, trade in services statistics) to improve trade in services and the business environment for trade in services.

In December 2016, it was announced that these negotiations had been completed an agreement reached, but it had still not been adopted in October 2017 and hence the adopted document was not available to the public. If this agreement is based on GATS plus principle, it would be an important breakthrough for CEFTA and the Western Balkan countries. In a recent paper, Sanfey et al. (2016) identify trade integration, and in particular regional integration, as one of the most important sources of growth for Western Balkan countries. The analysis in this chapter shows that the services sectors of the Western Balkan countries have plenty of

[12]http://cefta.int/structures/subcommittee-on-trade-in-services/negotiation-group-on-services/

development potentials and that a successful CEFTA negotiation in services may provide an important impetus to the overall integration process. Creating a free trade area for services will make it easier for small and medium domestic service providers to export within the region, while larger suppliers who may already be successful exporters of services will reap the advantages of a larger market. In addition, foreign suppliers would have more interest to relocate to the region. Liberalising the trade in services within the region will help to foster economic development and bring the countries of the Western Balkans closer to the EU.

Trade in Services: Evidence from the Data

The data used in this analysis are taken from the United Nations Conference on Trade and Development (UNCTAD) online database and the World Bank World Development Indicators online database. Since all trade data in these databases are denominated in current US$, a country-specific GDP deflator was used to recalculate the data in terms of constant 2010 US$. This enables a better comparison of data from different years and is needed because there were significant fluctuations in the exchange rate of the US$ over the period of analysis from 2008 to 2015. This trend is particularly visible in 2015, which is the reference year in this analysis.

Since the development goal of the Western Balkan countries is EU membership, evidence of results achieved by these economies will be compared against the same indicators for EU countries. In particular, the reference point will be a cluster of new member states (NMS) of the EU without the Baltic countries.[13] This cluster will be called 'non-Baltic NMS' and will be used as a benchmark to assess the progress of the Western Balkan economies.

Domestic Economy

The population size of Western Balkan countries varies from around 600,000 in Montenegro to around 7 million in Serbia (Table 2). In total, Western Balkans had around 18 million inhabitants in 2015. Gross domestic product (GDP) per capita in current US$ in 2015 was highest in Montenegro at 6400 US$, and almost half of that in Kosovo, where GDP per capita was lowest. Montenegro had a similar GDP per capita as does the lowest positioned among non-Baltic NMS, Bulgaria (6820 US$ in 2015). Still, these countries have a long way to go: the average value of GDP per

[13]The reason the Baltic countries were excluded from this cluster is that their economies have had a very different dynamics during the observed period compared to the Western Balkan countries as well as the other NMS.

Table 2 Population, GDP and GDP per capita in current and constant 2010 US$

Country	Population, thousands, 2015	GDP, current US$ millions, 2015	GDP per capita, current US$, 2015	GDP per capita, constant 2010 US$		
					Annual growth rate, %	
				2015	Average 2001–2008	Average 2009–2015
Montenegro	622	3993	6415	7276	4.8	0.7
Serbia	7098	36,513	5144	5659	6.2	0.4
Macedonia	2078	10,086	4853	5094	3.1	2.0
BiH	3810	15,995	4198	4808	5.5	0.8
Albania	2889	11,456	3965	4541	6.7	2.7
Kosovo	1797	6386	3553	3786	6.6	2.8
WBC			4688	5194	5	2
Non-B. NMS			13,249	15,394	5.2	0.8
EU			31,843	34,861	1.7	0.1

Source: UNCTAD, World Bank WDI or calculated from that data

capita for the Western Balkan countries[14] was around a third of the non-Baltic NMS average in 2015, while the EU's GDP per capita was almost seven times larger than the Western Balkan country average.

As explained above, the data in current US$ for 2015 are particularly susceptible to changes in the value of the US$, so Table 2 also provides GDP per capita 2015 data in constant 2010 US$. The data clearly show two phases of GDP growth: high precrisis levels and modest postcrisis levels (see two last columns in Table 2). Before the crisis, the average annual growth rate for the Western Balkan countries (over period 2001–2008) was 5%. This compares well with the EU growth rate in the same period and supports the catch-up argument. However, this is not quite so when compared to the non-Baltic NMS, whose average precrisis growth was at least as high (5.2%). Postcrisis growth rates in the Western Balkan countries, although modest, are higher on average over the period 2008–2015 than those of the EU or the non-Baltic NMS. One could argue that even the modest rates of growth in the Western Balkan countries may be high enough to preserve the process of catching up.

The value-added composition of GDP in the Western Balkan countries shows a relatively high share of services (see Fig. 1). Services (including construction[15])

[14]This is a simple average, i.e. each country is assigned equal weight. The same applies for the NMS cluster average. On the other hand, EU data in this table are provided for the whole EU territory, i.e. they are a weighted average, where each country is weighted by its size.

[15]In GDP statistics, construction is an item in industry category, together with mining, manufacturing and utilities. However, under WTO classification construction is a service. Furthermore, construction is calculated as an integral part of services trade in countries balance of payment

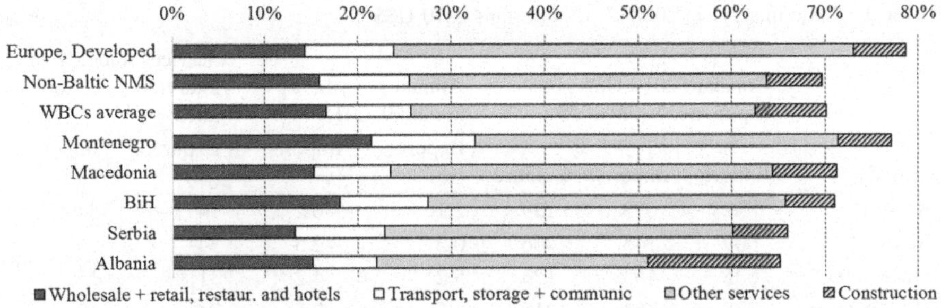

Fig. 1 GDP: value added in services, average for 2008–2014, % GDP. Source: Calculated from UNCTAD and World Bank WDI databases

comprise 77% of total GDP in Montenegro, which is close to the average for the developed European countries (79% of GDP). Services have the lowest share in Albania and Serbia, where only 65% and 66% of value added was achieved in services sectors during the period 2008–2014. On average, the share of services in GDP in the Western Balkan countries (70%) is the same as that of the non-Baltic NMS.

The service share in GDP in the Western Balkan country average is much below that of the developed EU countries and similar to that of the non-Baltic NMS country average (70% of GDP). Western Balkan countries also have a smaller share of 'other services' than in the developed EU and larger shares of more traditional services sectors listed in Fig. 1. Furthermore, the composition of other services is different in the Western Balkans having a far lower share (and per capita level) of high value-added 'business services' among other services than either the developed EU or the non-Baltic NMS, as will be discussed further below.

Trade Data

In comparing Western Balkan country trade performance, differences in the size of their market should be taken into account. This is usually done by comparing trade volumes as a percentage of GDP. In this chapter, instead, trade volumes will be presented as per capita values. This gives a better control for country size in cases where population size is less volatile than GDP, as is the case in the Western Balkans over the observed period. This measure has additional advantages in that it is easier to interpret and provides a clearer comparison across countries over a period of years.

statistics. Indeed, trade in construction sector is performed not via customs, and limitations on its trade cannot be expressed in terms of tariff rates but rather in the same manner as for all the other services. Since services trade is the scope of this analysis, construction sector has been included in the analysis of the domestic services market as well.

Table 3 Trade in service, 2008–2015, constant 2010 US$

Country	Constant 2010 US$ per capita, av. 2008–2015			Annual growth, %, av. 2009–2015		Services trade, % of total trade, av. 2008–2015	
	Exports	Imports	Balance	Exports (%)	Imports (%)	Exports (%)	Imports (%)
Albania	832	673	159	2.1	−0.2	74	34
BiH	609	143	466	0.3	−2.5	34	6
Macedonia	635	463	173	5.2	4.2	31	15
Montenegro	1978	764	1215	4.5	−0.5	71	17
Serbia	623	551	73	6.1	2.5	31	19
WBC	935	519	417	3.6	0.7		
Non-Baltic NMS	1881	1301	581	2.5	1.6		
Europe	4293	3772	522	2.9	3.0		

Source: Calculated from data available in UNCTAD and World Bank WDI databases

Total services trade (exports and imports) per capita in Western Balkan countries is lower than that of the non-Baltic NMS, and much lower than European levels (Table 3), but they still achieve fairly high levels of trade in services and have positive trade balances. Particularly striking is the case of Montenegro, which exported services worth 2000 US$ per capita in 2008–2015 (of which 1300 US$ per capita was travel services) and achieved a surplus in trade in services of 1200 US $ per capita. These levels are higher than in the non-Baltic NMS, but far below developed EU countries. Other Western Balkan countries have lower levels of per capita exports of services. The highest is 830 US$ per capita in Albania, while all the other Western Balkan countries have per capita exports just above 600 US$, far less than the levels achieved by non-Baltic NMS.

The annual growth of exports of services per capita (Table 3) in Western Balkan countries has been modest, but higher than the rates of growth of GDP per capita (compare with Table 2), indicating stronger export performance. The annual growth of exports of services in Western Balkan countries has also been higher than the growth of non-Baltic NMS and developed EU countries' exports of services per capita. Similarly, imports in Western Balkans have been growing at a lower rate than in non-Baltic NMS or Europe.

The highest growth in exports of services took place in Serbia (6% in 2008–2015) and in Montenegro and Macedonia (5%). Imports of services in BiH fell by 3% per annum over the same period; imports also fell in Montenegro and Albania. This may indicate a slowing of domestic activity in the affected sectors or a substitution of imports by the domestic supply of services. Imports of services have grown fastest in Macedonia (4%) and Serbia (3%). BiH had the lowest growth of trade in services, while the highest growth was in Serbia and Macedonia.

Exports of services account for 74% of total exports in Albania and 71% in Montenegro over the period 2008–2015 compared to just 34% in BiH and 31% in Macedonia and Serbia. The high shares of services exports in total exports in Albania

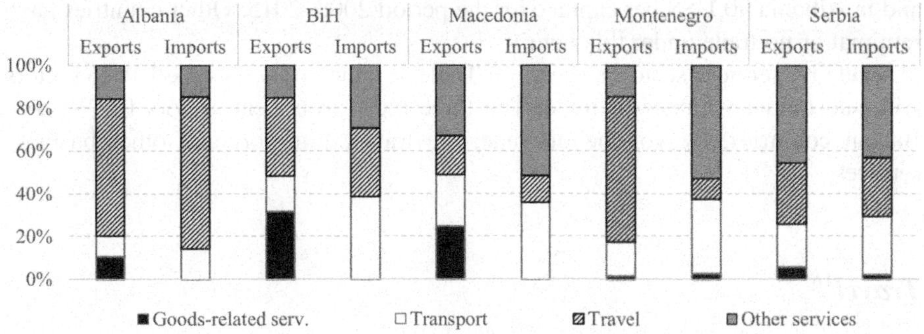

Fig. 2 Composition of exports and imports of services, average for 2008–2015 (%). Source: Calculated from data available in UNCTAD and World Bank WDI databases

and Montenegro are due to their high level of per capita exports in tourism (see Fig. 2) and low exports of goods.

Imports of services are not a large part of total imports, except in Albania, where they account for 34% of total imports, mainly due to the high imports of travel services (see Fig. 2). Albania has uncommonly high per capita import levels in tourism compared to the other Western Balkan countries, as will be shown below.

The GDP share of services in the Western Balkan countries compares well to that of the non-Baltic NMS cluster. However, this result is masked by high per capita volumes of travel services in Montenegro, which is an outlier with a high weight in the Western Balkan countries' average. Without travel services, Western Balkan countries do not compare so well against the non-Baltic NMS, as the sector analysis below will show. Also, Fig. 1 shows that only Serbia and Macedonia have substantial exports in the category 'other services',[16] which includes many high value-added services, indicating a rather low overall level of development of services trade in the other Western Balkan countries.

The trade in services data analysed here have been based on the latest International Monetary Fund's (IMF) Balance of Payments and International Investment Position Manual, 6th Edition (BPM6). According to BPM6 'goods-related services'[17] that were previously classified as trade in goods have now been reclassified as trade in services. The goods-related services category covers two items: manufacturing services on physical inputs owned by others and maintenance and repair services not included elsewhere (n.i.e.). Some of the Western Balkan countries have high levels of exports in this category, but imports are minimal or non-existent. In Macedonia exports were on average around 160 US$ per capita, in BiH 140 US$

[16]This category covers the following sectors: construction, insurance and pension services, financial services, charges for the use of intellectual property not included elsewhere (n.i.e.), telecommunications, computer and information services, other business services, personal, cultural and recreational services, government goods and services (n.i.e.) and services not allocated.

[17]Goods-related services category covers two items: manufacturing services on physical inputs owned by others and maintenance and repair services (n.i.e).

and in Albania 90 US$ per capita over the period 2008–2015. Other countries have minimal or no trade under this item.

Trade by services sector is shown in Table 4, which only lists the BPM6 sectors with substantial volumes of trade. The three most prominent sectors for Western Balkan countries, by volume of trade, are travel, transport and other business services.

Travel[18]

Of all services sectors, travel services have the largest per capita trade volumes in the Western Balkan countries. They also have the highest impact on the balance of trade in services. Montenegro achieves by far the highest results in per capita terms in travel services trade: during 2008–2015 Montenegro had by far the highest per capita travel services trade, and during 2008–2015 it exported annually US$1300 of travel services per capita. Within the non-Baltic NMS cluster, Slovenia had a similar level, while Croatia had much higher per capita level (US$2100). Since Croatia has similar natural resources attracting the tourists as Montenegro, this indicates that Montenegro could further expand its tourism trade.

All Western Balkan countries are net exporters of travel services—they receive more inbound travel than they travel abroad. Only Albania has higher per capita levels of imports of travel services, indicating that its residents travel abroad much more than other Western Balkan countries' residents. This is the single highest export figure of all Western Balkan countries and across all services sectors in Table 4. Albanian exports in the travel category are impressive (US$530 per capita), but pale in comparison to Montenegro (US$1340 per capita). Bearing in mind that Albania's natural tourist potential is comparable to that of Montenegro, this gap shows how big a potential for trade in travel services is lost in Albania due to lack of development of tourist and related infrastructure necessary to boost its travel exports.

Transport[19]

Transport services have the highest per capita levels in Montenegro, for both of exports (US$318) and imports (US$268) compared to other Western Balkan

---

[18]This category according to BPM6 classification encompasses 'goods and services for own use or to give away acquired from an economy by non-residents during visits to that economy', on the side of exports, and 'goods and services for own use or to give away acquired from other economies by residents during visits to these other economies', on the side of imports IMF (2009).

[19]BPM6 'transport' category includes 'all transport services involving the carriage of people and objects from one location to another' and related supporting and auxiliary services, as well as postal and courier services IMF (2009).

Table 4 BPM6 trade in services by sector, av. 2008–2015, constant 2010 US$ per capita

	Transport services		Travel services		Other business services		Telecomm, computer and information services		Construction		Financial services and insurance and pension	
	Exp.	Imp.	Exp.	Imp.	Exp.	Imp.	Exp.	Imp.	Exp.	Imp.	Exp.	Imp.
Western Balkan economies												
Albania	80	95	532	479	41	23	47	23	10	2	7	27
BiH	80	54	173	45	2	5	33	19	31	6	1	6
Kosovo	69	30	257	71	n.a.	n.a.	146	98	n.a.	n.a.	15	24
Macedonia	155	164	113	58	88	104	65	45	32	33	2	15
Montenegro	318	268	1339	72	84	161	77	69	81	77	14	28
Serbia	126	150	180	151	129	108	69	46	37	18	12	23
Country av.	*138*	*127*	*432*	*146*	*69*	*80*	*73*	*50*	*38*	*27*	*8*	*20*
New member states without Baltics												
Bulgaria	208	178	466	141	104	114	86	36	16	27	27	31
Croatia	301	197	2113	206	257	236	113	87	32	3	17	60
Czech R.	539	448	707	457	465	462	230	177	71	46	65	133
Hungary	479	365	568	229	425	583	177	140	41	27	28	48
Poland	290	180	276	225	249	198	75	63	42	23	25	51
Romania	190	101	71	89	148	128	101	59	23	17	17	36
Slovakia	429	382	445	402	248	266	128	104	38	65	38	110
Slovenia	890	492	1289	533	458	551	258	278	152	90	101	117
Country av.	*416*	*293*	*742*	*285*	*294*	*317*	*146*	*118*	*52*	*37*	*40*	*73*
Selected European economies												
France	724	743	812	640	1045	1016	248	245	53	47	251	167
Germany	673	823	456	1010	826	903	287	268	15	11	382	221
Greece	1694	893	1419	265	167	145	85	85	69	28	59	174
UK	555	486	588	941	1271	810	344	217	39	39	1606	296
Europe	*875*	*751*	*831*	*840*	*967*	*n.a.*	*482*	*n.a.*	*72*	*n.a.*	*605*	*n.a.*

Source: Calculated based on data from UNCTAD and World Bank WDI database

countries. These per capita levels are higher than in Bulgaria, Croatia, Poland and Romania but are lower than the non-Baltic NMS average.

Trade in transport services in Macedonia and Serbia is only half that in Montenegro. Both Serbia and Macedonia are net importers of transport services (trade balances are around −US$24 and −US$10 per capita), while Montenegro achieves around US$50 per capita surplus from trade in transport services. The trade levels of transport services for Montenegro and Serbia are around the level of Romania, the lowest positioned within the non-Baltic NMS cluster, but are significantly lower than in Bulgaria.

Other Business Services

The BPM6 category 'other business services' encompasses the following service activities: research and development, professional and management consulting and technical, trade-related and other business services (IMF 2009). These higher value-added services are necessary for the working of a successful market economy. For example, the developed European economies of the UK, France and Germany have more trade in other business services than in transport services or travel, as opposed to Greece who has high trade levels only in travel and transport.

Among the non-Baltic NMS cluster, high levels of trade are found in the Czech Republic, Hungary and Slovenia, for both exports (around US$450 per capita) and imports (around US$550). The next level is that of Croatia and Slovakia with roughly half the trade levels of Czech Republic, Hungary and Slovenia. The worst among the NMS are Romania and Bulgaria, whose average per capita trade levels are lower than those of Montenegro and Serbia, best positioned among the Western Balkan countries. Macedonia also has volumes of trade in other business services that are comparable to those of Montenegro and Serbia. Serbia has a surplus in trade in other business services of about US$20 per capita on average annually over the period, while both Macedonia and Montenegro are net importers of these services with trade deficits of around 20 US$ and 80 US$ per capita, respectively.

Of the remaining three sectors in Table 4, the sector of telecommunication, computer and information services has the highest trade levels. Here particularly striking are exports from Kosovo of 150 US$ per capita. The other sectors are not so important for total services trade in Western Balkan economies.

Looking at results from Table 4, one could roughly say that the higher the GDP of the country, the more activity can be seen in services sectors such as other business services, telecommunications, computer and information services or financial services. In this respect Serbia, Montenegro and Macedonia show progress, as all have significant volume of trade in other business services, although exceptionally Kosovo has also made progress in trade in telecommunications, computer and information services, mainly in outsourced call centres.

Conclusions

The process of services trade liberalisation in the Western Balkan countries has been driven by their need to integrate into international markets in order to develop strong market economies and achieve EU membership. A prerequisite for this is WTO membership. Albania, Macedonia and Montenegro are already WTO members, Bosnia and Herzegovina and Serbia are still negotiating their accession, and Kosovo has not yet applied for membership but is expected to do so. All countries have signed an SAA with the EU and are at various stages of their EU approximation process. Finally, all countries are members of CEFTA, a regional trade agreement that aims at further liberalisation and improvement of the business environment for trade in services.

The negotiations for the WTO accession of BiH and Serbia have reached a stalemate. The negotiating requests by some WTO members require them to liberalise more than they can. This is especially problematic bearing in mind that if they wish to become EU members, the WTO commitments that they negotiate may not be more liberal than are the WTO commitments of EU. Otherwise, if a new EU member country had WTO commitments that were more liberal, then the EU itself would have to negotiate and agree with the other WTO members' additional concessions for the resulting loss of market access. This procedure may be just too impractical and costly. In short, until the situation changes, the WTO accession of BiH and Serbia cannot go forward, and they will not be able to complete their EU accession either.

Compared to the non-Baltic NMS and Europe, the Western Balkan services sectors are smaller in size and have a more adverse composition, with traditional services sectors being dominant over sectors with a higher value added. The biggest exports of services in the region come from tourism, followed by transport, while only a few countries (Serbia, Montenegro and Macedonia) realise some trade volumes in 'other business services', one of the higher value-added services. Even if modest, the rate of growth of Western Balkan exports in services is higher than that of non-Baltic NMS, and higher than their own GDP growth, which indicates an improving export performance and allows for a process of gradual catch-up.

CEFTA has almost concluded its services negotiations and may liberalise services trade on a 'GATS plus' level in one schedule for the whole region. This would be of immense benefit for increasing the competitiveness of the services sectors in the region and improve the business climate in the region. For small and medium domestic service providers, it would be easier to export in the region, larger suppliers will reap the advantages of a larger market, and foreign suppliers would have more interest to relocate to the region. This would allow Western Balkan economies to improve the regional business climate for foreign investors in services and contribute to the development of vibrant modern economies.

References

Bjelić, P., & Dragutinović Mitrović, R. (2012). The effects of competing trade regimes on bilateral trade flows: Case of Serbia. *Proceedings of Rijeka School of Economics, 30*(2), 267–294.

Gervais, A. (2015). *The impact of policy restrictions on services trade*. mimeo, University of Notre Dame.

IMF. (2009). *Balance of payment and international investment position manual* (6th ed.). Washington DC: International Monetary Fund.

Kurtović, S., & Talović, S. (2015). Impact of trade agreements with eu on the reduction in trade balance deficit of Bosnia and Herzegovina. *Journal of International and Global Economic Studies, 8*(1).

Mojsoska-Blazevski, N., & Petreski, M. (2012). *Western Balkan's trade with the EU and CEFTA-2006: Evidence from Macedonian data* (Munich Personal RePEc Archive, MPRA Paper No. 41942).

Nordas, H. K., & Rouzet, D. (2016). The impact of services trade restrictiveness on trade flows. *The World Economy, 40*(6).

Sanfey, P., Milatović, J., & Krešić, A. (2016). How the Western Balkans can catch up (EBRD Working Paper No. 186).

Van der Marel, E., & Shepherd, B. (2013). Services trade, regulation and regional integration: evidence from sectoral data. *The World Economy, 36*(11), 1393–1405.

Higher Education and the Graduate Labour Market in the Western Balkans

Will Bartlett and Milica Uvalić

Introduction

In recent years, the Western Balkan countries have been badly affected by the spillover effects of recession in the Eurozone, and the economic recovery that is underway has been subject to a series of setbacks. Weak economic performance has been reflected in low employment rates, high levels of unemployment and the attendant risk of a depreciation of the human capital of unemployed and inactive workers. The conventional wisdom is that structural reforms are a key element of the policies that are needed to support recovery, and upgrading the labour force skills is an essential part of this process. A recent study carried out by the authors and colleagues has sought to contribute to this debate by considering the contribution of higher education systems to upgrading labour force skills, analysing the problems facing higher education graduates in accessing the labour market and the problems facing employers in dealing with skill gaps among their new graduate employees (Bartlett et al. 2016). The data used in the study were collected through two cross-country surveys carried out from March to August 2015. The first of these was targeted at recent HE graduates who had completed their studies since 2010 (4602 respondents); the second was targeted at private companies and public organisations that employ HE graduates (1074 respondents). In addition, semi-structured interviews were carried out with HEI management staff, employer associations, ministries, trade unions and EU delegations. This chapter summarises the findings of the study.

W. Bartlett (✉)
LSEE, European Institute, London School of Economics and Political Science, London, UK
e-mail: w.j.bartlett@lse.ac.uk

M. Uvalić
Department of Economics, University of Perugia, Perugia, Italy
e-mail: milica.uvalic@unipg.it

R. Osbild, W. Bartlett (eds.), *Western Balkan Economies in Transition*, Societies and Political Orders in Transition, https://doi.org/10.1007/978-3-319-93665-9_4

Table 1 HEIs in the Western Balkans, 2015

	HEIs	Public HEIs	Private HEIs	HEIs per 100,000 population
Albania	39	16	23	1.3
Bosnia and Herzegovina	47	10	37	1.2
Kosovo	41	12	29	2.2
Macedonia	16	5	11	0.8
Montenegro	12	1	11	2.1
Serbia	85	51	34	1.2
Western Balkans	240	95	145	1.3

Source: project database

The Provision of Higher Education

Over the last two decades, the number of higher education institutions (HEIs) in the Western Balkans has increased in response to growing demand for higher education, especially in the early to mid-2000s when many new graduate-level jobs were created.[1] There are now 240 active HEIs in the Western Balkans, or 1.3 HEIs per 100,000 of the population (see Table 1), delivering over 5000 study programmes—half at Bachelor level and two fifths at Master level. Almost one third of study programmes are delivered by private HEIs, which account for about three fifths of all HEIs in the region, though public HEIs remain dominant in terms of student enrolments. The Bologna reforms have succeeded in introducing the three-cycle system of study programmes in many HEIs, most commonly through 3-year study programmes at "first cycle" level (Bachelor), although many HEIs still offer 4-year study programmes. Almost half of "second cycle" study programmes (Master) are of 2-year duration, but there are also many 1-year and 1.5-year programmes. In Serbia, most HEIs have opted for the 4+1 model (GoRS 2012: 103).[2] Of 664 Bachelor level study programmes identified in the database, 37% are 3-year programmes, while of 605 Master level programmes only 8% are 2-year programmes (aligned with 3-year bachelor programmes). This variety of solutions complicates the HE system. Students who complete a 3-year Bachelor degree but wish to continue studying at a university that offers a 1-year Master degree have to pass additional exams to obtain a full set of ECTS credits.[3] The different ways of organising studies also create difficulties in obtaining reliable statistics on student enrolments and completion rates at different levels of higher education in Serbia.

[1]Higher education institutions (HEIs) include universities, faculties and a range of tertiary level colleges.

[2]After the adoption of the Law on HE in 2005, there was uncertainty about the financial resources that would be available for the new MA study programmes at public HEIs. This led many HEIs to adopt the 4+1 model to be on the safe side (Interview, public HEI).

[3]This problem is recognised in the *Strategy for the Development of Education in Serbia until 2020* (2012, p. 103): "Having various possibilities for organising studies hampers the continuation of studies at the Master's level when students move from the 3+2 model to 4+1 and vice versa".

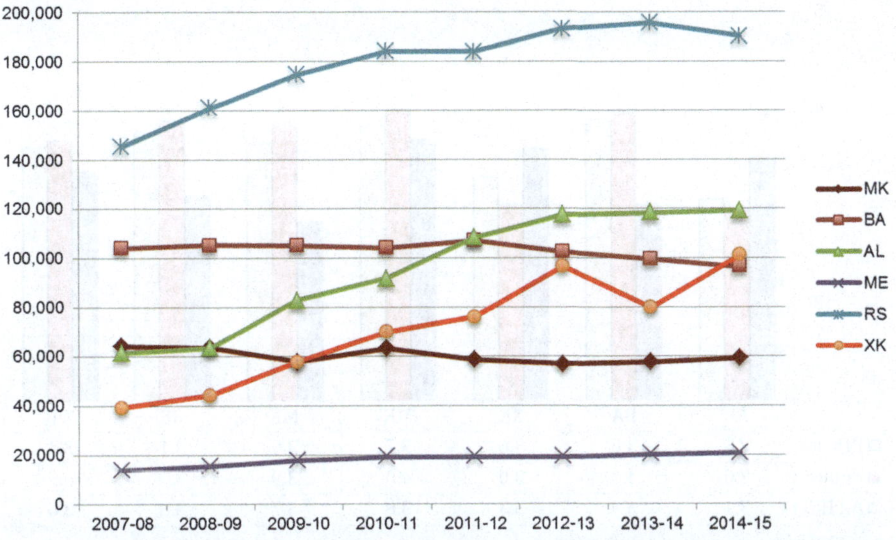

Fig. 1 Number of registered Bachelor students (first cycle), 2004–2015. Source: Country reports. Note: Note: AL = Albania, BA = Bosnia and Herzegovina, XK = Kosovo, MK = the former Yugoslav Republic of Macedonia, ME = Montenegro, RS = Serbia and WB = Western Balkans as a whole. The data show the total number of students currently registered to study at all HEIs at all years within Bachelor programmes. Data for Albania are estimates based on the share of the total number of students enrolling in Bachelor studies; data for Kosovo for 2014–2015 are estimated

Student numbers have grown rapidly over the last decade as demand for higher education has increased. By 2015, about three quarters of a million students were registered to study at HEIs in the Western Balkans at all levels of study (see Fig. 1). The increase in student numbers is now beginning to level off, except in Kosovo where growth continues.

Almost half of students in the region, on average, enrol in Humanities, Social Science, Business and Law (HSS) subjects (compared to only 43% in the EU-28), while 24% enrol in Science, Technology, Engineering and Mathematics (STEM) subjects (compared to 23% in the EU-28). In Serbia, a relatively lower proportion (40%) of students enrol in HSS study fields,[4] and a relatively higher proportion (30%) of students enrol in STEM subjects.[5] This likely reflects the relatively higher demand for graduates in engineering and science fields in Serbia than in other Western Balkan countries. In the Western Balkans as a whole, most students enrol in public HEIs, but about one fifth of students enrol in private HEIs, not much different to the situation in the EU. In the 2013–2014 academic year, about 220,000 students were newly enrolled, while fewer than 116,000 students completed their

[4]Within this total, 83% of students completed HSS study fields at private HEIs, compared to 36% at public HEIs.

[5]Within this total, 6% of students completed STEM study fields at private HEIs, compared to 33% at public HEIs.

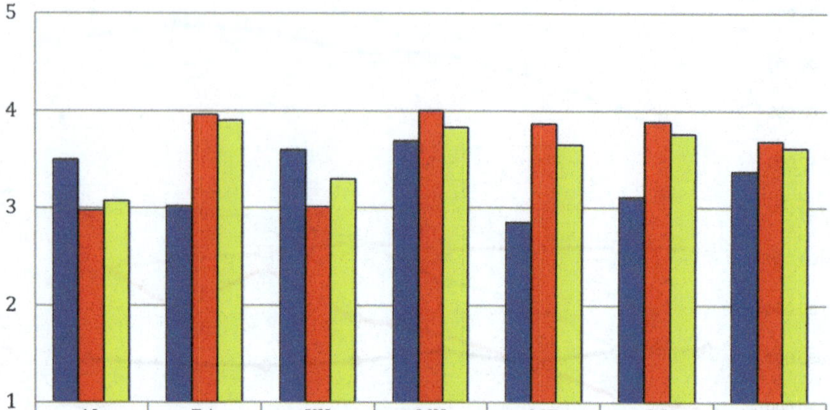

	AL	BA	XK	MK	ME	RS	WB
Private	3.5	3.0	3.6	3.7	2.9	3.1	3.4
Public	3.0	4.0	3.0	4.0	3.9	3.9	3.7
All HEI	3.1	3.9	3.3	3.8	3.7	3.8	3.6

Fig. 2 Whether improvements in teaching methods are needed to improve job prospects, by ownership of HEIs. Source: Graduate survey. Note: AL = Albania, BA = Bosnia and Herzegovina, XK = Kosovo, MK = The former Yugoslav Republic of Macedonia, ME = Montenegro, RS = Serbia. The question is scored on a scale 1 = "no improvement needed" to 5 = "very much improvement needed". Differences between public and private HEIs are statistically significant at 1% level, $N = 3758$

study programmes, giving an overall "completion ratio" of only 53% across the region, similar to the lowest completion rates in the European Higher Education Area (found in Italy and Hungary).

It has been widely observed that HEIs in post-socialist countries typically fail to respond sufficiently to labour market changes through curricula reform or the adoption of new teaching methods. Many HEIs practice traditional modes of teaching and use out-dated curricula, and those who try to introduce change are often perceived as a threat to established structures. Due to poor teaching methods, many HE graduates lack skills that are relevant to the needs of the labour market (Sondergaard and Murthi 2012).

The graduate survey shows that graduates in the Western Balkans are only moderately satisfied with the quality of higher education they receive. Those lucky enough to be taught in small classes and to have access to an internship or work experience during studies report significantly higher levels of satisfaction with the quality of their higher education. Many graduates consider that their job prospects would have been improved by better teaching methods, by a more relevant curriculum and by having better qualified professors. They also consider that HEIs make too little use of analytical and problem-solving teaching methods.

Graduates hold a strong view that teaching methods should be improved and that this would improve their job prospects (see Fig. 2). In Albania and Kosovo, the greatest improvement is considered necessary at private HEIs. In recognition of their

Table 2 Unemployment and employment rates of HE graduates and whole labour force, 2015 (%)

	Unemployment rate, total (a)	Unemployment rate of all HE graduates (a)	Unemployment rate of recent HE graduates (b)
Albania	17.5	17.2	27.7
Bosnia	27.7	18.4	40.1
Kosovo	35.3	14.7	50.7
Macedonia	26.1	21.4	37.2
Montenegro	17.6	10.3	25.9
Serbia	19.4	15.0	42.4
Western Balkans	23.9	16.2	37.1
EU-28	9.4	5.6	n/a

Source: (a) Labour Force Surveys from National Statistical Offices and Eurostat, (b) data from graduate survey, calculated by the authors. Note: data for Western Balkan countries are for the 15+ age group, and for EU-28 are for the 15–74 age group (Eurostat variable code lfsa_urgaed)

failings, the Albanian government has recently closed down many poorly performing private HEIs, and similar measures may be needed in Kosovo too. Elsewhere in the region, graduates consider that the greatest need for improved teaching methods is in public HEIs.

In the employer survey, respondents were asked their opinions about the most useful modes of teaching and learning. In their opinion, the most useful teaching methods are internship and work placement, which scored 4.5 on a scale from 1 = "not at all important" to 5 = "very important", followed by problem-solving and creative thinking teaching methods (scoring 4.4). Classes in small groups (3.9) are thought by employers to be more useful than lectures in large groups (2.7). Rote learning of facts is considered by employers to be of little value (2.0) in imparting the skills needed by business.

Transition from Higher Education to the Labour Market

The countries in the Western Balkan region have among the highest unemployment rates in Europe (see Table 2). Having a higher education provides some protection against unemployment: the average graduate unemployment rate in the Western Balkans was 16.2%, almost eight percentage points below the general unemployment rate. However, the graduate survey shows that the unemployment rate among *recent* graduates was 37.1% for the region as a whole, ranging from as high as 50.7% in Kosovo to a low but still alarming unemployment rate of 25.9% in Montenegro. This indicates the extremely difficult prospects facing new HE graduates in labour markets in the region.

HE graduates in the Western Balkans face a precarious transition to stable employment. The graduate survey shows that currently employed graduates take 9 months to find their first job. On average, they have held two different jobs since leaving their HEI, and 57% have experienced at least one period of unemployment since entering the labour market. Currently unemployed graduates have a worse experience, having on average been unemployed for 1 year and 4 months, while one half has held at least one job; on average they took 7 months to find their first job. These data reveal that the transition from HEI to the labour market is far from being a smooth process for many graduates.

A major barrier facing students in their transition from higher education to the labour market is their lack of work experience. In a competitive market, employers often prefer graduates with work experience, which handicaps graduates who have not had any work experience during their studies. More than half of employers believe that previous work experience is important to them in graduate recruitment decisions. The graduate survey shows that graduates with work experience are more likely to find a job, and one well matched to their level of qualification, than graduates without any work experience. Various initiatives in the region to introduce internships during studies have often failed due to a lack of willingness by private employers to offer internships to final year students.

In searching for a job when they exit the HE system, graduates receive relatively little support from formal career guidance institutions either within or outside their HEI. Consequently graduates are more reliant on their friends or family to assist in their job search, a factor that hinders a level playing field in the job market and promotes clientelism and nepotism in graduate recruitment. The graduate survey shows that, throughout the Western Balkans, the family is the main source of assistance in finding a job, closely followed by friends (see Fig. 3). This highlights the importance of personal connections, and to a certain extent, nepotism, in the job

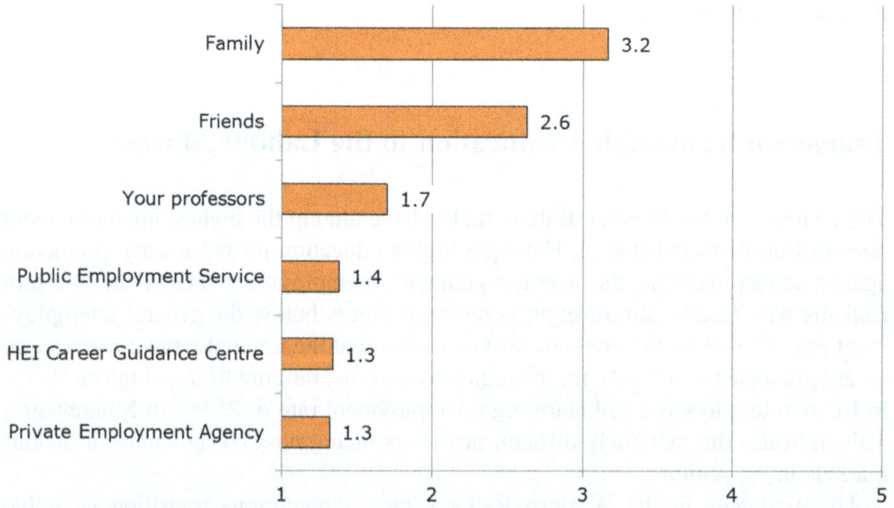

Fig. 3 Help received in finding a job from various sources. Source: Graduate survey. Note answers are scored on a scale of 1–5 where 1 = "no help at all" to 5 = "very much help"

search process. In contrast, assistance from graduates' professors or careers services at HEIs or from public or private employment agencies is extremely low.

Some HEIs in the Western Balkans have a career centre that aims to provide information to students and graduates about suitable careers and internships. Some career centres provide training in writing a CV, organise trial interviews with companies and organise career days and job fairs. However, most HEIs fail to monitor the effectiveness of their career centres or identify which of their activities are most effective in helping graduates find a job. This suggests that the activities of career centres should be upgraded and monitored so that HEIs can become more aware of their successes and failures in order to better assist their students find a job upon graduation.

Graduates' transition to the labour market is hindered by a low level of cooperation between HEIs and employers in relation to curriculum design and recruitment. Few employers discuss curricula with HEIs on a regular basis. Yet, most employers say that such cooperation would improve the matching of graduates to the job. This suggests that there is a role for public policy to provide incentives and support for improved HEI-business cooperation over recruitment since this could provide gains to both parties that they are unwilling or unable to achieve by themselves.

Graduate Skill Gaps

About one third of employers are dissatisfied with the skills of their new graduate recruits, although employers in high technology industries and employers that cooperate relatively more with HEIs tend to be more satisfied with the skills of graduates than others. Most employers perceive graduates' interactive skills, such as decision-making skills, analytical skills, team working skills and planning and organisational skills to be relatively weak, and graduate skill gaps are correspondingly high in these areas. Such skills are often neglected in HE systems where traditional teaching methods emphasise rote learning rather than student-centred approaches. The employer survey shows that employers think that HEIs could better support the development of interactive skills among graduates by modernising their teaching methods, using small interactive class groups rather than large anonymous lecture rooms for more of the teaching than is currently practiced and adopting practical problem-solving approaches rather than purely theoretical learning. In addition, all types of skill gaps are expected to increase in the future, as technological development is likely to outstrip the ability of HE systems as currently configured to adapt to changing labour market needs.

The limited possibilities that students have to engage in internships or relevant work experience during their studies also create obstacles to graduate employment. Employers frequently complain about the skills of HE graduates, emphasising their lack of work experience, practical knowledge and even lack of motivation to find a job in certain cases. The employer survey shows that 52% of employers in the Western Balkans attach "a lot" or "very much" importance to having previous work experience when making a decision to recruit a new graduate. Having some work experience is therefore important for HE graduates' labour market outcomes. This view is supported by the findings from the graduate survey, which shows that 55% of respondents who had at least some work experience held a job, compared to 46% of those who had had no work experience ($p < 0.01$).[6] Work experience also supports matching to the job by level of qualification: while 52% of those who have at least some work experience (or internship) hold a job that is well matched to their level of qualification, only 40% of those with no work experience hold a job that is well matched in this sense ($p < 0.01$).

The employer survey asked about the importance of different types of skills for business activity and the skills that graduates actually have. The difference between the importance of the *desired* skills and graduates' *actual* skills provides a measure of the current skill gap among graduate employees. Skill gaps in the Western Balkans are found in all dimensions of skills.[7] We distinguish between "cognitive" and "interactive" skills. Cognitive skills include numeracy, literacy, foreign language skills, computer skills and sector-specific skills (e.g. engineering skills); interactive skills include communication skills, analytical and problem-solving skills, ability to adapt to and act in new situations, decision-making skills, team working skills and planning and organisational skills.

Figure 4 reveals relatively high skill gaps in interactive skills such as planning and organisational skills, decision-making skills, analytical and problem-solving skills and adaptability. All types of skill gaps are expected to increase in the future (i.e. over the 3 years following the survey, up to 2018). The greatest expected increase in skill gaps is in foreign language and decision-making skills. All this points to deficiencies in the quality of HE systems, especially in relation to teaching interactive skills.

The general pattern is that (i) current interactive skill gaps are greater than current cognitive skill gaps, (ii) future expected skill gaps of all types are greater than current skill gaps (i.e. the problem is expected to become greater over time) and (iii) future interactive skill gaps are expected to be greater than future cognitive skill gaps. Graduates' skill gaps of all types seem to be large and growing in relation to employer needs. The problem is more serious in relation to interactive skill gaps than cognitive skill gaps, reflecting the emphasis among HEIs on imparting theoretical knowledge, rather than the practical knowledge that might better assist the graduates in their future careers. The policy implication is that HEIs should restructure their learning pathways so that a larger proportion of student time is spent on developing their interactive skills. This needs to be built into the curricula in cooperation with employers so that HEIs provide a new mix of skills, more

[6]The terminology "$p < 0.01$" indicates that the probability that the differences in proportions observed in the sample do *not* represent true differences in the underlying population is less than 1%.

[7]We refer to a distinction between "cognitive" and "interactive" skills, rather than the commonly used terms "hard" and "soft" skills as more accurate descriptors of the different classes of skills involved. This terminology is proposed in Green (2013: 23–24).

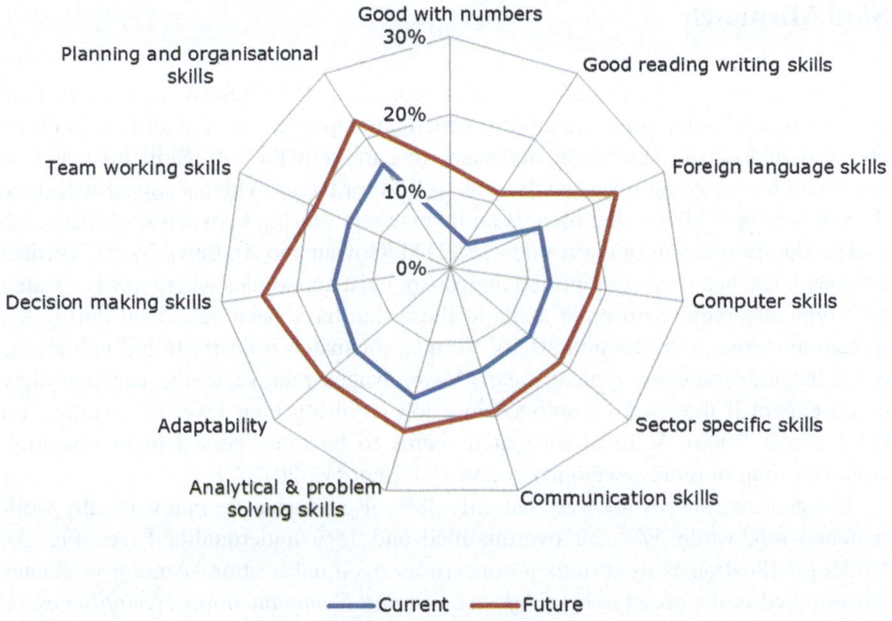

Fig. 4 Graduate skill gaps in the Western Balkans (%). Source: Employer survey. Note: data represent difference between answers on a 1–5 scale to a question about whether graduates have the skills required and a question about the skills employers need. Differences are scaled to a percentage gap

appropriate to the changing labour markets. This should not imply a reduction in HE quality, rather a greater appreciation of the role of interactive skills as a key feature of modern graduate jobs.

These findings reflect research carried out elsewhere in Europe, where interactive skills are becoming increasingly important for graduate employability. Such skills can rarely be compensated by high grades or by a relevant study field, since such achievements may be outweighed by the negative effect of poor interpersonal skills on work teams and organisational goals (Humburg et al. 2013). A number of "employability" initiatives have been developed in EU countries to address this issue and improve the provision of interactive skills of graduates. The most common initiatives include codesign of curricula between HEIs and employers, project-based learning, sandwich courses[8] and placement periods as well as exchange of staff between academia and business.

[8]A "sandwich course" is an undergraduate programme during which spells of work experience outside the HEI in a company are a mandatory part of the curriculum. Such work experience can be for an entire academic year, for example, as the third year of a 4-year Bachelor programme or for shorter spells depending on the course content and objectives.

Skill Mismatch

Skill mismatch[9] is widespread in market economies (McGuiness 2006). "Vertical skill mismatch" refers to a situation in which an employee has a qualification either above or below the skill level necessary to carry out the job. Skill mismatch is important for the economy as a whole as well as for the individuals concerned, since there is strong evidence that there is an inverse relationship between skill mismatch and productivity levels at the country level (McGowan and Andrews 2015). Vertical mismatch has been widely reported in post-socialist economies where newly created jobs typically require different skills to those that have been destroyed during the transition (Lamo and Messina 2010). Vertical mismatch is costly to individuals, as overeducated graduates typically earn lower wages relative to the earnings they could expect if they were employed in a job requiring their level of qualification (McGuiness 2006). Vertical mismatch seems to be more persistent in transition countries than in more developed countries (Kiersztyn 2013).

The graduate survey showed that only 48% of graduates are in a vertically well-matched job, while 37% are overqualified and 15% underqualified (see Fig. 5). Underqualification is as serious a concern as overqualification. Among graduates who studied in the broad field of *Information and Communication Technologies*, as many as 30% are underqualified in relation to the skills needed by their job. This is a worrying finding, suggesting that HE systems fail to impart the skills needed in a key field contributing to high value-added employment.

Having a well-matched job has implications for earnings. The graduate survey shows that graduates who are well matched have higher initial earnings than those who are mismatched, with median monthly earnings of €300, compared to €250 for overqualified graduates and €240 for underqualified graduates. The differences persist, but narrow somewhat as graduates sort themselves into better-matched subsequent jobs: for the current job, well-matched graduates have median monthly earnings of €400, compared to €370 for overqualified graduates and €350 for underqualified graduates.[10] The differences in earnings may be a measure of the productivity gap between well-matched and poorly matched graduates, and therefore of the potential gain from ensuring that the matching process works more efficiently for HE graduates. In addition, graduates whose first job is not well matched are more likely to become unemployed or to drop out of the labour market than others.

Several factors affect the likelihood of a graduate achieving a good match on the labour market. Having above-average performance at HEI, studying in small class

[9]It should be noted that much of the discussion of skill mismatch is really framed within the context of "qualification mismatch". However, the term "skill mismatch" is commonly used throughout the literature, where "qualifications" is taken as a proxy for "skills". The OECD has recently begun to carry out skill surveys that get around this problem. In our graduate survey, for vertical mismatch we ask whether the qualifications of the graduate match the skills needed by the job, in order to pin down the "skill" aspect of the issue.

[10]Other studies of skill mismatch in transition countries also find a wage penalty associated with overqualification; see, e.g. Lamo and Messina (2010).

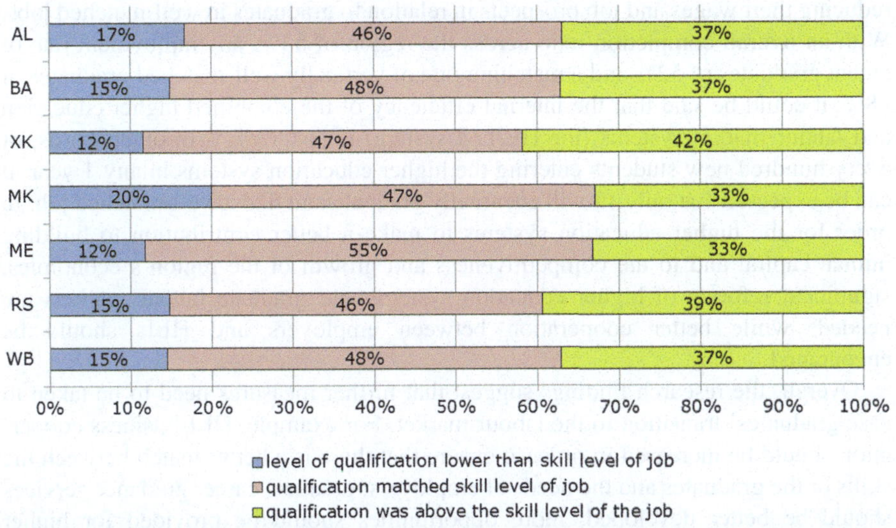

Fig. 5 Vertical matching: whether qualification level matched the requirements of the job (%). Source: Graduate survey. Note: AL = Albania, BA = Bosnia and Herzegovina, XK = Kosovo, MK = the former Yugoslav Republic of Macedonia, ME = Montenegro, RS = Serbia and WB = Western Balkans as a whole

groups, being exposed to teaching methods that use problem-solving and creative thinking methods, having an internship or work experience during studies and receiving support from professors or from the public employment service all increase the likelihood of finding a well-matched job. A major cause of mismatch is the overall lack of jobs, which provides an incentive for graduates to take up any job that is available. Yet simply increasing the number of jobs without tackling the underlying causes of mismatch, improving skill attainment and raising the quality of HE provision is unlikely to secure a more effective utilisation of the available human capital.

Conclusions: Reforms of HE Systems Are Badly Needed

The findings of the research cast a worrying perspective on the ability of higher education systems in the Western Balkans to deliver the qualified personnel that are needed to support future economic growth. The higher education systems produce too many graduates relative to the needs of the labour market, leading to high graduate unemployment rates throughout the region. There is an oversupply of graduates from most study fields but especially from *Business, Administration and Law*. Many students drop out of studies leading to a low completion rate; of those students who do graduate, many face the prospect of unemployment; of those who do find a job, many are in jobs that are not matched to their level of qualification, reducing their wages and job prospects in relation to graduates in well-matched jobs. With an overall completion ratio across the region of 53%, an employment rate of recent graduates of 52% and a matching rate of vertically well-matched graduates of 48%, it could be said that the internal efficiency of the combined higher education and labour market systems (the HE-LM system) is just 13%.[11] In other words, of every hundred new students entering the higher education systems in any 1 year, it can be expected that only 13 will eventually graduate and find a well-matched job. In order for the higher education systems to make a better contribution to building human capital and to the competitiveness and growth of the region's economies, significant reforms of higher education systems and graduate labour markets are needed, while better cooperation between employers and HEIs should be encouraged.

Overall, the research findings suggest that further measures need to be taken to ease graduates' transition to the labour market. For example, HEI-business cooperation should be increased in order to ensure that there is a better match between the skills of the graduates and the needs of employers; graduate career guidance services should be better developed; more opportunities should be provided for higher education students to gain work experience before entering the labour market after graduation; teaching methods within higher education systems should be modernised to provide graduates with more interactive skills; and on-the-job post-graduate training opportunities should be made more widely available in coordination with employers' training policies.

Acknowledgement The research on which this chapter is based was carried out within a project on "Higher Education provision and Labour Market Opportunities in the Western Balkans" funded under the Framework Service Contract No EAC/02/2010 of the European Commission DG Education and Culture. We are grateful to the European Commission for funding this research. However, the chapter reflects the views of only the authors, and any errors or omissions are entirely our own responsibility. An earlier version of this chapter was published in Quarterly Monitor, a publication of the FREN research unit at the Faculty of Economics in Belgrade, Serbia.

References

Bartlett, W., Uvalić, M., Durazzi, N., Monastiriotis, V., & Sene, T. (2016). *From university to employment: higher education provision and labour market needs in the Western Balkans synthesis report*. Brussels: European Commission, Directorate General for Education and Culture https://ec.europa.eu/education/sites/education/files/2016-higher-education-labour-market-balkans_en.pdf

GoRS. (2012). *Strategy for the development of education in Serbia until 2020*. Belgrade: Government of the Republic of Serbia.

Green, F. (2013). *Skills and skilled work: An economic and social analysis*. Oxford: Oxford University Press.

[11]The efficiency of the HE-LM system can be assessed as the product of these three proportions: $0.53 \times 0.52 \times 0.48 = 0.13$.

Humburg, M., van der Velden, R., & Verhagen, A. (2013). *The employability of higher education graduates: The employers' perspective: Final report.* Brussels: European Commission.

Kiersztyn, A. (2013). Stuck in a mismatch? The persistence of overeducation during twenty years of post-communist transition in Poland. *Economics of Education Review, 32*, 78–91.

Lamo, A., & Messina, J. (2010). Formal education, mismatch and wages after transition: Assessing the impact of unobserved heterogeneity using matching estimators. *Economics of Education Review, 29*, 1086–1099.

McGowan, M. A., & Andrews, D. (2015). *Labour market mismatch and labour productivity* (OECD Economics Department Working Papers No. 1209). Paris: OECD Publishing.

McGuiness, S. (2006). Overeducation in the labour market. *Journal of Economic Surveys, 20*(3), 387–418.

Sondergaard, L., & Murthi, M. (2012). *Skills not just diplomas: Managing education for results in Eastern Europe and Central Asia.* Washington: The World Bank.

The Labour Market, Social Inequality and the Role of Emigration: The Case of the Western Balkan Economies

Mehmed Ganić

Introduction

The last two decades have been very turbulent in the Western Balkan region. Since the beginning of the economic and political transformation in the early 1990s, the problem of growing social and economic inequalities has been a major concern for the governments of transition economies. In a strict sense, given the complexity and nature of the transition process, it is evident that certain primary factors of the transition were not taken seriously in the early stages of this process. The history of the transition process in the Western Balkans involved a long period of political and economic crisis in the 1990s, followed by wars and armed conflicts which caused needless human suffering and economic losses (Bartlett 2008). Today, Croatia has already become an EU member, Montenegro and Serbia have opened a few chapters in EU membership negotiations, and Albania and Macedonia have been granted EU candidate status, while Bosnia and Herzegovina and Kosovo are recognised as potential candidates.

Many interrelated issues that have affected the region during the last two decades have been domestically generated. The problems of macroeconomic instability, poor economic management and political constraints during the transition towards a market economy should also be noted. While mostly being ignored by many governments of the region, these issues mean that most countries are still at a lower level of economic development than in the pre-transition period.

At the macroeconomic level, the post-war period has been characterised by key transition problems such as internal and external imbalances and high levels of unemployment and poverty. The Western Balkan countries have largely completed

M. Ganić (✉)
Faculty of Business Administration, International University of Sarajevo, Ilidža, Bosnia and Herzegovina
e-mail: mganic@ius.edu.ba

R. Osbild, W. Bartlett (eds.), *Western Balkan Economies in Transition*, Societies and Political Orders in Transition, https://doi.org/10.1007/978-3-319-93665-9_5

the privatisation of state-owned enterprises in the financial sector. However, they are lagging behind advanced transition countries regarding public sector management reform (the restructuring and privatisation of public enterprises, the reform of public services and public administration) and judicial reform. This chapter makes a comparative analysis of five countries of the Western Balkans (Albania, Bosnia and Herzegovina, Macedonia, Montenegro and Serbia). First of all, the economic outlook is analysed based on several indicators including real GDP growth rates, the level of GDP per capita, the long-term unemployment rate, income inequality and migration trends.

Transition as a Necessity

Of all the communist countries, former Yugoslavia had the fastest growing in the Eastern Europe. It was expected that its path of economic reform and the transition to a market economy would progress more rapidly than it did. More importantly, its private sector generated 25% of GDP, and Yugoslavia's living standard was high in comparison to other Eastern Bloc countries. Also, it was expected that Yugoslavia would become the first member of the European Union, of all Eastern Europe communist countries, given that it had open borders that enabled its citizens to travel freely abroad and to become acquainted with practices in Western countries. Unfortunately, conflict, violence and war destroyed the country's economy, thus leaving the Yugoslav successor states behind in comparison to almost all other communist countries in the transition process (Ganić et al. 2014).

In the early stages of the transition, the institutions and mechanisms for the regulation of regional development in the newly established countries of the region were dismantled. Many companies were unable to survive due to the altered conditions caused by global economic changes, as well as their weak competitive positions. The export activities were characterised by exports of raw materials and semi-finished goods. Over the transition period, a number of complex economic policy measures were adopted such as the liberalisation of prices and trade, financial stabilisation, establishment of currency convertibility, enterprise restructuring and the development of an institutional and legal framework for a market economy. Taking 1989 as the base year, the economic development of the Western Balkan countries has been very limited compared to the more developed European countries—most specifically the EU member states. Even after more than two decades of transition, only Albania (2000), Croatia (2005) and Macedonia (2008) reached their pre-transition level of GDP of 1989 (Ganić et al. 2014).

A comparative overview of the basic indicators of the Western Balkan countries reveals the intensity of the transition at different transition stages, with many economic similarities. In recent years, upward movements in the leading economic indicators have confirmed that the region has experienced favourable trends. Table 1 compares real GDP growth rates of five Western Balkan countries with the EU28 between 2000 and 2016. The first column shows that the annual GDP growth rates of

Table 1 Real GDP growth rates, 2000–2016

	Average	Maximum	Minimum
Albania	4.4	7.9	0.5
Bosnia and Herzegovina	3.0	6.3	−2.7
Macedonia	2.9	6.5	−3.1
Montenegro	3.2	10.7	−5.7
Serbia	3.4	9.0	−3.1
Average (five Western Balkan countries)	3.4	7.0	−1.7
European Union (28 countries)	1.4	3.9	−4.4

Source: author's elaboration of data from World Bank World Development Indicators (2016)

the individual Western Balkan countries exceeded the average annual GDP rate of the EU28. All the Western Balkan countries (with the exception of Macedonia and Montenegro) grew at over 5% between 2000 and 2007 before the region was hit by the recession. The GDP growth rate was positive in all five countries until 2009 when the effects of the global financial crisis were felt. Since then, the economies of the region have been faced with a slowdown in their rates of growth (with the exception of Albania). The GDP growth rate of the Western Balkan region has been well below the growth rates necessary for significant economic progress. The economies of the region were stabilised in 2013, followed by a recovery leading to real growth.

Real GDP growth rates in Albania averaged 4.4% from 2000 to 2016, reaching a maximum in 2001 (7.9%) and a minimum in 2013 (0.5%). Between 2000 and 2016, the economies of Albania and Serbia grew at annual 4.4% and 3.4%, respectively. Out of these five Western Balkan countries, Albania and Serbia achieved higher GDP growth rates than Bosnia and Herzegovina, Macedonia and Montenegro (see Table 1). The average real GDP of the five Western Balkan countries increased by around 3.4% from 2000 to 2016, faster than the EU28 average (1.4%). Overall, the growth rates Western Balkan region were more than double that of the EU28; but the low base for this growth should be kept in mind.

Despite this success, the economic performance of the Western Balkan countries has been weaker than three neighbouring transition economies of the EU (the "EU3" countries), while the gap with these economies increased over the period from 2002 to 2016 measured by GDP per capita (constant 2010 US$). In relation to the size of their economies, the Western Balkan countries have a different position, and progress varies substantially from country to country (see Table 2).[1]

The differences in the rate of growth of individual countries of the Western Balkans can be also explained by political and administrative constraints including incomplete political democracy, weak institutional capacity to formulate and

[1]Benchmark indicator EU3 measures the gap between selected Western Balkan countries and average of EU3 countries (Bulgaria, Romania and Croatia). This average is equal to the index of 100, and the value of selected Western Balkans represents a share in that value. Index 100 represents the "moving average", for the EU 3 average, which is calculated separately for each year.

Table 2 GDP per capita 2002–2016

	2002	2006	2007	2008	2009	2010	2011	2012	2013	2014	2015	2016
Bulgaria	63.8	67.1	68.12	68.9	70.7	71.7	71.8	72.55	72.7	73.0	73.6	73.5
Romania	77.7	81.6	82.8	86.7	86.6	86.9	86.1	87.45	89.9	91.7	92.5	93.4
Croatia	158.5	151.3	149.0	144.4	142.7	141.4	142.1	140.0	137.4	135.3	133.9	133.1
Average EU3	**100**	**100**	**100**	**100**	**100**	**100**	**100**	**100**	**100**	**100**	**100**	**100**
Albania	35.5	35.9	35.8	36.9	40.9	42.8	43.0	43.9	43.9	44.2	43.9	43.6
Bosnia and Herzegovina	45.5	45.7	45.3	45.5	47.3	48.3	48.0	48.3	49.5	49.8	50.0	49.1
Macedonia	27.1	36.6	41.5	46.8	47.3	47.6	51.7	48.2	52.9	54.7	46.7	48.5
Montenegro	67.8	64.7	66.9	67.8	71.1	69.9	70.4	68.8	70.3	70.5	70.4	69.1
Serbia	53.1	53.8	53.5	52.7	55.8	56.7	56.5	56.5	57.6	55.9	54.7	51.7

Source: author's elaboration from World Bank World Development Indicators (2016)

implement the economic reform programmes and constraints on implementing structural reforms. Furthermore, the convergence of per capita incomes across of the Western Balkans has been disappointing. In particular, the new EU member states (EU3) have grown much faster than Western Balkans. Interestingly, none of the Western Balkan countries did GDP per capita approach 70% of EU average with the exception of Montenegro. Table 2 shows a disparity between the Western Balkan countries and the EU3. Among all the Western Balkan countries, Montenegro has the highest relative GDP per capita at 69% of the EU3 average, followed by Serbia (51.7%), Bosnia and Herzegovina (49.1%), Albania (43.6%) and Macedonia (48.5%).

Unemployment: A Problem that Must Be Managed

Businesses in the Western Balkans operate in difficult economic conditions with relatively poor economic management, resulting in a high rate of unemployment in these countries. The problem of high unemployment is further aggravated by the high share of structural and long-term unemployment in total unemployment. Active labour market policies (ALMPs) are often considered the most effective response to structural unemployment, but in the Western Balkans, they are underdeveloped and inefficient and only include a relatively small number of the unemployed. Unemployment has been one of the major economic and social problems for more than two decades throughout the region. Youth unemployment and the high share of long-term unemployed have reached historically high levels. In addition, the mismatch of demand and supply of labour and qualification mismatch has increased during the transition period, creating barriers to the inward flow of foreign direct investment (FDI) and to the development of new industries. The education system in public universities is of poor quality, and many study programmes are out of date, while public expenditure on education is significantly below the EU average. The share of long-term unemployed is above 50% in Albania (50.5%) and Montenegro (50.4%) (see Table 3).

The continuing high levels of unemployment are a key problem for all Western Balkan countries and express deep concerned people in the region. After the break-up of the former Yugoslavia and the unsuccessful privatisation process in almost all countries in the region, there has been an enormous increase in unemployment. After the last economic crisis in 2008, the percentage of unemployed in the region has been increased significantly. Generally speaking, unemployment in the Western Balkans has three extremely unfavourable characteristics. Firstly, it is among the highest in Europe; secondly, long-term unemployment rate in percentage of the active labour force by countries has grown at very rapid rate over 20% in some countries (Bosnia and Herzegovina and Macedonia); and thirdly, youth unemployment rate is also a record high.

In comparison, the unemployment rate measured by long-term unemployment in percentage of the active labour force is much higher in the Western Balkan countries

Table 3 Long-term unemployment rates 2007–2015 (% of active labour force)

	Nominal indicators							Benchmark (EU3)						
Indicator/year	2007	2010	2011	2012	2013	2014	2015	2007	2010	2011	2012	2013	2014	2015
EU3														
Bulgaria	4.0	4.7	6.3	6.8	7.4	6.9	5.6	110.0	97.2	93.1	98.0	97.3	95.7	111.9
Romania	3.2	2.4	2.9	3.0	3.2	2.8	3.0	137.5	190.3	202.3	222.2	225.0	235.7	208.9
Croatia	**6.0**	6.6	8.4	10.2	11.0	10.1	10.2	73.3	69.2	69.8	65.4	65.5	65.3	61.4
Average EU3	100.0	100.0	100.0	100.0	100.0	100.0	100.0	100.0	100.0	100.0	100.0	100.0	100.0	100.0
Bosnia and Herzegovina	25.1	22.3	22.3	23.1	22.9	23.4	22.8	17.5	20.5	26.3	28.9	31.4	28.2	27.5
Albania	9.4	15.5	10.2	11.5	11.5	11.2	11.3	46.8	29.5	57.5	58.0	62.6	58.9	55.5
Macedonia	28.7	26.7	25.5	25.5	23.9	23.4	21.3	15.3	17.1	23.0	26.1	30.1	28.2	29.4
Serbia	14.6	13.3	16.9	18.7	16.8	12.8	11.3	30.1	34.3	34.7	35.7	42.9	51.6	55.5
Montenegro	14.2	15.7	15.6	15.6	16.0	14.0	13.6	31.0	29.1	37.6	42.7	45.0	47.1	46.1

Source: author's elaboration on LFS (EUROSTAT)

Note: Long-term unemployment refers to the number of people who are out of work and have been actively seeking employment for at least a year

than in Romania (3%), Bulgaria (5.6%) and Croatia (10.2%). The highest long-term unemployment in percentage of the active labour force was recorded in Bosnia and Herzegovina (22.8% in 2015) and Macedonia (21.3% in 2015) followed Montenegro (13.6% in 2015) and Serbia and Albania (11.3% in 2015).

The negative repercussions of high youth unemployment cannot be understated. Perhaps the biggest mistake of the economic model of the Western Balkans is a chronic problem of underutilisation of human resources and the underutilisation of training capacity. Unemployment in the Western Balkans is quite different from the modern unemployment in industrialised countries and in developed countries.

There is a noticeable gap in long-term unemployment rates between EU3 and Western Balkan countries, although this gap has narrowed significantly over the last decade. Some countries of the Western Balkans have the highest long-term unemployment rates in Europe (Bosnia and Herzegovina and Macedonia), significantly higher than the EU3 average. Despite the recent positive economic outlook in the region, long-term unemployment rates remain high. Long-term unemployment rates in the Western Balkan region averaged 16% of active labour force in 2015, in the range from 11.3% in Albania and Serbia to 22.8% in Bosnia and Herzegovina Bosnia and Herzegovina.

The long-term unemployment rate in Bosnia and Herzegovina was 27.5% followed by Macedonia with 29.4%. Between 2007 and 2015, the most substantial progress in terms of decreasing the long-term unemployment rates were made by Macedonia and Serbia by 7.4 percentage points and 3.3 and percentage points, respectively.

Income Inequality in Western Balkan Countries

Poverty in the Western Balkans is largely caused by the non-participation of individuals in the formal labour market and low overall labour mobility. The IMF notes that the biggest problem of the economic model applied in Western Balkan countries is the underutilisation of human resources and high unemployment. Furthermore, the unemployment rate in the region is at least 10% higher than in the other new member states of the European Union, and this is a key reason for their economic backwardness (IMF 2015). Moreover, the high unemployment rate and the high level of income inequality undermine social cohesion. Measured by the national absolute poverty line, poverty in the Western Balkans is relatively high.[2]

Furthermore, according to this defined poverty line (which is specific to each country), between 8 and 25% of the population in the Western Balkans are living in poverty.

[2]This poverty line is determined by estimates of household consumption at which families, after paying basic non-food costs, maintain minimum nutritional requirements. Minimal nutritional needs are determined in accordance with the nutritional requirements of FAO and follow the consumption patterns of the national population.

Table 4 Income inequality by Western Balkan countries (2010–2015)

	Gini coefficient (average)		Quintile ratio (average)
	2000–2010	2010–2015	2010–2015
Albania	33.0	29.0	4.3
Bosnia and Herzegovina	36.3	33.8	5.7
Macedonia	44.8	44.1	9.3
Montenegro	36.9	31.9	4.8
Serbia	28.2	29.1	4.4
EU28*		30.7	5.05

Source: UNDP Human Development Report (2016); data for EU28 from Eurostat (2016)

Macedonia is the only country in the region that does not measure poverty according to an absolute poverty line. There are about four million poor people in the Western Balkans, or over 17% of the total population, making the Western Balkans one of the poorest regions in Europe. The largest numbers of poor people currently live in Bosnia and Herzegovina, Serbia, Albania and Kosovo. In each of these countries, between 800,000 and 1,000,000 people cannot meet the minimum national standards of basic food and non-food needs (Papić et al. 2012, p. 21).

Table 4 shows a comparison between two basic indicators for measuring income inequality in the region. In the past decade, almost all countries had different experiences with the transition from socialist to a market economy which leads to diversity in the extent of inequality. Of the various measures of inequality, this study analyses the two most widely used indicators, the Gini coefficient and the Quintile ratio. The Gini coefficient is used to measure the inequality of consumption, and the second indicator measures the inequality between the richest quintile and poorest quintile.[3] Measured by the Gini coefficient over the period between 2010 and 2015, Macedonia has the highest income inequality (44.1%), while Albania has the lowest (29%). In almost all countries of the region, the Gini coefficient has decreased over the years, indicating a gradual decrease of income inequality (see Table 4).

In the past, income inequality in Bosnia and Herzegovina measured by the Gini coefficient increased over the period from 2010 to 2015 from 36.3 to 33.8. Moreover, income inequality in Serbia, measured by the Gini coefficient, increased slightly from 28.2 (2000–2010) to 29.1 (2010–2015). Accordingly, Albania and Serbia have the most equal income distribution in comparison to other countries in the region. Inequality in income distribution as measured by the Gini coefficient in the Western Balkans is not large compared to EU28 (30.7%), with the exception of Macedonia.

The second indicator for measure of income inequality is expressed by Quintile ratio, which measures changes in the top and the bottom quintile of the income distribution (80/20). On this measure, income inequality is quite high in the region and is greatest in Macedonia (9.3%) and Bosnia and Herzegovina (6.4%). This means that, in Macedonia, the richest 20% of households consumed 9.3 times

[3]A "quintile" is a 20% section of the population ordered by income level, so the poorest quintile is the bottom 20% of households by income level.

more than the poorest 20%, and 5.7 times more in the case of Bosnia and Herzegovina. Finally, it should be mentioned that inequality is much lower in Serbia (4.4), Albania (4.3) and in Montenegro (4.8).

Migration Trends

Almost all the Western Balkan countries are faced with large numbers of emigrants. In the past the migration flows moved to Germany, Austria, Italy and Greece, but also across the region due to cultural similarities and commercial and family ties, especially in the former Yugoslavia. In the early 1990s, due to bilateral agreements between the former Yugoslavia countries and many receiving countries, the final destinations of most Yugoslav emigrants were EU countries. Many former emigrants from the Western Balkans have social and family ties in these countries, providing a further incentive for emigration.

During the 1990s, migration flows between the countries of the Western Balkans were related to internally displaced persons and refugees as a result of armed conflict and internal disturbances. From 1992 to 1995, more than a million people were displaced by interethnic violence, human rights violations and armed conflict between Serb, Croatian and Bosnian armed forces and militias (Global Overview 2014). With the beginning of armed conflict in Western Balkans, the character, the intensity and to some extent the direction of migration flows from the region again abruptly changed. The educational structure of migrants has changed due to the large number of highly educated immigrants. Immigration flows were often forced for people of all ages due to the armed conflicts in the Balkans, which caused large-scale migrant movements, both across the Western Balkans and outside its borders.

More recently, given the economic situation, emigration has been motivated by economic insecurity and a sense of hopelessness. Individual decisions to emigrate are often related to factors such as family links abroad and the level of education and the search for a better life. More generally emigration is driven by the low level of economic development in the region and political instability. According to UN estimates (UN 2015), net migration flows have been decreasing over the last 15 years. In Table 5, net migration per 1000 people and the net number of migrants are used as the benchmark indicators to analyse trends in migration flows in three subperiods. Almost all Western Balkan countries recorded net emigration (net migration plus population decline) between 2000 and 2015. The only exception is Bosnia and Herzegovina in the period of 2000–2010 due to return migration after the end of the war, although in 2010–2015 Bosnia and Herzegovina recorded net emigration too.

The highest rates of emigration were recorded in Albania (6.3 emigrants per 1000 persons in the subperiod from 2010 to 2015), while the rest of the countries in the region experienced emigration rates between −4.4 and −0.1 per 1000 people. It has been proposed that, apart from the wars, the main reasons for these negative trends have been the loss of social benefits; paid holidays; free health insurance and paid

Table 5 Migration trends and population by the Western Balkan countries

Country	Total population (000s)			Net migration rate (per 1000 population)[a]			Net number of migrants (000s)[b]		
	2000–2005	2005–2010	2010–2015	2000–2005	2005–2010	2010–2015	2000–2005	2005–2010	2010–2015
Bulgaria	7839	7515	7253	−2.1	−2.2	−1.4	−83	−83	−50
Romania	21,779	20,747	19,803	−4.5	−8.4	−4.4	−490	−874	−437
Albania	3112	2972	2887	−11.3	−16.9	−6.3	−175	−253	−92
Bosnia and Herzegovina	3883	3838	3822	1.8	0.2	−0.1	35	4	-3
Croatia	4369	4343	4271	−0.1	−1.0	−0.9	−3	−23	−20
Montenegro	617	620	625	−2.6	−1.0	−0.8	−8	−3	−2
Serbia	9155	9108	8938	−5.9	−0.8	−2.2	−276	−38	−100
Macedonia	2047	2055	2072	−1.5	−0.5	−0.5	−15	−5	−5

Source: UN (2015)

[a]Migration Data balance obtained as a residual, by subtracting the natural growth rate of the increase in the total population, with variations that occur due to imprecise population estimates and data on population changes

[b]Serbia including Kosovo

vacations, which the populations of these countries enjoyed under socialism (Vladimirova 2003, pp. 274–5); and political instability and the consequences of economic transition from a socialist to a private market economy, accompanied by widespread corruption, job losses and the collapse of many state enterprises (Segert 2009, p. 10).

Due to welfare benefits and economic opportunity, the migratory flows are mainly directed to Germany, Austria and other EU countries but also to overseas countries (USA). Generally, in the Western Balkans as a whole, most people emigrated to traditional immigration countries such as Germany and Austria (see Table 6). In contrast, emigrants from Albania mainly went to Greece and Italy. The stabilisation of the political situation and improvements of the economic situation in recent years has led to a decreasing rate of emigration although it remains at a high level from all Western Balkan countries.

Conclusion

After a double-dip recession, the Western Balkan countries are now experiencing a weak but fragile recovery. The privatisation process in the Western Balkan countries caused the loss of many social benefits, and armed conflicts and wars in Croatia, Bosnia and Herzegovina, Kosovo and Macedonia resulted in a great number of internally displaced persons and refugees and a loss of human capital. Consequently, the Western Balkans today includes some of the poorest European countries. In fact, all countries in the region have a GDP per capita below that of the new EU member

Table 6 Stock of emigrants from Western Balkan, 2013

Country of birth-emigration country	Top three destination countries	Emigrant populations by destination countries	Total number of emigrants
Albania	Greece	574,840	1,264,185
	Italy	449,657	
	United States	84,665	
Bosnia and Herzegovina	Serbia	298,835	1,699,893
	Germany	166,000	
	Austria	151,700	
Montenegro	Serbia	69,127	281,812
	Turkey	54,850	
	Croatia	39,357	
Serbia	Germany	216,000	1,292,910
	Switzerland	128,392	
	Austria	132,400	
Macedonia	Germany	114,083	626,312
	United States	89,837	
	Turkey	83,000	

Source: The World Bank (2013)

states, including Bulgaria and Romania. For example, the GDP per capita of Albania is 30% of EU28 average and of Bosnia and Herzegovina is 29% of the EU28 average, well below the standards achieved in Croatia at 59% of EU28 average and Romania at 55% of the EU28 average. Poverty in the region has drastically increased especially after the onset of the global economic crises. Poverty is greatest in Macedonia, Bosnia and Herzegovina and Albania. Nowadays, the impact of the economic crisis is visible in almost every aspect of social and economic life.

Economic trends over the last two decades have had extremely negative consequences. The main challenge over the coming decade will be economic recovery and the implementation of structural reforms. Moreover, the reduction in GDP levels, the high unemployment rate and the lack of investment indicate a need to adopt stimulus measures that should be better coordinated and aligned to reduce administrative burden and to accelerate the process of transition and economic recovery from the recessions of recent years. The level of employment has stagnated well below the EU average. In particular, the high rate of long-term unemployment and the high rate of youth unemployment have affected all countries of the region. Although unemployment has decreased in the last two years, this has often been associated with an increase in the share of precarious jobs. One of the main concerns in this initial recovery period is that the new jobs may not be created fast enough to absorb all the young people entering the labour market.

The region has made modest but uneven progress towards becoming a functioning market economy. The persistence of a high unemployment remains a major cause of concern for the citizens of the region, many of whom consider leaving their countries and moving to Western Europe and the USA. The migration of people from the Western Balkans towards the EU and the USA has a stronger intensity than to the region or within the region. In recent years, most migrants have been less educated low-skilled workers. Therefore, adequate measures should be taken to create a favourable economic environment through the implementation of suitable macroeconomic measures that would stimulate economic growth and development in the long term. Otherwise, each year outside of EU membership, together with the historical instability in the region, leaves the door open for the continuation of large-scale emigration to the EU.

References

Bartlett, W. (2008). *Europe's troubled region: Economic development, institutional reform and social welfare in the Western Balkans*. London: Routledge.

Eurostat. (2016). *European Union Labor Force Survey (EU LFS)*. Metadata for official statistics

Ganić, M., Sarajčić, S., Omerhodžić, S. (2014). *Lessons from transitional economies' failures: Why is Bosnia and Herzegovina a transitional (Non) success story?* Paper presented at the First Sarajevo international conference on "Global crisis and countries in transition", International University of Sarajevo, pp. 9–22.

IMF. (2015). *Regional economic issues: The Western Balkans 15 years of economic transition*. Washington, DC: International Monetary Fund.

Norwegian Refugee Council/Internal Displacement Monitoring Centre (NRC/IDMC). (2014, May 14). *Global Overview 2014: People internally displaced by conflict and violence* – Bangladesh. http://www.refworld.org/docid/5374748d17.html

Papić, Ž., Slijepčević, T., Dmitrović, T., Vuković, D., Delovamiladinova P, Ninković, R. (2012). *Ko, kako, zašto? Regionalna saradnja NVO-a u smanjenju socijalne isključenosti i siromaštva*. Foundation Open Society Institute (OSI-ZUG).

Segert, D. (2009). Dilemmas of the simultaneous transformation of politics and economics in East-Central Europe between 1989 and 2008. *Political Studies, 1–2*, 3–16.

UN. (2015). World population prospects: The 2015 revision, methodology of the United Nations population estimates and projections (Working Paper No. ESA/P/WP 242). United Nations, Department of Economic and Social Affairs, Population Division.

UNDP. (2016). *Human development report 2016*. New York: United Nations Development Programme.

Vladimirova, K. (2003). Employment and security in market economy transition years in Bulgaria. In K. Vladimirova (Ed.), *Employment status, labour contracts and security* (pp. 271–298). Sofia: Stopanstvo University Publishing.

World Bank. (2013). *World development report: Jobs*. Washington, DC: World Bank.

On the Way to Europe: Economic and Social Developments in Albania

Engjëll Pere and Will Bartlett

Introduction

Albania became a candidate for EU membership in 2014, having signed a Stabilisation and Association Agreement with the EU in 2006.[1] Writing 1 year after the SAA was signed, Bogdani and Laughlin (2007) identified two potential obstacles to Albania having a smooth accession path. Firstly, they observed that the Albanian political class and leadership at that time lacked the necessary commitment to implement the reforms needed to fulfil the conditions for membership—the so-called Copenhagen criteria. These require that as a condition of future membership, candidate countries develop institutions that underpin democracy, the rule of law and human rights as well as having a functioning market economy. Secondly, they observed the onset of enlargement fatigue by the EU. Since then, Albania has made great strides in securing a democratic political system and a functioning market economy but, as this chapter demonstrates, still has some way to go. On the EU side, the recently introduced Berlin Process has injected some new energy and optimism into the enlargement process, albeit with the caveat that this is expected to still take several more years to achieve.

After the collapse of communist system in the early 1990s, the state-owned enterprises in Albania were privatised, and the previous state-owned, autarkic command economy was transformed into a private market economy (Hashi and

[1]The interim agreement covering trade aspects entered into force in 2006, while the full SAA entered into force in 2009.

E. Pere (✉)
European University of Tirana, Tirana, Albania
e-mail: engjell.pere@uet.edu.al

W. Bartlett
LSEE, London School of Economics and Political Science, London, UK
e-mail: w.j.bartlett@lse.ac.uk

R. Osbild, W. Bartlett (eds.), *Western Balkan Economies in Transition*, Societies and Political Orders in Transition, https://doi.org/10.1007/978-3-319-93665-9_6

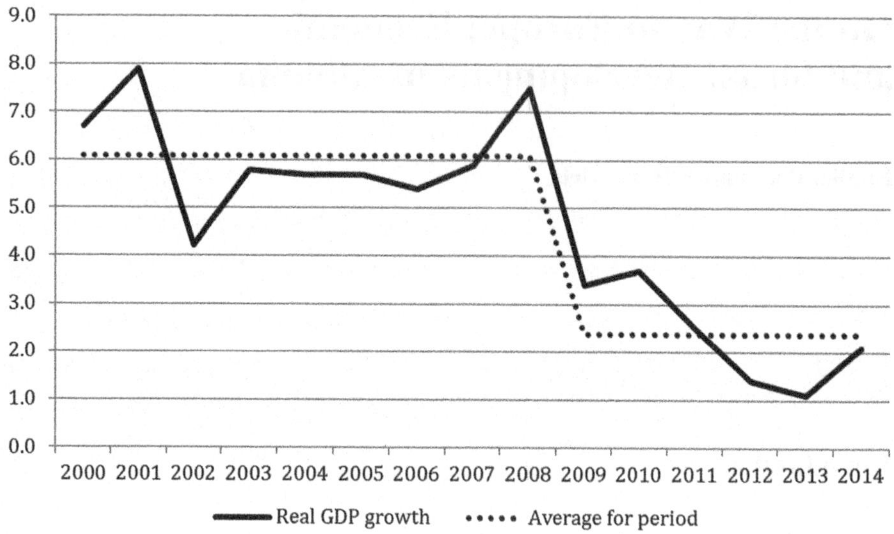

Fig. 1 Real GDP growth (% per annum). Source: Eurostat online data and authors' calculations

Xhillari 1999). Following a period of crisis in 1997 when a number of pyramid savings banks collapsed (Jarvis 2000), the economy entered a period of rapid economic growth, at 6.2% per year from 2000 to 2008 (see Fig. 1). An important factor supporting growth was large-scale emigration and the associated income from remittances from abroad (Gërmenji and Milo 2011). By 2007, the value of these remittances reached about 14% of the country's GDP (about €1 billion) and was one of the most important financial resources for economic development (Duval and Wolff 2010). However, following the onset of the Eurozone crisis and the loss of emigrant workers' jobs in Greece and Italy, the flow of remittances fell, reaching about 9% of GDP by 2016.[2]

The Albanian economy experienced the effects of the economic crisis in the Eurozone later than most other countries. The rate of growth of real GDP fell to 3.7% in 2010, 2.5% in 2011 and 1.6% in 2012 (NBA 2014). Towards the end of 2013, economic growth turned negative before recovering in early 2014 with a growth of 1.65% per annum during the first quarter of 2014 (NBA 2014). Over the period from 2009 to 2015, the average rate of economic growth was just 2.4% per year. Instead of adjusting to the new external environment by introducing reforms to improve the competitiveness and productivity of the economy, businesses and the government relied on ever-increasing amounts of external borrowing and debt. By 2015, external debt had risen to 73% of GDP, up from 26% in 2007. Low growth has put pressure on tax revenues and has led to increased levels of public sector debt. In early 2013 the IMF reported that: "... public debt at over 60% of GDP is among the highest in

[2]World Bank World Development Indicators database online data.

Southeast Europe and fiscal buffers are largely exhausted".[3] In response, the government has pursued a policy of fiscal consolidation. This is expected to continue over the next few years due to commitments under a 36-month €330 million IMF Extended Fund Facility agreed in 2014, conditional on fiscal consolidation and a reduction in the budget deficit. This was achieved through an increase in tax revenues and cuts in public expenditure that mainly affected capital expenditure. This is likely to exert a continuing downward influence on economic growth in the coming years.

Over the period of transition, the economy has turned from an agricultural and industrial economy into a primarily service economy. Industrial production (excluding construction) as a share of gross value added has been falling over time, reaching 14% in 2014, while the share of construction was 11%.[4] The share of agriculture has also fallen but is still a fairly substantial component of the economy at 23% of gross value added in 2014. Meanwhile, the economy has become steadily more and more oriented to the provision of services, the share of which in gross value added reached 52% in 2014.[5] It should be expected that as the economy further develops, the share of agriculture will fall further, while the share of the services sector would increase. This is likely to involve further labour shedding in agriculture and additional net migration from rural to urban areas, creating further pressure on the provision of public services such as housing, transport, education and health services in the towns and especially in the capital city, Tirana.

Governance and the Quality of Institutions

It is increasingly recognised that the quality of institutions and the way these institutions manage economic governance play an important role in supporting economic growth and development (Rodrik et al. 2004; Acemoglu et al. 2014; Bartlett et al. 2016). Prominently among institutions, economic freedom is often held to support economic growth (Gwartney et al. 1999). Yet economic freedom can be adversely impacted by weaknesses in democratic consolidation, a factor that has influenced the development of the political system in Albania in the 1990s (Pano 1997; Pettifer 2000; Feilcke-Tiemann 2006). Fortunately, the orderly transfer of power in the 2013 election suggests that EU conditionality has had a positive impact on the evolution of democratic institutions (Bajrovic and Satter 2014).

On the road to European integration, the quality of institutions has emerged as an important aspect of governance. In addition to alignment with European norms, its potential positive impact on growth is one of the reasons why the Copenhagen

[3]IMF News Release, Tirana, 15 February 2013.

[4]Eurostat online data variable code [cpc_ecnabrk].

[5]For the EU-28 countries, the structure mentioned above is as follows: 23.5% industrial manufacturing (15% manufacture), 1.5% agriculture, and 75% services.

accession conditions place such a heavy emphasis on institutional reform and governance arrangements. Over the last few years, the EU has introduced a process of new economic governance that requires Western Balkan countries to produce annual Economic Reform Programmes (ERPs). The ERP for 2016–2018 envisages a set of measures related to fiscal consolidation and structural reform, prioritising the improvement of public finance management and the business environment.

The European Commission also devotes considerable attention to governance and institutional issues. In its annual report on Albania for 2016, the Commission emphasised the need for greater transparency and accountability in public institutions and the need to tackle the politicisation of the judiciary. The latter is especially important since weaknesses in the rule of law adversely affect institutional quality (Mavrikos-Adamou 2014). In addition, it is difficult for businesses to enforce property rights, a feature of the institutional framework that is thought to hinder investment and sustainable economic growth. Reviewing the quality of institutions regulating the economy, the report points out that "inefficient contract enforcement, uncertain property rights and the prevalence of corruption are major concerns repeatedly expressed by businesses". Moreover, clientelism is a pervasive feature of the political and economic system in Albania, as ruling parties make use of their powers of patronage to award jobs to their political supporters (Bogdani and Loughlin 2007; Xhaferaj 2013).

The World Bank also monitors the institutions governing the business environment through its Ease of Doing Business survey; in 2016 Albania ranked 90th out of 190 countries on the "ease of doing business index". However, recent reforms have brought about a dramatic improvement, and in 2017 the index improved to place Albania in 58th position. This was largely due to a reform that made it easier to obtain construction permits for business investments.[6] The World Bank provides governance indicators with six subindices giving information on the level of governance in respective fields of voice and accountability, political stability and absence of violence, government effectiveness, regulatory quality, rule of law and control of corruption. These indices are evaluated on a scale from −2.5 to +2.5, where 0 is the international average. The indices have been continuously improving, although there was some backsliding between 2010 and 2013. The most positive indicators relate to voice, accountability and regulatory quality, while the most negative aspects relate to the rule of law and the control of corruption.

Over time, most of the governance indicators have improved, especially those relating to regulatory quality, political stability and control of corruption (see Fig. 2). However, there has been a notable decline in voice and accountability, which has fallen below the international average in recent years. The rule of law, although improving, also remains below the international average. The poor performance on the rule of law and on voice and accountability reflects the slow pace of democratisation and indeed some backsliding in relation to democratic participation

[6]Albania had been near the bottom of the list in this regard at 186th position, but improved to 106th position in 2017.

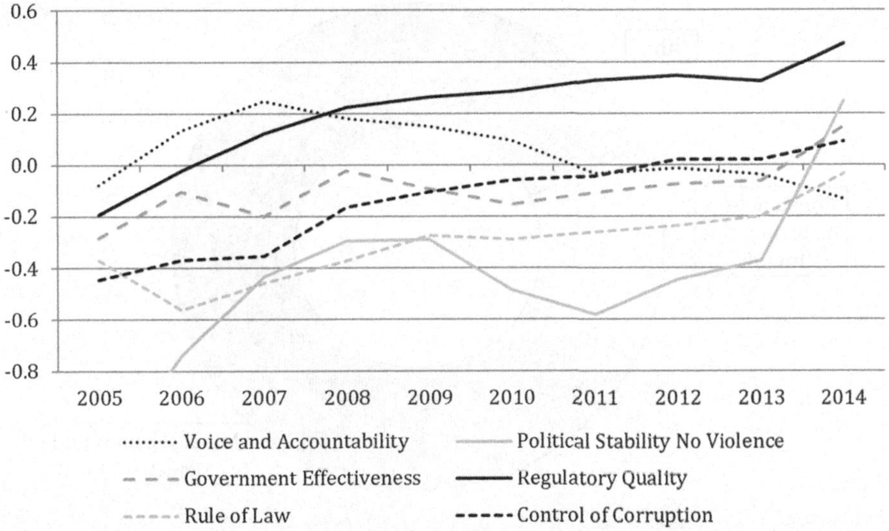

Fig. 2 Governance indicators. Source: World Bank, Worldwide Governance Indicators, 2015

in the affairs of state. The major emphasis on the rule of law in EU accession conditionality suggests that Albania still has some way to go before there are realistic prospects for future EU membership.

Foreign Trade

An important factor of economic development and integration is the opening of the economy and intensification of foreign trade. In this regard, international trade is seen as an essential driver of economic development and international integration. Before the 1990s, the country followed an autarchic trade policy based on the dogmatic principle of producing everything based only on the country's own resources. Until 1990, foreign trade policy was based on political and ideological criteria, governed by a conservative form of socialism. The competitiveness of Albanian products was very low, and exports were limited to raw minerals such as chromium and iron. Trade was mainly with the Soviet Bloc, based mainly on the "clearing" method. The political changes in the early 1990s opened the country and led to a significant growth of foreign trade. In 2014 the sum of exports and imports amounted to about €5.6 billion (up from €2.6 in 2005), while the trade openness index (the share of exports and imports in GDP) was 57% in 2014 (up from 39% in

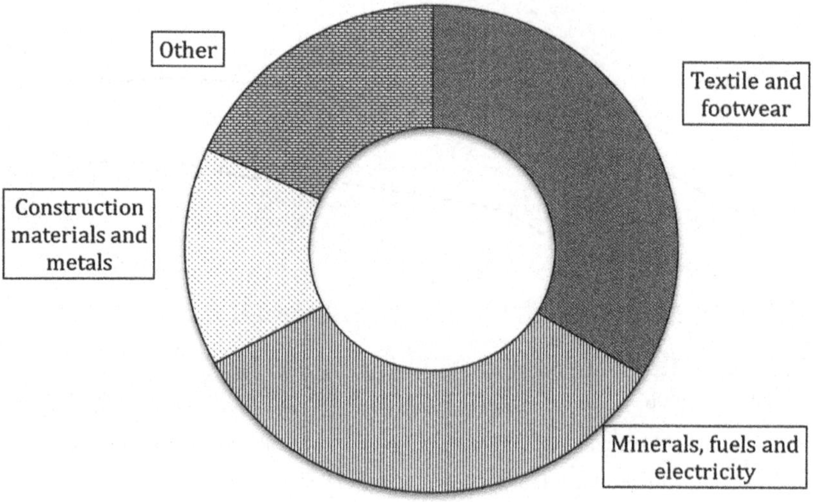

Fig. 3 Main export product groups (% of total exports, 2015). Source: INSTAT online data

2005). However, the balance of trade was persistently negative, although the coverage of exports by imports improved from 26% in 2005 to 47% in 2014.[7]

The most important exports are textiles and footwear products (36%), followed by minerals, fuels and electricity (27%) and construction materials and metals (15%) (see Fig. 3). The large emphasis on textile products is mainly due to reprocessing activities for the Italian market. In general, exports have a low value-added composition and although they generate a substantial number of jobs do not contribute much to the innovative potential of the Albanian economy or to productivity improvements that would support long-run economic growth. On the side of imports, Albania imports mainly machinery and equipment (21%), followed by food and beverages (18%) and construction, materials and metals (15%).

Italy is Albania's main export's partner, accounting for 52% of all exports in 2014. Apart from Italy, Albania's main export partners are Kosovo, Spain, Malta, Turkey and Greece. Exports to these countries account for 80% of the total. Although most exports of goods are with EU countries, the share declined from 91% in 2003 to around 65–75% in the period 2007–2014. Trade with the Western Balkans accounted for about 11.7% of exports in 2014. After 2003, Kosovo became an important partner with a share in exports of 7.3% in 2014.

Italy is also Albania's main partner in imports, although its share decreased from 44% in 1998 to around 30% in 2014 and 2015. Greece is the second import partner, although this has decreased too from 28% in 1998 to 9% in 2014. After 2003, imports from China have increased. Albania's top five import partners include Turkey and Germany, whose share has been fairly constant at 6–7% of the total.

[7]World Bank World Development Indicators online database.

Imports from EU countries declined from about 82–72% before 2004 to around 61–68% from 2005 to 2015. Imports from within the region do not have an important role, amounting to just 3% of total imports mainly from Serbia and Macedonia.

Albania has a large current account deficit, which on average since 2007 has exceeded 10% of GDP, though on a falling trend to reach 7.6% of GDP in 2016.[8] This deficit was partly offset by large inflows of remittances from Albanian citizens working abroad. The value of net remittances was about 11% of GDP in 2016.[9] More than one fifth of the households in Albania receive remittance incomes, which are mainly spent on basic consumption goods or on housing construction (Castaldo and Reilly 2007). Remittances are negatively correlated with both the donor's and the recipient's level of education (Duval and Wolff 2010). Remittances have been falling in recent years, not just as a proportion of GDP but also in absolute value as Albanian migrants living in Greece have been badly affected by the economic crisis in that country and many have lost their jobs and returned home. The impact of this on social conditions is significant, as many of Albania's poorest people depend for their subsistence on the inflow of remittances from family members working abroad (Shimamoto 2014). For example, in the town of Puke, in the north of Albania, "the amount of money that the migrants send home has dwindled in the last few years. The debts owed by their families—already struggling on the edge of the poverty line—have grown".[10] Many families are only able to survive by running up debts with local grocery store and pharmacy.

Competitiveness

Albania is ranked at 93rd place globally on the World Economic Forum's competitiveness index (WEF 2016). For 2015–2016, Albania performed similarly to emerging market economies as a whole, but worse in relation to technology and financial market development. As shown above, the export structure of the economy is mainly in the low value-added industries, and this is reflected in the poor performance of the economy in relation to technological development. Investment is a major driver of economic growth and competitiveness. Albania records a relatively high share of gross fixed capital formation (the investment rate) at 26.3% of GDP, compared to 19.5% in the EU.[11] Foreign investment inflows are also relatively strong at 8.9% of GDP.[12]

---

[8]World Bank World Development Indicators online data.

[9]Ibid.

[10]Klodiana Kapo, "Drop in remittances hits poor Albanian hard", *Balkan Insight*, 29/09/2014.

[11]Eurostat online data variable code [nama_10_gdp].

[12]UNCTAD online data.

Another major driver of competitiveness is the productivity and skills of the workforce. Public expenditure on education in Albania is 3.4% of GDP.[13] Without further raising the resources available to the education sector, it is unlikely that effective measures to promote inclusive education will succeed. Access to preuniversity education in Albania is relatively low compared to EU countries. In 2012 only 16.8% of 30–34-year-olds had received a tertiary education compared to 37.1% in the EU. There are substantial differences in the length of education in different parts of the country; for example, a young person raised in Tirana attends school approximately 3.5 years more than the average.

In recent years the number of pupils attending public sector primary schools has decreased, while attendance at private primary schools has increased. In 2011, 140 primary schools were in the private sector (9.4% of primary schools), enrolling 5% of students and employing 7.4% of teachers. There has been a worrying trend of decline in the share of girls graduating from primary education. The trend is similar in both urban and rural areas.

Secondary general education is not compulsory; it starts after finishing primary education at age 16. In recent years, the number of private secondary schools has increased, reaching 117 in 2011 and enrolling 4112 students. The cost of sending a child to a private school is such that only the children of middle-class or wealthy parents are able to attend such schools.[14] The gross enrolment ratio in upper secondary education is relatively high, at 82.5% in 2012, although almost a quarter of girls did not enrol for upper secondary education. The lower enrolment of girls puts them at greater risk of social exclusion compared to boys. Enrolment in vocational secondary schools has fallen over time from a peak in 1992 of 62% of all students enrolled in upper secondary education to just 7% in 2012. This negative trend reflects the falling demand for skilled workers in the economy following the collapse in industrial output in the 1990s. Nevertheless, if Albania is to re-engage with high productivity growth industries, there will be a need to reverse this fall in enrolment in vocational education. The vocational education system will need to be completely revitalised if it is to play a significant role in the Albanian education system and provide qualified graduates to meet the needs of future growth in the economy. Relatively few students continue their education to tertiary level in universities and other higher education institutions. In 2012, the tertiary completion rate (the proportion of young people of the relevant age group that completed university studies) was just 16.8%, less than half of the Europe 2020 target of at least 40% of 30–34-year-olds completing third-level education.[15]

The overall educational attainment of the working age population has been improving over the last decade. According to the results of the 2011 census,

---

[13]Eurostat online data variable code [cpc_pseduc].

[14]See M. Rukaj "Albania: the boom of private schools" Osservatorio balcani e caucaso, 2nd October 2012, available at http://www.balcanicaucaso.org/eng/Regions-and-countries/Albania/Albania-the-boom-of-private-schools-122645

[15]See http://ec.europa.eu/europe2020/targets/eu-targets/

compared with the situation recorded by the 2001 census, the proportion of the working age population having completed tertiary level education doubled from 6.2 to 12.0%. The proportion of the population without any educational qualification fell from 7.1 to 5.0%, and the proportion with only a primary education fell from 13.1 to 9.0% (between 2001 and 2011). Yet, the highest level of qualification of about half of the working age population is still only a lower secondary diploma. There are striking differences between urban and rural areas in the probability of having a tertiary education. For instance, among working age people, more than three times as many urban residents have a tertiary education compared to rural residents (17.8% against 4.7%, respectively) (INSTAT 2014a). Lack of education is often associated with low-skill employment, with low wages and low job security. As a result, less educated individuals are at a higher risk of exclusion from the labour market. The working poor has on average 9.6 years of education, compared to 11.5 years for the working nonpoor (MSWY 2014). A lack of education reinforces social exclusion on the labour market. People with a low level of education are more likely to be unemployed than individuals with secondary and tertiary education. In 2012, according to the Labour Force Survey, the employment rate of people with lower secondary education was 53.5% compared to 57.4% of those with upper secondary education and 66.9% for those with university and above (MSWY 2014).

The Labour Market

Having paid employment is one of the most important ways in which households in market economies earn their livelihood and avoid falling into poverty. Yet the Albanian economy, with an employment rate of just 50%, is extremely weak at creating jobs, and as a result hundreds of thousands of people have left the country in search of work abroad. Over two fifths (41%) of people in employment are not regular employees, but have "self-employment" status (INSTAT 2014a). In the second quarter of 2014, self-employed (employers or self-employed without employees) account for 25%, and unpaid family workers represent 34% of the total employment (INSTAT 2014b). The self-employed have a lower likelihood than regular employees of having formal work arrangements and so are less likely to have access to social security system or trade union representation. Informal employment is widespread, accounting for about 30% of GDP in 2013 (Boka and Torluccio 2013). The extent of informality has increased in recent years as a consequence of the economic crisis, which has affected the formal economy more than the informal economy. The likelihood of participation in the informal economy is inversely related to a person's level of education (Gerxhani and de Werfhorst 2013). Informal sector workers are not covered by labour legislation or social insurance, nor do they contribute to the social insurance system. Informal employment is important to the welfare of many households, but it is also significantly correlated with low earnings, poverty and vulnerability (INSTAT 2014a).

Table 1 Employment rate and unemployment rate

	Employment rate (%)	Total unemployment rate (%)
2007	62.7	13.5
2011	64.9	14.0
2015	59.3	17.1

Source: Eurostat online data

From 2007 to 2011, the employment rate followed an increasing trend, but has since begun to fall in 2013 as economic growth has slowed (see Table 1). Correspondingly, the unemployment rate increased to 17.1% at the end of 2015, although this may well be an underestimate, as the 2011 census recorded an unemployment rate of 29.4% in the census year (28.2% for men and 31.4% for women). According to the census, the unemployment rate among people aged 15–24 years is 53%. Youth unemployment can have serious consequences for their future social inclusion chances as it may lead to a loss of human and social capital and make it more difficult for them to find a formal sector job in the future.

Significant gender differences exist in the labour market with women experiencing far lower employment rates than men across all age groups. On average the gap is around 15 percentage points, as the employment rate for women between the ages of 15–64 years is 40.7% compared to 55.4% for men (in Q1 2014). The gap is narrower among younger workers aged 15–29 years, for whom it is just 10 percentage points, but much wider for those aged between 30 and 64 years for whom it reaches almost 20 percentage points. This means that older women are more likely to be differentially excluded from the labour market compared to men (even though the employment rate for older women is higher than for younger women). This may be because older women are more likely to drop out of the labour market as they take on family responsibilities. It also suggests that women may face difficulties to re-enter the labour market after having children. The gender gap is narrower between men and women with a higher level of education, suggesting that educated women find it easier to enter or re-enter the labour market. Therefore the provision of pre-school education facilities or kindergarten facilities may be especially important for less educated women to support their return to work. Female labour force participation is higher in households that receive remittances, have a higher level of educational attainment and are larger, where the males are employed and where the woman is the head of the household and has children. It is lower in wealthier households (Shehaj and Adnett 2014). When women do obtain employment, they tend to earn less. Although women have on average about 1.3 years more education compared to men, they receive on average one fifth (20%) lower wages, and the gender wage gap seems to be increasing (MSWY 2014). The increase of the gender wage gap may be due in part to the effects of the economic crisis.

Poverty

Despite the rapid growth rates of GDP per capita, at least up until the onset of the economic crisis at the end of the last decade, income levels in Albania remain very low, at just €3,440 per capita, or 28% of the average in the EU in terms of purchasing power parity.[16] Due to the rapid growth of the economy, the extent of poverty fell up until 2008 but has begun to increase since then following the onset of the economic crisis (MSWY 2014). Information on the extent of poverty is given by the Living Standards Measurement Survey (LSMS). This showed that 25.4% of people lived below the poverty line in 2002, while due to economic growth and development, the proportion of poor people had fallen to 12.5% by 2008 (INSTAT 2015). However, the extent poverty began to increase again following the economic crisis to reach 14.3% in 2012. In addition, relative poverty has increased, suggesting that growth has mainly benefited the better of sections of the society (Mastromarco et al. 2014). This worsening of relative poverty was especially pronounced in rural areas.

People living in rural areas, especially in remote rural areas and mountainous areas, have lower standards of living than people living in other parts of the country, as employment opportunities are few and incomes from employment are relatively low. It is especially concerning that there are few employment opportunities for young people in rural areas.[17] Women also are especially disadvantaged in rural areas often working as unpaid family farm labour, which limits their economic independence and empowerment (UNDP 2013). In 2008 the poverty headcount was highest in mountain regions, but has since fallen from 26.6% to just 15.3%; by 2012 the poverty rate was the highest in the coastal regions. These regional changes may be linked to the internal migration of the population from rural to urban areas.

Poverty is linked to a variety of causes, including labour market status, unemployment or inactivity, age, geographical location, ethnicity, level of education and other factors (UNDP 2011). Available data indicate that the population groups facing higher risk of poverty are the unemployed, the less educated, people living in rural areas and those engaged in own account farming (MSWY 2014). One fifth (20%) of children live in poor families that rely on social assistance for their survival, many of whom spend their time on the street working in informal jobs, selling small items or begging. A recent study identified over 2500 "children of the street" of whom two thirds were between the ages of 4 and 14, three quarters of whom were from the Roma and Egyptian communities (UNICEF 2014). Poverty can also be attributed to people in work who receive very low wages. In Albania, the "working poor" earn about 17% less than the working nonpoor and if informally employed also lack social security entitlements and access to old-age pensions (MSWY 2014).

---

[16]Eurostat online data variable code [cpc_ecnagdp].

[17]See *Government Program: Public Services*, available at http://www.kryeministria.al/en/program/public-service

Table 2 Gini coefficient (%)

	Albania	Germany
2005	30.6	26.1
2006	n/a	26.8
2007	n/a	30.4
2008	30.0	30.2
2009	n/a	29.1
2010	n/a	29.3
2011	n/a	29.0
2012	29.0	28.3

Source: World Bank, Worldwide Development Indicators (Albania) and Eurostat (Germany) indicator label [ilc_di12]

Albania introduced a social assistance scheme for poor people in 1993. This system, known as "Ndihma ekonomike", is funded by the central government but delivered by local authorities on a discretionary basis. According to a recent study, it fails to protect poor people form social exclusion and is incapable of reducing inequalities between households and social groups (Ymeraj 2007).

Inequality

In view of social welfare and equity, an important point is also income distribution. Table 2 shows the Gini coefficient for Albania compared with Germany. Albania inherited a high degree of equality from the communist period, yet the table shows that Gini coefficient for Albania has increased to that of Germany. In 2012, based on the Living Standards Measurement Survey, inequality in Albania measured by the Gini coefficient reached 29.0%; in Germany the Gini coefficient of equivalised disposable household income was about the same at 28.3%. In terms of income distribution, in 2012 the lowest 10% of income earners received only 3.7% of total income, while the highest 10% of income earners received about 23% of the total income of the country.[18] This distribution is similar to countries such as the Netherlands or Austria.

Regional inequalities in Albania are significant. In the central region, GDP per capita in 2012 was 22.7% above the national average, while in the north region, it was 19.3% below the national average, and in south region, it was 8.5% below the national average.[19] The highest level of GDP per capita in level 3 regions (*qarks*) was in Tirana at 41% above the national average, in Fier it was 13% above average, and in Durrës 4.5% above average. The GDP per capita of all the other *qarks* was below the national average. The lowest was in Dibër at 33% below average, followed by Kukës (30.5% below average) and Korça (30% below average).

[18]World Bank World Development Indicators online database.

[19]INSTAT, "Gross Domestic Product according to Statistical Regions in Albania, 2012", *Press Release*, 31/7/2014.

These disparities are reflected in the distribution of poverty rates across regions, which are significantly higher in the north of the country than in the central region (UNDP 2010). Regional inequalities are also reflected in variations in the provision of public services such as education and healthcare services. In the education sector, the high rate of migration from rural to urban areas has led to a decline in the number of children in some of the poorer quarks such as Dibër and Kukës and an increase in the teacher pupil ratio, which has correspondingly decreased in Tirana and other urban centres (UNDP 2010).

Conclusions

After the democratic change in 1990, Albania achieved robust economic growth particularly during the decade from 1997 to 2008. Growth has decreased since 2009 due to the spillover from the Eurozone crisis and the reduction of emigrants' remittances. Competitiveness is important for economic development. The overall index of competitiveness is low, ranking the country at 93rd position in 2015–2016. Backwardness is seen in particular in technological development, while the main obstacles to progress concern weaknesses in governance and the quality of institutions especially in the rule of law and democratic participation through mechanisms of voice and accountability. Albania has made a significant progress in economic integration with the EU. The growth rate of export and imports has been high, and the economy is open to foreign trade and investment. However, it has a negative balance of trade, and exports are focused on low value-added products including textiles and footwear, minerals, fuels, electricity, metals and construction materials.

Despite economic growth, income per capita is relatively low compared with other European countries, and poverty remains relatively high. The extent of poverty has been increasing in recent years, after a long period of falling poverty levels. In 2012, about 14.3% of population were below the absolute poverty line. The high level of poverty can be explained by the high unemployment rate, especially among young people. Inequality of incomes has widened during the transition from communism and today has reached levels similar to that in Germany, i.e. inequality is rather normal for the institutions of a market economy.

Overall, Albania has made great strides over the last two and a half decades since the fall of communism, and the living standards of the population have greatly improved. However, many remain in poverty, and inequality has increased although not excessively. Albania is well on the path of European accession, but many institutional reforms need to be completed, including in particular an improvement in the quality of institutions, the rule of law being one of the most prominent issues. Albania managed to avoid some of the worst effects of the global economic crisis and the spillovers from the Eurozone crisis but only at the expense of a steady increase in public and external indebtedness. In 2014, the country had to appeal to the IMF for financial support, which was given on condition that the country pursues a path of fiscal consolidation. The EU has also brought Albania within the purview of its system of new economic governance, with the requirement to prepare regular Economic Reform Programmes which are vetted by the European Commission. The policies of fiscal consolidation may make it more difficult to expand redistributive social assistance programmes for the relief of poverty. In order to overcome these limitations, critical policy decisions will need to be made to improve the competitiveness of the economy, facilitate and encourage a faster rate of technological development and move towards a path of high value-added production and export activities to support sustainable economic growth that relies on the full utilisation of domestic resources rather than foreign borrowing to support the future development of the economy.

References

Acemoglu, D., Gallego, F. A., & Robinson, J. A. (2014). Institutions, human capital and development. *American Economic Review, 6*, 875–912.

Bajrovic, I. C., & Satter, J. R. (2014). Albania: From bunkers to ballots. *Journal of Democracy, 25* (1), 142–153.

Bartlett, W., Čučković, N., & Jurlin, K. (2016). A comparative perspective on institutional quality in countries at different stages of European integration. *Tijdschrift voor Economische en Sociale Geografie, 108*(1), 92–108.

Bogdani, M., & Laughlin, J. (2007). *Albania and the European Union: The tumultuous journey towards integration and accession*. London: GB, I.B. Tauris.

Boka, M., & Torluccio, G. (2013). Informal economy in Albania. *Academic Journal of Interdisciplinary Studies, 2*(8), 212–221.

Castaldo, A., & Reilly, B. (2007). How do migrant remittances affect the expenditure patterns of Albanian Household? *Journal of Economics, 1*, 25–54.

Duval, L., & Wolff, F. (2010). Remittances matter: Longitudinal evidence from Albania. *Post-Communist Economies, 22*(1), 73–97.

Feilcke-Tiemann, A. (2006). Albania: Gradual consolidation limited by internal political struggles. *Southeastern and Black Sea Studies, 6*(1), 25–41.

Gërmenji, E., & Milo, L. (2011). Migration of the skilled from Albania: Brain drain or brain gain? *Journal of Balkan and Near Eastern Studies, 13*(3), 339–356.

Gerxhani, K., & de Werfhorst, H. G. (2013). The effect of education on informal sector participation in a post-communist economy. *European Sociological Review, 29*(3), 464–476.

Gwartney, D., Lawson, R. A., & Holcombe, R. G. (1999). Economic freedom and the environment for economic growth. *Journal of Theoretical and Institutional Economics, 15*(4), 643–663.

Hashi, I., & Xhillari, L. (1999). Privatisation and transition in Albania. *Post-Communist Economies, 11*(1), 99–125.

INSTAT. (2014a). *Albanian labour market dynamics 2001–2011*. Trana: Institute of Statistics.

INSTAT. (2014b). *Quarterly labour force survey, second quarter 2014*. Tirana: Institute of Statistics.

INSTAT. (2015). *Albania: Trends in poverty, 2002–2005–2008–2012*. Tirana: Institute of Statistics.

Jarvis, C. (2000). The rise and fall of the pyramid schemes in Albania. *IMF Staff Papers, 47*(1), 1–29.

Mastromarco, C., Peragine, V., Russo, F., & Serlenga, L. (2014). Poverty, inequality and growth in Albania: Empirical evidence, 2002–05. *Economics of Transition, 22*(4), 635–682.

Mavrikos-Adamou, T. (2014). Rule of law and the democratization process: The case of Albania. *Democratization, 21*(6), 1153–1171.

MSWY. (2014). *Employment and skills strategy 2014–2020*. Tirana: Ministry of Social Welfare and Youth.

NBA. (2014). *Monetary policy report, second quarter*. Tirana: National Bank of Albania.

Pano, N. (1997). The process of democratization in Albania. In K. Dawisha & B. Parrott (Eds.), *Politics, power and the struggle for democracy in South-East Europe* (pp. 285–352). Cambridge: Cambridge University Press.

Pettifer, J. (2000). Albania: The democratic deficit in the post-communist period. In G. Pridham & T. Gallagher (Eds.), *Experimenting with democracy: Regime change in the Balkans* (pp. 237–248). London: Routledge.

Rodrik, D., Subramanian, A., & Trebbi, F. (2004). Institutions rule: The primacy of institutions over geography and integration in economic development. *Journal of Economic Growth, 9*, 131–165.

Shehaj, E., & Adnett, N. (2014). Modelling the drivers of female labour force participation: The case of Albania. Paper presented at the 2nd Biannual conference of the LSEE Research Network on Social Cohesion, *Post-crisis recovery in Southeast Europe and beyond: Policy challenges for social and economic inclusion*. London: LSEE – LSE Research on South East Europe, 27–28 March.

Shimamoto, D. (2014). *Motivation behind remittance from migrants: Evidence from Albania* (Discussion Papers in Economics and Business no. 14-05). Osaka: Osaka School of International Public Policy.

UNDP. (2010). *Regional disparities in Albania*. Tirana: United Nations Development Programme.

UNDP. (2011). *Report on vulnerable groups excluded from the labour market*. Tirana: United Nations Development Programme.

UNDP. (2013). *National study on the rural labour market*. Tirana: United Nations Development Programme.

UNICEF. (2014). *National study on children in street situation in Albania*. Tirana: United Nations Children's Fund.

WEF. (2016). *Global competitiveness report 2015–2016*. Geneva: World Economic Forum.

Xhaferaj, A. (2013). Appointed elites in the political parties: Albania case. *Academic Journal of Interdisciplinary Studies, 2*(3), 307.

Ymeraj, A. (2007). Albania. In B. Deacon & P. Stubbs (Eds.), *Social policy and international interventions in South East Europe* (pp. 187–202). Cheltenham: Edward Elgar.

Public and Private Debt: Recent Developments in Bosnia and Herzegovina

Jelena Poljašević and Jelena Trivić

Introduction

The economy of Bosnia and Herzegovina relies heavily on the export of metals, energy, textiles and furniture and is also reliant on remittances and foreign aid. Due to its highly decentralised government, economic policy coordination and reform is difficult, while the bureaucracy does little to promote foreign investment. The economy slowly recovered after the end of the war in 1995, and growth accelerated in the following decade. During the period 2003–2008, the growth of gross domestic product (GDP) exceeded 5% per annum. However, in 2009, the country was affected by the global economic crisis and GDP declined. It declined again in 2012 due to the spillover from the Eurozone crisis, while the floods that hit the country in May 2014 reduced the pace of economic recovery.

The country has a central government—the "Institutions of Bosnia and Herzegovina"—two regional levels of government or "Entities" with a high degree of autonomy—the Federation of Bosnia and Herzegovina and the Republika Srpska—and the small District of Brčko. Furthermore, the Federation of Bosnia and Herzegovina is comprised of ten highly autonomous cantons. The Entities and District have their own policy of direct taxation, while responsibility for indirect taxation is held at state level. The pension, social and health funds function at the level of the Entities.

The main weaknesses are the high budget deficit, growth of public debt, complex public sector, non-productive public expenses, weak economic recovery and weak

J. Poljašević (✉)
Faculty of Economics, University of Banja Luka, Republic of Srpska, Bosnia and Herzegovina
e-mail: jelena.poljasevic@ef.unibl.org

J. Trivić
Faculty of Economics, University of Banja Luka, Banja Luka, Bosnia and Herzegovina
e-mail: jelena.trivic@ef.unibl.org

R. Osbild, W. Bartlett (eds.), *Western Balkan Economies in Transition*, Societies and Political Orders in Transition, https://doi.org/10.1007/978-3-319-93665-9_7

domestic demand. The growth of the budget deficit and slow implementation of structural reforms have led to an increase in borrowing. Because of the abovementioned fiscal weaknesses and the overall political situation, the country's credit rating is very low.

Public Debt

In the literature, the terms "public debt", "sovereign debt" and "national debt" are often used as synonyms. The shortest definition of sovereign debt is a debt issued by a national government. But this definition does not specify the level of government that issues the debt. Public debt as defined in the Maastricht Treaty is the nominal value of the consolidated general government gross debt, outstanding at the end of the year. Data for the general government sector are consolidated between subsectors at the national level. Public debt in the sense of Maastricht covers all general governments in the context of the national accounts: the state, other government bodies, local governments and social security administrations.[1] Public debt should not be confused with the external debt, which is owed by the state or the private sector to foreign creditors. In general, public debt can be composed of both internal and external debts. In this chapter, the sovereign, public or national debt of Bosnia and Herzegovina is defined according to national reports on public debt. Thus, public debt comprises a sum of external and internal debt that is owed by the state, entities, cantons, municipalities and social security funds.[2]

Brief Methodology of Sovereign Debt Analysis

In the European Union, the criteria set out in the Maastricht Treaty prescribe certain thresholds for macroeconomic indicators of public finances: (1) the ratio of the annual government deficit to GDP must not exceed 3% at the end of the preceding financial year, and (2) the ratio of gross public debt-to-GDP must not exceed 60% at the end of the preceding financial year.

There have been several efforts to measure the seriousness of indebtedness, particularly in less developed countries and developing countries. The World Bank classifies indebtedness based on two ratios: the ratio of the present value of total debt service to gross national product (GNP) and the ratio of the present value of total debt service to exports. These indicators are shown in Table 1 according to countries' income classification. In 1998, the World Bank published a comprehensive

---

[1]See http://www.insee.fr/en/methodes/default.asp?page=definitions/dette-sens-maastricht.htm

[2]Internal debt thus includes old foreign currency savings war claims, general obligations, long-term bonds, credits, treasury bills and activated warranties (Ministry of Finance 2015).

Table 1 Indebtedness and income criteria

	Indebtedness classification		
Income classification	PV/XGS higher than 220% or PV/GNP higher than 80%	PV/XGS less than 220% but higher than 132%or PV/GNP less than 80% but higher than 48%	PV/XGS less than 132 and PV/GNP less than 48%
Low income: GNP per capita less than $785	Severely indebted low-income countries	Moderately indebted low-income countries	Less indebted low-income countries
Middle income: GNP per capita between $786 and $9635	Severely indebted middle-income countries	Moderately indebted middle-income countries	Less indebted middle-income countries

Source: World Bank (1998)
Note: *PV*, present value of the debt; *XGS*, exports of goods and services

study in which it established a set of indicators by which countries are classified into "less indebted", "moderately indebted" or "overindebted" groups.

However, these thresholds are now obsolete because of the commonly accepted view that there are no uniform thresholds for all countries—or even for groups of countries. Therefore, the modern methodology for assessing public finances is based on the recommendations of the IMF in its *Guidelines for Public Debt Management* from 2014 (IMF 2014). The IMF's *Guidelines* do not define a precise threshold of debt burden indicators to classify countries as more or less indebted. Instead, the IMF recommends a set of indicators that should be followed in order to assess the quality and dynamics of public finances.

The part of the public debt more often analysed for developing countries is external debt, i.e. the debt that is created by borrowing abroad. The IMF's document *External Debt Statistics: Guide for Compilers and Users* precisely defines external debt, how it is measured and which institutional sectors and instruments are considered to be public. Debt sustainability is assessed on the basis of indicators of the debt stock or debt service relative to various measures of repayment capacity (GDP, exports or government revenues). The basic equation is:

$$\text{Debt indicator} = \text{Indebtedness}/\text{Repayment capacity}$$

Indicators based on debt stocks (gross external debt position) are used to identify possible solvency problems. Such indicators include the debt-to-GDP ratio and the debt-to-exports ratio. Indicators based on debt service (interest payments and amortisation) are typically used to assess liquidity problems. Such an indicator is the debt service-to-export ratio. Based on the methodology given in IMF's *Guidelines*, we present some indicators of the debt burden in Bosnia and Herzegovina from 2008 to 2014.

Table 2 shows that while the external debt-to-GDP ratio, which represents the flow position, is rather modest at 31.7% in 2015 (although having doubled since 2008), the external debt-to-exports ratio has reached rather high levels at 88.7% in

Table 2 Indicators of external debt (%)

	2008	2009	2010	2011	2012	2013	2014	2015
External debt-to-exports	61.2	83.8	83.0	79.3	84.6	82.4	88.9	88.7
External debt-to-GDP	16.4	21.0	24.7	25.4	27.2	27.7	30.1	31.7
External debt-to-revenue	38.5	50.3	57.5	58.6	62.2	64.9	68.7	n.a.
External debt service-to-exports	3.4	4.0	4.0	4.0	4.9	7.6	8.2	n.a.
External debt service-to-(government) revenues	0.9	1.0	2.8	3.0	3.6	6.0	6.4	n.a.
Total debt-to-export	107.3	132.8	125.5	118.7	124.1	115.9	124.5	132.7
Total debt-to-GDP	28.8	33.2	37.3	38.1	39.9	39.0	42.2	43.5
Total debt-to-revenues	67.5	79.6	87.0	87.8	91.3	91.4	96.3	n.a.

2015. At the same time, the external debt service-to-export ratio has almost tripled from 3.4% in 2008 to 8.2% in 2015. This indicates a deteriorating capacity to service the external debt, although the actual ratio is still rather low. This suggests that the current level of export earnings can rather easily service the external debt, at least for now.

In addition to external debt analysis, we have also performed an analysis of the total debt indicators in Bosnia and Herzegovina, as internal debt represents a huge part of overall debt, especially in Republika Srpska. Table 2 shows that the total debt-to-GDP and ratio, which represents the stock position, has also increased from about 29% of GDP in 2008 to 43.5% in 2015. This is not in itself a worrying development, as the level of this ratio is low. However, when it comes to total debt stock, the total debt-to-export ratio has increased rather alarmingly to about 133% of GDP, which suggests that there may be difficulties arising in the future in relation to the capacity to repay the debt.

Private Sector Debt

The private sector debt is the stock of liabilities held by the nonfinancial corporate sector,[3] households and non-profit institutions serving households.[4] The main indicator is the stock of private sector debt as a percentage of GDP where the indicative

[3]The nonfinancial corporations sector comprises all private and public corporate enterprises that produce goods or provide nonfinancial services to the market [European System of Accounts ESA 2010, paragraphs 2.45 to 2.54]. See Eurostat (2013).

[4]The instruments that are taken into account to compile private sector debt are debt securities and loans. Data are presented in consolidated terms, i.e. do not take into account transactions within the same sector and expressed in % of GDP and million of national currency. Definitions regarding sectors and instruments are based on ESA 2010. The indicator is calculated as [PSDt/GDPt]×100.

Table 3 Domestic credit to private sector (% of GDP)

	2008	2009	2010	2011	2012	2013	2014	2015
Short-term loans	2667	2551	2722	3017	3273	3252	3053	3066
Long-term loans	4681	4730	4967	4869	4949	5098	5183	5120
Total	7349	7281	7689	7886	8222	8350	8236	8186
Percent of total loans								
Short-term loans	36	35	35	38	40	39	37	37
Long-term loans	64	65	65	62	60	61	63	63
Total	100	100	100	100	100	100	100	100
Change in loans (%)								
	2009	2010	2011	2012	2013	2014	2015	
Short-term loans	−4.4	6.7	10.8	8.5	−0.6	−6.1	0.4	
Long-term loans	1	5	−2	1.6	3	1.7	−1.2	
Total loans	−0.9	5.6	2.6	4.3	1.6	−1.4	−0.6	

Source: World Bank online data

threshold is 133% of GDP.[5] The total amount of loans provided by the commercial banks in Bosnia and Herzegovina was BAM[6] 16.9 billion at the end of 2015. Loans to the private sector amounted to 93% of total outstanding loans by commercial banks (down from 97% in 2008). Loans to households represent approximately half of total private debt and accounted for 42% of newly approved loans to the domestic private sector. Credit to the household sector grew by 4.7% in 2015, while loans to companies decreased.

The growth of total loans was modest in 2015, at about 2% per month. Mikerevic (2015) suggests that the reasons behind this low level of credit growth were the low demand for loans, the lack of quality projects, the poor investment climate, the high risks, the high taxes and the social contributions (Mikerevic 2015). Due to the situation in the banking sector, commercial banks largely use domestic sources to finance new loans, while their use of funds from abroad continues to decrease. At the same time, total deposits in the banking sector continue to rise, reaching BAM 15.6 billion at the end of 2015.

Domestic credit to the private sector decreased from 2008 to 2010 and increased from 2011 to 2013 (see Table 3). Private and public nonfinancial companies do not issue debt securities, so their debt consists only of loans. At the same time, 99% of companies are small and medium sized and do not have access to foreign sources of lending. In Bosnia and Herzegovina, general loans dominate in the loans structure.

[5]Defined by MIP scoreboard, European Commission. See https://ec.europa.eu/info/business-economy-euro/economic-and-fiscal-policy-coordination/eu-economic-governance-monitoring-prevention-correction/macroeconomic-imbalance-procedure/scoreboard_en

[6]The konvertibilna marka (convertible mark or BAM)—the national currency introduced in 1998—is pegged to the euro while central bank is organised as a currency board.

Table 4 Amount of short-term and long-term loans in millions of BAM

	2008	2009	2010	2011	2012	2013	2014	2015
Short-term loans	2667	2551	2722	3017	3273	3252	3053	3066
Long-term loans	4681	4730	4967	4869	4949	5098	5183	5120
Total loans	7349	7281	7689	7886	8222	8350	8236	8186

The Nonfinancial Sector

The main risk for the domestic macroeconomic environment is weak domestic demand as a result of the negative trends in the economy and the low level of competitiveness in foreign trade. The economic environment is unfavourable, which is the main reason behind the low level of investments. Industrial production increased only by a modest 0.2% in 2015. All these factors have led to a low demand for loans from the corporate sector. Over the last 2 years, the corporate sector has been characterised by stagnation in lending activity and a high level of credit risk.

The deflationary tendencies in Bosnia and Herzegovina and in the Eurozone have adversely influenced credit activity, and the high level of credit risk and the restrictive conditions for extending loans have limited credit growth in the nonfinancial sector. The decline in interest rates implies that the banks are ready to finance projects that have an economic justification. However, the growth in company deposits indicates that companies are keeping their money on account rather than investing it in new projects.

The total amount of loans to the corporate sector was BAM 8.2 million at the end of September 2015 (see Table 4). Short-term loans were between 35% and 40% of total loans.

Standard loans were 40% of long-term loans at the end of 2014. Standard and revolving loans are the most important part of total loans. The significant part of non-purpose loans was taken with aim to rescheduling of existing loans. The increasing trend in approved and used overdraft facilities based on revolving loans may indicate that companies are facing liquidity problems and are searching for additional sources of financing to maintain their liquidity.

Loans to private and public companies decreased in the third quarter of 2015, on both quarterly and annual levels, and total newly agreed loans to nonfinancial companies amounted to €412 million, which was equivalent to the level of new loans in the third quarter of 2013 (CBBIH 2015a). Such a trend has been present for a long time, and there are no signs of recovery in bank lending activity.

The rate of return on equity of companies fell from 1.6% in 2013 to 1.2% in 2014. Losses increased from BAM 2.5 billion in 2013 to BAM 3.5 billion in 2014 or by 40%. In recent years companies took non-purpose or revolving loans. As profitability is very low and losses have increased, interest expenses significantly burden businesses. This indicates that more new loans will be used to reschedule existing loans.

Households

High unemployment and low wages are major characteristics of the labour market in Bosnia and Herzegovina. The unemployment rate according to ILO methodology is less than the official registered unemployment rate because a significant number of the registered unemployed work in the shadow economy. Remittances provide an important source of income for many households and may result in higher reservation wages.

Household prosperity indicators such as individual consumption per capita and GDP per capita did not change much in recent years and have remained at low level. Individual consumption per capita was 37% of the average of the EU member states measured in purchasing power standard (PPS).[7] The largest part of individual consumption is used for basic needs, primarily food, non-alcoholic drinks and housing. The low level of wages and their stagnation over a long period of time, together with the high rate of unemployment, have weakened consumer purchase power and domestic aggregate demand (CBBIH 2014). In 2014, the registered unemployment rate fell. In 2015, the average wage was €422, the same as in 2014.

The highest risk for household financial stability is low domestic demand. While household loans have increased, households have increased their saving more than their consumption. In September 2015, the total amount of household loans was BAM 7750 million or BAM 1955 per person (CBBIH 2015b). At the end of 2015, 75.7% of loans were general consumption loans including credit card claims, while housing loans accounted for 21% of total loans. Housing loans declined by 1.2%, while general consumption loans increased in 2015 by 7%. The decline in housing loans even though the interest rate on these loans fell, and the growth in general consumption loans, indicate the low standard of living of households. In previous years, households increased their borrowing in order to solve their housing problems due to uncertainty about their ability to service their debts and due to expectations of further falls in real estate prices (CBBIH 2014). The growth of general consumption loans was mainly due to the low disposable incomes, which caused increased borrowing to meet basic needs of living. During the last quarter of 2015, the growth in loans approved was fairly uneven by their maturity structure. Long-term loans increased by 5.8%, while short-term loans decreased by 2.7%. During this quarter, new loans totalling BAM 588 million were approved to the household sector, which accounts for 42% of newly approved loans to the domestic private sector. This indicates that banks' lending activities are to a large extent focused on the household sector. The share of non-performing loans to in total loans increased sharply in 2009–2011 as result of the financial crisis, but since then they have been on a declining trend (CCBH 2015b).

Deposits of households accounted for 50% of total bank deposits, while they were equivalent to about 85% of total loans to households in 2014–2015. The quarterly

[7] PPS is the term used by Eurostat for the common currency in which national account aggregates are expressed when adjusted for price level differences.

growth of deposits was mostly related to other deposits, reflecting a desire to save. The growth of deposits cannot be explained as an indicator of a better standard of living, but instead reflects uncertainty about future economic conditions.

Conclusion

All the indicators of public debt in Bosnia and Herzegovina have been on a sharp upward trend since 2008. Denial and comparison with developed countries where these indicators maybe even higher are only excuses for not solving the problem. Normally, developed countries have a relatively larger share of debt because the way in which they borrow is different; they have access to international capital markets and stronger economies that are able to carry the burden of debts.

With serious macroeconomic problems including an unemployment rate of around 30% and a persistent current account deficit of around 9% of GDP, debts are an additional problem that the economy can hardly cope with. Without attempting to provide a solution on ways to stop negative trends of borrowing in Bosnia and Herzegovina or its Entities, we would address some issues such as how to reduce the budget deficits at all levels in order to avoid further debts, what should be done with the most vulnerable people and whether further indebtedness is leading Bosnia and Herzegovina towards a Greek scenario. These are not only economic issues; these also have political and general social aspects. The health of the public finances in Bosnia and Herzegovina, and especially in the Republika Srpska, has become a widely discussed topic in the media, but the authorities lack a clear vision on how to solve these problems.

In the conditions of stagnant or slow-growing public revenues, while debts are growing rapidly, an excessively large public administration that threatens private sector production and investment, an uncompetitive economy with low levels of foreign and domestic investments and a poor business environment, debts are just another issue that threatens further progress. Recent negotiations with the IMF on a new loan under an Extended Fund Facility have revealed that the government budgets depend heavily on foreign loans and have also demonstrated that lenders set their own requirements that threaten the sovereignty of the country (through privatisation of the strategic sectors of the economy such as forestry and electric power production and distribution). However, it should be said that under public ownership, these sectors are inefficient and reduce the competitiveness of the economy.

The private sector debt, at about 55% of GDP, is less problematic than public debt. The main characteristic of private debt is a weak demand for loans because of weak business activity and the low standard of living. The stagnation of lending activities and the high credit risk have been the main features of the corporate sector in recent years. Even with low interest rates, companies have few profitable projects because of the low level of demand; if they have liquid assets they often prefer to hold them as idle deposits in the banks. A major concern is that a significant part of additional loans have been taken out with the sole aim of rescheduling existing loans. This may be an indicator that companies are facing serious liquidity problems. At the same time, the profitability of companies is very low, while losses of capital have increased.

In the household sector, the low levels of wages and their stagnation over a long period of time and the high rate of unemployment have weakened consumer purchasing power. In consequence, domestic demand has been relatively weak in recent years. Loans for housing and business activity have decreased, while general consumption loans have been on a growing trend. The continuous decline in housing loans even as interest rates have fallen and the growth of general consumption loans are indicators of the low standard of living of households. The growth of general consumption loans is a direct result of the low level of personal disposable income, which has caused households to borrow increased amounts just in order to meet their basic needs.

References

CBBIH. (2014). *Financial stability report for 2014*. Sarajevo: Central Bank of Bosnia and Herzegovina.

CBBIH. (2015a). *Bulletin no. 3*. Sarajevo: Central Bank of Bosnia and Herzegovina.

CBBIH. (2015b). *Financial stability report for 2015*. Sarajevo: Central Bank of Bosnia and Herzegovina.

EUROSTAT. (2013). *The European system of accounts, ESA 2010*. Luxembourg: Publication Office of the European Union.

IMF. (2014). *Guidelines for public debt management*. Washington: International Monetary Fund.

Mikerevic, D. (2015). Comparative analysis of yield, assets and financial position of the Republic of Srpska economy in 2014. *Financing, 6*(4), 7–24.

Ministry of Finance. (2015). *Information on state of the public debt, various issues from 2008–2014*. Sarajevo: Ministry of Finance and Treasury of Bosnia and Herzegovina.

World Bank. (1998). *Global development finance*. Washington: World Bank.

Trade and Industrial Development in Kosovo

Petrit Gashi

Introduction

A persistent negative trade balance has posed a severe challenge for policymakers in post-war Kosovo. The proposed remedies have mainly focused on liberalising trade with its major trade partners. However, the evidence shows that free trade did not produce significant results for the economy; growth is minute, and exports are low, while unemployment is high and persistent. In line with the other research in the developing world (OECD/WTO/World Bank 2014), recent evidence for Kosovo shows that the effects of a Stabilisation and Association Agreement (SAA), and for that matter the trade liberalisation in general, are conditional on supply-side factors (Gashi et al. 2016). In addition, there are fears that the recent signing of an SAA with the EU, and an FTA with Turkey, may further worsen the position of the slowly emerging small-scale manufacturing activities.

Following years of underinvestment, neglect, and looting, Kosovo's industrial base has been almost completely depleted. After the war, the mining, energy, and manufacturing sectors, which provided the backbone of Kosovo economy in socialist times, were in a state of complete collapse, while technologies and skills had become obsolete. In the early days of the international protectorate, significant steps were taken to turn the tide and revive the industrial sector. UNMIK (the UN body governing Kosovo until 2008) embarked on all-encompassing privatisation programme of the former socially owned enterprises (SOEs). Whether privatisation has supported the industrialisation of Kosovo remains questionable largely due to the lack of hard evidence. However, one can draw some conclusions about the outcomes of the privatisation process, first, by analysing the underlying conditions

P. Gashi (✉)
Faculty of Economics, University of Prishtina, Prishtina, Kosovo

Privatisation Agency of Kosovo, Prishtina, Kosovo
e-mail: petrit.gashi@uni-pr.edu

R. Osbild, W. Bartlett (eds.), *Western Balkan Economies in Transition*, Societies and Political Orders in Transition, https://doi.org/10.1007/978-3-319-93665-9_8

on which the privatisation programme was established, including institutional and legal constraints, the adopted methods of transformation, and other related processes, policies, and institutions, and, second, by analysing the underpinnings of the success of privatisation in other transition countries. This assessment is relevant today, as after almost a decade and a half since the process commenced, more than 50% of the assets have still not been privatised. Some assets in the agriculture sector (i.e. cooperative land) and mining (including Trepça—a large former mining combine) are strategic to the future development of the country. Hence, there is still a significant portion of SOE assets that could potentially support industrialisation and enhance manufacturing capacity.

Firstly, this chapter will look into the developments related to the external sector. Analysing the latest data and the recent literature, it will identify the major constraints to increasing the competitiveness of Kosovo's industries in the international market. In this regard, trade policies and institutions and other related aspects will be reviewed. Secondly, the past and current industrial structure in Kosovo will be discussed. Although Kosovo has not designed a comprehensive industrial policy, specific measures to support local industries have been implemented. These will be highlighted and their effects briefly discussed. Thirdly, the process of privatisation and its legal and institutional framework will be analysed in the context of industrialisation. The underlying constraints that have shaped the process will be examined, including the methods and outcomes of privatisation. Finally, the discussion will centre on the effects of the process of privatisation in the context of its contribution to the industrialisation of the country and its overall development.

The Economy and Trade

In December 2015, the IMF's first review under the stand-by arrangement for Kosovo concluded that the economy was on a sustainable growth path. In addition, the report argued that growth rates were above the regional average, while the macroeconomic environment was stable and the financial sector sound. However, the report also highlighted the persistent shortcomings of the economy, arguing that:

> Kosovo needs stronger- and higher-quality growth to raise incomes and employment. This means moving away from its current remittance- and consumption-driven growth model to one driven by the productive and tradable sectors. This in turn requires strong steps to improve competitiveness and develop a more dynamic private sector. (IMF 2016: 16)

Along the same lines, an MTI (2015) report explained that growth in the early post-war years had been driven by high inflows of development aid. In the latter years, the role of aid as a source of growth had gradually diminished, while the share of remittances had steadily grown. From 2000 to 2013, the joint contribution of aid and remittances amounted to an average of 46% of GDP (MTI 2015). The high share of aid and remittances triggered a consumption boom by both households and government making the latter the main source of growth over the last 15 years.

The MTI report highlighted that between 2010 and 2013, final consumption expenditure reached an average of 109% of GDP.

Similarly, other macro-ingredients paint a picture of a heavily consumption-dependent Kosovo economy. For instance, the credit market is heavily skewed towards consumption, as banks favour households and SMEs in the service sectors (CBK 2015). Furthermore, the overwhelming share of FDI goes into non-tradable sectors, particularly in services and construction. Even the structure of tax receipts reflects the consumption-oriented character of the economy; for instance, consumption taxes (VAT and customs duties) constitute the largest share of government revenues.

The structure of external trade gives additional indications of Kosovo's import-dependent consumption pattern and the low production capacities (on the latter, see the discussion below). The data show that food and other consumption goods have dominated the import structure. The breakdown of imports by sectors shows that even the imports of intermediate goods and technology have not been used to develop the production capabilities of the country but rather to sustain high levels of consumption. For instance, the most important import products in the category of machinery and appliances are boilers for domestic use and home appliances.[1] On the other hand, exports are heavily concentrated on basic metals and other low-value-added products. Iron and steel, ores and concentrates, electrical energy, coal and bitumen, and related products are among the typical exports from post-war Kosovo. The low level of diversification of exports makes Kosovo's economy particularly vulnerable to external price and demand shocks (MTI 2015).

Overall, while there are some positive trends in the export sector, the situation remains challenging. Together with the high level of unemployment, imbalances in the external sector remain one of the most pressing issues facing Kosovo. Despite a good performance of the service sector, the overall trade deficit remains huge (see Table 1). Since 2000, services have performed much better than goods, largely owing to the demand stemming from the presence of international institutions and a significant movement of Kosovo migrants in and out of the country. Moreover, the gap created by goods imports has not been covered by services exports. As a result, the trade deficit in 2014 was over €1.8 billion, or 35% of GDP, while the share of total imports in GDP has been constantly over 50%.

The situation with goods exports remains particularly challenging, and a number of indicators provide more insight into developments in the sector (see Table 2). The first index in the table shows that export earning covered between 5% and 13% of import costs between 2005 and 2014. While exports of goods increased at a significant rate (albeit from a low base and with significant oscillations), imports of goods also increased by 9% over the same period. The depth of imbalances between exports and imports of goods is shown by the normalised trade balance (the ratio of the difference between exports and imports to total external trade). This indicates that while the degree of integration into international markets is high, it

[1]Based on HS nomenclature, Chapter 84.

Table 1 External trade indicators

	2008	2011	2014
Exports of goods and services (current, € millions)	595.4	944.4	1095.2
Goods exports (current, € million)	198.5	319.2	324.6
Service exports (current, € millions)	396.9	625.2	770.6
Exports of goods and services (% of GDP)	15.1	19.8	19.9
Imports of goods and services (current, € millions)	2178.5	2861.2	2972.7
Goods imports (current, € millions)	1928.2	2492.4	2538.2
Service imports (current, € millions)	250.3	368.9	434.5
Imports of goods and services (% of GDP)	55.3	59.9	54.0
Trade balance on goods and services (current, € millions)	−1583.2	−1916.9	−1877.6
Trade balance in goods (current, € millions)	−1729.8	−2173.2	−2213.7
Trade balance in services (current, € millions)	146.6	256.3	336.1
Trade balance (% of GDP)	−41.1	−42.8	−35.1

Source: MTI (2015)

Table 2 Goods exports indexes

	2005–2014
Export-import coverage ratio	Between 5% and 13%
Normalised trade balance	Around −85%
Export propensity index	Around 5%
Import dependency index	Around 30%
Marginal propensity to import index	Over 70%
HH index of sectorial concentration—exports	Between 0.25 and 0.47
HH index of sectorial concentration—imports	Around 0.13
Grubel-Lloyd index	Between 0.030 and 0.065
HH index of geographic concentration—exports	Around 0.35
HH index of geographic concentration—imports	Around 0.27

Source: MTI (2015) and author's calculations based on KAS data. Note: Data are averages, unless otherwise stated

results primarily from goods imports rather than exports—a rather alarming conclusion.

While the low value of the export propensity index (the share of goods exports in GDP) indicates the lack of export orientation of the manufacturing sector, the import dependency index (a measure of the proportion of domestic demand satisfied by imports) remained at around 30%. Bearing on the earlier discussion of the import-driven consumption bias in Kosovo, this index is likely to be much higher for consumption goods. The next index (marginal propensity to import) is of particular relevance, as it measures the increase in imports in a given period of time for a given increase in GDP. The index has decreased slightly in recent years, but on average remains very high. It suggests that between 2005 and 2014, on average 73% of the annual GDP increase is spent on imports.

The next five indices reveal the sectoral and geographic distribution of Kosovo's external trade. The sectoral Herfindahl-Hirschman (HH) index is around three times higher for exports relative to imports. As the index approaches unity, it shows a greater degree of concentration of exports, while a number closer to zero shows a higher degree of diversification. The high degree of concentration into a few exported goods makes Kosovo particularly vulnerable to external demand and price shocks, as was the case during the financial crisis of 2008–2009. Another sector-related indicator is the Grubel-Lloyd index, which shows the degree of intra-/inter-industry trade. Unsurprisingly, there is very little overlap between exported and imported goods, i.e. most of the trade is conducted in goods from different industries. The values of the Grubel-Lloyd index give an indication that Kosovo is narrowly specialising along its static comparative advantages, while product differentiation and economies of scale do not play a significant role in the international competitiveness of Kosovo's businesses.

Finally, the HH index can be applied to analyse the degree of geographical concentration of trade. Again, as in the case of sectoral HH index, a greater geographic concentration of trade partners is associated with a higher degree of vulnerability to shocks. And again, exports are concentrated in fewer destinations than imports. In any case, export and import partners are more or less the same: EU countries, CEFTA (Central European Free Trade Agreement) countries, Turkey and China.

This review of macroeconomic indicators has revealed the strong bias of the economy towards consumption. This bias has been evidenced by the structure of external trade and capital inflows and by the structure of credit and tax receipts. As the MTI concluded, Kosovo has failed to channel its economic resources into productive uses, as consumption bias has diverted resources away from manufacturing, thus limiting employment growth and increasing the poverty rate. As a result, the share of the industry has changed little in the post-war years, remaining at roughly 16% of GDP, while construction and services have increased to 53% of GDP, indicating a continuing process of tertiarisation of the economy.

Trade-Related Constraints and Policy Measures

So, what have been the policy responses to this situation? Contrary to some recommendations,[2] the adopted policy was to increase competitiveness in export markets through an all-encompassing liberalisation.[3] Kosovo liberalised trade with

[2]For instance, Bartlett (2003) suggested that rather than going for complete trade liberalisation, Kosovo should develop an integrated export policy that would rest on three major pillars: competitiveness of domestic companies (border-in policies), trade facilitation programmes (border-related policies), and export promotion programmes (border-out policies).

[3]Kosovo institutions have adopted formally two trade policies, the first in 2005 while the second in 2009. Both policies focus on the need for trade liberalisation as a promoter of export growth.

its major partners. During the period of the UN protectorate, Kosovo negotiated CEFTA agreement with the neighbouring countries, which entered into force in 2007. Member countries have agreed to abolish all import duties on goods, and negotiations are underway on the liberalisation of services. Another major undertaking, in terms of trade liberalisation, was the signing of the Stabilisation and Association Agreement (SAA) with the EU. Before the SAA entered into force, since 2000 Kosovo had already enjoyed a rather free access to the EU market through the so-called autonomous trade measures. However, the SAA is a much deeper integration, ensuring a more stable and predictable trade and investment setting in Kosovo. It also has an additional, very important dimension, since along with the free movement of goods, it requires that Kosovo should undertake substantial institutional reforms during the EU accession process. The Agreement entered into force in April 2016, providing duty free access to the EU for almost all products produced in Kosovo. The Agreement is asymmetric, as Kosovo has not been required to be so generous with the concessions it provides to the EU due to the small size of the economy. The SAA only covers services partially, as it details only the provisions on the rights to establishment.

In addition, Kosovo has negotiated a free trade agreement with Turkey. Although the negotiations were concluded some time ago, the deal is still not in place due to the hesitation of Kosovo institutions to ratify the Agreement from fear that it may adversely affect domestic producers. In addition, Kosovo has signed GSPs (Generalised System of Preferences) with a number of partners, such as the United States, Norway, Japan, and Switzerland. Kosovo has made the first contacts with EFTA mechanisms to look into prospects for signing a trade deal. Finally, Kosovo is assessing the options for WTO membership.

Shielding domestic production was not an option for Kosovo policymakers, local and international alike. Even the import duties that were applied had a fiscal rather than a protective character. Kosovo applies a double import duty rate of 10% and 0%. Currently, most imported goods qualify for the latter rate (machinery, equipment, and certain raw materials are exempted from duties regardless of the country of origin). There are few non-tariff instruments.

In recent years, significant progress has been achieved in trade facilitation reforms. This progress has been recognised by the World Bank Doing Business 2017 report, which ranks Kosovo at 51 out of 190 economies on the ease of trading across borders (an indicator recording the time and cost associated with the logistical process of exporting and importing goods) down from 118 in 2015.[4] Partially, the drop is related to the change in the methodology of estimating the time and costs of international transactions; however, substantive steps have been taken by the government to cut red tape and simplify the procedures at border crossings. Still, problems persist in the form of excessive controls and physical inspections, harmonisation and standardisation of documentary requirements, corruption, lack

[4]http://www.doingbusiness.org/reports/global-reports/doing-business-2017 (accessed on: October 20, 2016).

of coordination between border agencies, insufficient information and data exchange with the border agencies of other countries, and so on. How smoothly goods can flow from one country to another depends also on the measures taken by partner countries in terms of easing the process of clearing goods, the infrastructure in partner countries, and the extent of red tape. In the case of Kosovo, significant problems arise because the processes are not streamlined in the partner countries.

The policy outcomes have been rather negligible, and trade liberalisation is becoming hugely unpopular because it has failed to enhance the competitiveness of the ailing domestic manufacturing sectors, while it has opened the floodgates to imports. This outcome comes as no surprise. For a long time, research has emphasised the fact that liberalisation is a necessary but not a sufficient mechanism to boost exports. As a recent study has argued:

> Actual experience and studies place a greater emphasis on domestic measures taken to enhance countries' production capacities . . . Trade liberalisation may thus be important, but it is only one ingredient among many others. A trade agreement by itself cannot put a given country on the right path, regardless of its ambitions or content; this can be achieved only by the country itself, acting on an understanding of what must be done and the political will to do it. (OECD/WTO/World Bank 2014: 12–13)

Indeed, a series of papers analysing the determinants of Kosovo's external trade highlight the constraints on the supply-side as a determining factor in the growth of exports (see Table 3 for a summary). These studies rely on contemporary trade theories to develop research hypotheses and utilise advanced techniques and data available at both firm and aggregate level to identify the determinants of external trade in general or export behaviour in particular.

Based on aggregate- and sector-level data, Gashi et al. (2016) empirically establish that Kosovo's export performance is largely constrained by supply-side factors. They analyse trade exchanges between Kosovo and the EU from 2005 to 2013 to inform policymakers about the potential benefits of the FTA signed within the framework of the SAA. The study uses a gravity model as a theoretical platform and a dynamic Poisson regression model to address a number of competing methodological issues.[5] The econometric model includes GDP and geographical distance, but excludes some typical gravity model control variables due to the specificities of Kosovo and the EU. The only policy variable that the model incorporates is the effect of the common currency. Uncommon in gravity models of trade is the inclusion of the effect of diaspora in trade exchanges, which has been incorporated in the model on the assumption that it can positively affect trade through the reduction of transaction costs or simply by increasing the demand for native goods. The results are robust to a number of specifications. Low and uniformly insignificant estimated income elasticities of demand for Kosovo's exports suggest that Kosovo produces goods for which EU demand grows little or not at all with

[5]Specifically, the issue of zeros, of which there are many in the Kosovo trade matrix and especially in sectorial databases as well as the prospect of accounting for historical patterns in the trade between Kosovo and the EU.

Table 3 Studies investigating determinants of trade in the context of Kosovo

Study	Theoretical framework	Data	Dependent and independent variables (DV and IV)	Econometric model	Geography	Results
Gashi et al. (2014)	Melitz's dynamic model of export participation	Micro-level data of SMEs (cross section and panel) for 2002, 2005, and 2009	*DV:* The share of total sales generated by exports *IV:* Factors related to human resources, technology, and productivity-enhancing spillovers	Censored regression models; logistic regression	All former socialist countries, including Kosovo	Estimates highlight the particular importance of the human- and technology-related factors to the export behaviour of SMEs in transition countries. Other important factors for SME exporting activities are productivity-enhancing spillovers from industry, especially vertical linkages, firm size, ownership type, type of activity, the availability of external finance, networking through business associations, and market share. In addition, significant period and country differences are identified
Gashi (2014)	Melitz's dynamic model of export participation	A cross section of micro-level data surveyed in 2013	*DV:* [a] Exporters vs. -non-exporters; [b] export experience of firms *IV:* Human resource-related variables, as well as firm growth, technology, and other control variables	Probit regression; censored regression models	Kosovo	Estimates provide mixed results on the relationship between export behaviour and workforce education, while the outcome for the investment in training variable shows a consistent positive and statistically significant relationship with the export propensity and longevity of serving export markets Other factors that affect the decisions of firms to enter and

						serve export markets are found to be firm size, experience, past growth levels, and adoption of quality standards
Gashi et al. (2016)	Gravity model specification	Panel aggregate export and import data between 2005 and 2013 Panel HS-2 digit sectoral export and import data between 2005 and 2013	*DV:* [a] Exports from Kosovo to the EU; [b] imports from the EU to Kosovo *IV:* GDP of partners, distance, common currency, diaspora, and remittances	Dynamic Poisson estimation	Kosovo	The results show that together, persistent trade patterns and an unfavourable combination of demand and supply elasticities suggest that trade liberalisation in isolation is not sufficient to promote exports but may need to be incorporated within a wider policy and institutional framework. In addition, the findings suggest that trade costs should be a particular focus for policy: distance has a big negative influence on Kosovo's exports to EU countries, while diaspora communities promote Kosovo's exports to EU markets, most likely because they offset trade costs through networking

rising income. Conversely, in line with the earlier discussion on 'consumption bias', the paper finds indications of a very high-income elasticity of demand for imports in Kosovo. Further, the estimations identify high persistence in trade patterns.

As a result, the authors argue that the combined influence of persistent trade patterns and an unfavourable combination of demand and supply elasticities suggests that trade liberalisation in isolation is not sufficient to promote exports, but may need to be supplemented by a wider policy and institutional framework to enhance Kosovo's production capacities. Two other important conclusions are that the high level of transaction cost constrains trade and that there is a diaspora effect that greatly enhances trade between the partners.

The other two studies presented in Table 3 (Gashi et al. 2014; Gashi 2014) pinpoint the supply-side factors necessary for success in export markets. In terms of theoretical platforms, the studies acknowledge that no single theory of international trade is able to fully explain firms' international expansion. Both studies rely primarily on Melitz's framework—linking firm heterogeneity and participation in foreign markets—but the models are augmented to incorporate other strands of thought on international trade and other related fields, such as industrial organisation theory, the resource-based view, transaction costs theory, and so on. In terms of econometric techniques, the studies employ censored and binary regression models and use micro-level data: Gashi et al. (2014) utilise a large sample of firms from former socialist countries, while Gashi (2014) employs a sample of around 500 Kosovo SMEs. Results indicate that the constraints related to export expansion—i.e. propensity, intensity, and longevity in export markets—depend largely on a set of factors related to technology, human resources, and other productivity-enhancing factors. Technology-related factors that enhance export performance are related to the introduction of new products and new technologies and the implementation of quality standards. Related to human resources, the education of the workforce is consistently positive and significant in Gashi et al. (2014) in explaining the share of total sales generated by exports. Other skill-related variables that enhance export performance include on-the-job training (see Gashi 2014). Gashi et al. (2014) included a set of variables that identify the link between productivity-enhancing spillovers and export performance. These variables identify industry linkages, such as links between SMEs with foreign firms, large firms, and importers. These linkages are significant and enhance the export performance of SMEs. Finally, among others, these studies argue that size matters, that there are sectoral differences in export performance, that foreign capital, access to credit, and networking support the international expansion of SMEs, and that past firm growth is positively associated with current export performance.

To summarise, the evidence presented here overwhelmingly points to the need to undertake measures that would develop Kosovo's domestic production capacities. Yet, during the period of former Yugoslavia, Kosovo had a rather developed industrial base. In what follows, I look at how the industrial base of Kosovo was depleted during the 1990s. In addition, I examine a small set of policy measures enacted after 2000 to enhance industrial growth in Kosovo. Further in this context, the discussion concentrates on the process of privatising socially owned enterprises

Table 4 Level of development of Kosovo in socialist Yugoslavia

Indicators (% of Yugoslav average)	1984–1985
Territory	4.2
Population	7.6
Social product	2.4
Employment	3.3
Investments	4.6
Industrial production	2.3
Productivity in industry (Yugoslavia = 100)	65.1
Agriculture production	2.6
Exports	2.0
Imports	1.7

Source: Vjetari Statistikor i Kosovës (various years); Jugoslavija 1918–1988—Statistički Godišnjak (1989)

(SOEs), which has been an important mechanism of industrial growth in other transition countries. This discussion is still highly relevant, as more than 50% of the assets of former SOEs have not yet been sold or liquidated. The next section provides a short background on the privatisation process, covering the institutional and legislative framework, the methods of privatisation, and the current state of affairs. Finally, an assessment of the success or failure of the process is made.

Policy Measures to Enhance Industrial Development

Kosovo was the least developed part of the former Yugoslavia. It contributed only fractionally to Yugoslav social product,[6] industrial and agricultural production, and exports (see Table 4). In comparison to Slovenia, the richest part of Yugoslavia, Kosovo's per capita income was in a ratio of 1:9, to Vojvodina 1:4.6, to Macedonia 1:2.2, and to the average Yugoslav level 1:3.7. Kosovo had an extremely high rate of unemployment estimated at over 30%, while Slovenia enjoyed virtually full employment. Lydall (1989) reported that in Kosovo, there was more than one job seeker for every two workers employed in the social sector.[7] The level of productivity in Kosovo had historically been low, and between the early 1970s and the late 1980s, it was around 70% of the Yugoslav average. From the early 1980s, Kosovo absorbed a higher than proportional share of investments from the Federal Fund for the Less Developed Regions aimed at supporting the least developed parts of former Yugoslavia (it absorbed 46% of the total in 1984 and 40% in 1985). However,

[6]Social product was the Yugoslav version of GDP.

[7]In former Yugoslavia, the 'social sector' was the sector composed of socially owned enterprises together with the public sector. It excluded the quite widespread private sector of activity, mainly in agriculture.

Table 5 Industry and mining in Kosovo (% of total)

	1984–1985
Social product	43.2
Workforce	35.5
Investments	52.2
Exports	99.0
Imports	86.7

Source: Vjetari Statistikor i Kosovës (various years)

Kosovo's relative economic position did not change significantly, while the political situation gradually deteriorated throughout the 1980s.

Table 5 provides information on the importance of industry and mining in Kosovo in the mid-1980s. The contribution of industry to social product was over 40%, double than that of agriculture (which was just over 20%). In addition, industry employed over one third of Kosovo's workforce and absorbed over half of total investments. In the context of international trade, industry (including mining) was the only player, at least when it comes to exports. It covered around 99% of exports, while its share in total imports was slightly lower. Over 85% of industrial exports were in the form of raw materials, semi-finished products, and final products for further processing. Actually, in the mid-1980s the latter group generated the largest share of exports with over 60% of the total. The other exports were finished consumption goods, such as food and beverages, textile products, and pharmaceuticals. Europe was the most preferred destination for Kosovo's exports, taking almost 90% of the total. The former Soviet Union and other countries in the socialist block absorbed the largest share of Kosovo exports at 63% of the total.

As the political situation in Kosovo started to deteriorate in the early 1980s, the economy and its industrial base started to weaken. The biggest blow to the Kosovo economy took place in 1989 when, as a result of constitutional changes, Kosovo lost its position as an equal member within the federation and was subjected to direct rule from Belgrade. As a result, the economy collapsed, and with that a huge process of deindustrialisation ensued. Knudsen summarised the dramatic developments of 1989:

> Serbia's oppression of Kosovo in the 1990s included imposition of a 'discriminatory' privatisation regime, described as putting 'the whole of Kosova up for sale at bargain basement prices' whilst excluding Albanians from the right to take part or be consulted. Short-term soft loans from central authorities and domestic banks that had assisted Kosovo's SOEs until 1989 were discontinued, leaving enterprises 'at the mercy of long-term under-investment and capital depreciation [. . .] and cannibalisation of plant and equipment, which were transferred to SOEs based in Serbia'. Following the passing of the Markovic laws, most Kosovo SOEs came under emergency measures introduced by Belgrade. Along with large-scale dismissal of Albanians, these included forced takeovers and mergers of Kosovo's companies with Serbian ones, and sale of enterprises in a discriminatory manner excluding Albanians as well as other investors deemed unfavourable by the Belgrade regime. The fact that Kosovo's values became subject to several such 'illegal ownership transactions' in the 1990s was to have serious implications on international statebuilders' post-war privatisation. (Knudsen 2010: 30-31)

A summary of Palairet's study (2002) on Trepça—the biggest mining and metallurgical complex in Kosovo and one of the biggest in the former Yugoslavia—illustrates the depth of transformations that the industrial sector in Kosovo underwent during the 1990s (see Box 1). However, Trepça was lucky insofar as it managed to survive, while a large number of SOEs were either shut done or became inactive during the 1990s. A significant decrease in investments, widespread mismanagement, and theft from the early 1980s until the end of the war in 1999 caused an enormous reduction in the industrial base.

Box 1 Trepça During the 1990s

Established in 1929, the Trepça mining and metallurgical complex grew to become one of the largest combines in former Yugoslavia. During its heyday it not only operated major mines in Kosovo but also elsewhere in Yugoslavia. Trepça had 21 units with around 23,000 employees or around 10% of total employment in the social sector in Kosovo. In addition to smelting and refining capacities to process zinc, lead, silver, and gold, from the early 1970s, Trepça started to establish and acquire various operations in downstream industries, such as battery production, paint and varnish, ammunition, jewellery, galvanisation, and so on.

During Yugoslav times Trepça absorbed an enormous amount of investment, estimated at $4 billion between 1966 and 1988. Most of these funds were provided by the Federal Government directly or indirectly through banks. The large inflow of the external finance was responsible for the so-called 'Trepça's golden age', between the 1960s and 1980s. Once the inflow stopped, Trepça ran into major difficulties. Typical for socialist enterprises of the similar stature, most of this money was wasted and the investment never lived up to expectations. Apart from poor investment decisions, mismanagement, over-employment, and theft (e.g. the theft of large amounts of silver in the mid-1980s) was typical, and as a result, the business performance was dismal. Trepça 'as a rule' lost money under the Yugoslav system. Following the abolition of central institutions in Kosovo and the introduction of emergency measures, Trepça entered a new phase. Political developments in Kosovo and elsewhere in Yugoslavia were accompanied by the breakdown of the socialist system and a fall in industrial production. The structural changes required to establish a market economy hit heavy industries hard.

Attempts to stabilise the economy in 1989 included a set of monetary reforms that squeezed credit, exposing loss-making systems such as Trepça. As a result, Trepça's business collapsed in 1988–1994. Protesting the political changes in Kosovo and dissatisfied with the poor performance of the enterprise, Albanian employees went on strike. This resulted in their dismissal en masse. Refugees from Croatia and Bosnia as well as expats from Eastern European countries replaced Albanian workers, while government cronies took over the management of the enterprise.

(continued)

Box 1 (continued)

The early 1990s saw changes in the ownership and organisational structure of the company. In 1991, a decision was taken to integrate all 21 units, which enjoyed a high degree autonomy, into a single entity. In 1992, Trepça was transformed into a joint stock company, with the state and society owing just under 90% of shares, while the other shares were distributed among two state banks and nine enterprises. Although some debt was written off, the structure of the shares partially reflected the structure of creditor claims against Trepça. In 1995, the Serbian government tried to revive the enterprise by appointing new management. In 1996 the shares owned by the Serbian Development Fund were transferred to the two biggest state banks and four other corporate enterprises. The new management succeeded in securing new working capital either by selling scrap or by securing loans from state banks or the government development funds. The management started a new wave of acquisitions, integrating all lead and zinc capacities in the country, together with factories producing batteries, cooling equipment, construction, and even farming capacities. Although at the beginning, output recovered significantly, it was hard to maintain activity due to shortages of working capital and labour and worn-out and under-maintained equipment. The management secured contracts with Greek and Swedish and other partners to supply new equipment for the mines and metal processing activities. Even the partial modernisation of the equipment did not boost production, but only increased the level of indebtedness of the company. Several contracts were signed after 1995 with Greek, French, American, Soviet, Swiss, South Korean, and Czech partners. The management received payment in advance to secure working capital, which was repaid in exported metal. As some of these contracts were not honoured, these deals further increased the indebtedness of Trepça. In 2000, concerned with environmental degradation, UNMIK took over the control of Trepça, shutting down the latter's operations in the north of the country.

Source: Palairet (2002)

The first few years after the war were not that different from pre-war years; the depletion of industrial capacities continued as the process of privatisation of former SOEs was delayed due to disputes about ownership (see further discussion below). Two decades of underinvestment and inactivity had led to the obsolescence of technologies and skills. Although the employees returned to these enterprises after the war, the worn-out technologies and outdated skills hindered the revival of most SOEs.

Partially, the responsability for post-war deindustrialisation should be placed on the international institutions governing Kosovo, from whom the revival of industry required a more active and direct role. In contrast, as explained above they relied heavily on the liberal paradigm and pushed for a substantial liberalisation of the economy. It is likely that liberalisation further exacerbated the process of deindustrialisation. The same type of thinking was initially imposed on local leaders as they gradually took over the reins of the economy. However, in recent years dissatisfaction towards trade liberalisation has increased, especially following concerns raised by the business community and civil society about the CEFTA arrangements. The impression has arisen that economic liberalisation has not supported the economy or the welfare of the people. Steadily, a consensus is growing that a more proactive role of the government is required to support the industrial development of the country.

However, to this day the government has not designed a fully fledged industrial policy.[8] Rather, for a number of years, it has employed only scattered measures to revive manufacturing sector, including tax concessions for the manufacturing sector (e.g. reduced import duties for production equipment and raw materials); agricultural subsidies; human resources policies such as skills upgrading; developing industrial parks, and creating plans to develop economic zones; some measures related to the business environment; and so on. In this context, Stiglitz et al. (2013) were right to point out that 'all governments really do have an industrial policy!'. However, they argue further that:

> The only difference is between those who construct their industrial policy consciously and those who let it be shaped by others, typically by special interests, who vie with each other for hidden and open subsidies, for rules and regulations that favor them, usually at the expense of others. (Stiglitz et al. 2013: 7)

It is likely that the resistance of the UN mission in Kosovo and other policymakers towards industrial policy was related to the grave possibility of the second scenario coming to life in such a fragile institutional setting.

The most important policy affecting the industrial regeneration of post-1999 Kosovo was privatisation. It may well have also been the biggest endeavour for the economic development of the country. Although the transition literature has usually placed privatisation within the framework of structural policies, one can also treat the privatisation process in the context of industrial policy. As Sawyer explained:

> Industrial policies can range from changing the form of ownership of a firm or industry (i.e. nationalisation and privatisation), and the encouragement or discouragement mergers, through to legislation governing the relationship between firms (e.g. limiting collusion between firms). (Sawyer 2005: 164-165)

The next section therefore turns to an analysis of privatisation in Kosovo, its context, methods, and results.

[8]In 2014, the Ministry of Trade and Industry developed the 'Concept of Kosova Industrial Policy', a concept document that in general terms lays out the directions for the industrial development of Kosovo.

Privatisation in Kosovo

The privatisation process in Kosovo was shaped by its specific conditions. The first of these was related to the variant of socialism adopted in Yugoslavia, the so-called market socialism, while the second set of conditions was political in nature. Regarding the former, largely confined to ex-Yugoslavia, market socialism was characterised by an ambiguous system of property rights associated with a social property and workers' self-management.[9] Uvalić (2010) explained the complexities of the system of property rights as follows:

> In 1950, 'social property' was introduced as 'property of the whole society', replacing the more traditional concept of state property. 'Social property' gave enterprises only the right to use socially owned assets and to appropriate the proceeds (usus and usus fructus), but not full property rights" (p. 15). "Although Yugoslav enterprises were never given full property rights, the system of self-management ensured workers ample decision-making rights, to the extent that many workers felt they were the real owners of their firm." (p. 20). "There was no clear division of property rights between the state and the firm. Although the firm formally had the right to income generated by socially owned capital, the state remained in charge of 'the rules of the game' (p. 29)

As Knudsen (2010) explained, workers in socially owned enterprises (SOEs) possessed management rights and had a clear, direct stake in the operation and development of the enterprises in which they were employed. However, neither the workers nor the SOEs they managed were the owners of the SOE's assets but only the users of those assets, e.g. land, buildings, and equipment.

Social property, in combination with workers' self-management, raised specific problems regarding privatisation in all parts of former Yugoslavia (Uvalić 2010). Since enterprises were owned 'by everyone and no one', the critical question was who had the authority to sell them—the state, the enterprise, or the employed workers? And following that, who was entitled to the proceeds from privatisation? In addition, another question gave an even more complicated spin to the property issue: Who was entitled to privatise SOEs in Kosovo when it was an international protectorate legally bound to Serbia?[10] After significant delays, the following solutions were proposed. First, the right to administer and sell SOE assets was vested in the Kosovo Trust Agency (KTA). The KTA was established as an independent body entitled to 'administer SOEs as a trustee for their owners' and 'carry out ancillary activities to preserve or enhance the value, viability and

[9]Workers' self-management implied workers' participation in the process of enterprise decision-making, both directly at the workers' general assembly and through representatives in the workers' councils (Uvalić 2010).

[10]The UNSC Resolution 1244 formally ended Serbian rule in Kosovo with the establishment of the international protectorate. However, Kosovo remained legally bound to Serbia until the declaration of independence in 2008.

governance of SOEs'.[11] With the declaration of independence, the KTA was transformed into the Privatisation Agency of Kosovo (PAK) with much the same mandate.[12] Second, the proceeds from the sale of each SOE would be placed into a trust fund, and 20% of the sales revenue was to be awarded to the former employees,[13] while the rest was to be used to address creditors' claims.[14] During the period of governance by the KTA, it was unclear what was to be the fate of the remaining funds after the employees had been paid and creditor claims had been addressed. Under current legislation, the remaining funds are to be transferred to the state for development projects.

As already pointed out, political considerations also had to be addressed within the privatisation process. First, in order to avoid disputes over what belonged to whom (whether the property belonged to Kosovo or Serbia), it was determined that the Agency would administer the property of all SOEs that operated within Kosovo. Consequently, the Agency has administered all SOE property in Kosovo regardless of whether the SOE had been established in Kosovo or elsewhere in former Yugoslavia. Somewhat contradictorily, the law assigned to the Agency the responsibility for administering the property of Kosovar SOEs located abroad. Secondly, the Agency leased assets for 99 years rather than selling them, although the lessee obtained full ownership rights over the assets albeit on a time-limited basis. The law enabled the lessee to possess and use the assets and to transfer them to a third party. However, it stipulated that the length of a lease might only be extended by amending the existing legislation.[15] Finally, the international community in Kosovo was concerned that Kosovo officials or institutions would not treat fairly creditor claims originating from the Serb community in Kosovo or from Serbia. To avoid this, a few checks to the process were made legally binding. Firstly, no distribution of the proceeds from the trust fund was to take place before all claims had been settled. Secondly, a Special Chamber of the Supreme Court was established as the judicial arm of the privatisation process with primary jurisdiction to decide on creditor and other claims against SOEs or the Agency.[16] Thirdly, the law enabled the liquidation process to be subcontracted to an outside party.

---

[11]See UNMIK Regulation 2002/12 on the establishment of the Kosovo Trust Agency (http://kta-kosovo.org/html/index.php?module=htmlpages&func=display&pid=6; accessed on: October 23, 2016).

[12]Much of the current privatisation infrastructure—legal and institutional—is similar to the one establishing KTA. Hence, the designation 'Agency' is used interchangeably for both KTA and PAK, respectively.

[13]The 20% rule was included not as a compensation for the loss of ownership rights but rather as compensation for workers' loss of their management rights (see Knudsen 2010).

[14]A share of proceeds would go into maintaining Agency operations. Currently, it stands at 5%.

[15]See UNMIK Regulation 2003/13 on the Transformation of the Right of Use to Socially-Owned Immovable Property.

[16]The Special Chamber of the Supreme Court, and indeed the entire process of privatisation, has seen a heavy international involvement over the years. Until September 2014, the board of directors of the agency—the main decision-making body—was comprised of members appointed by

The need to fine-tune the process so as to respond to the specificities of the country delayed the process of privatisation significantly. It took almost 2 years after its establishment for the KTA to start a fully fledged privatisation process. Before these details were sorted out, the Department of Trade and Industry (DTI)[17] introduced a process of commercialisation of SOEs, under which they could be leased to investors for a period of 10 years. Much of the design of the commercialisation process was later replicated in the privatisation process, although in the former case ownership rights were not included in the agreements and investors did not gain the right to transfer or place encumbrances on the enterprises they acquired. Ten SOEs were leased under the commercialisation process with no noteworthy achievements. Eventually, these same SOEs underwent a full privatisation process.

The Methods

The KTA – and subsequently PAK – implemented the method of direct sale to privatise SOE assets in Kosovo and carried out privatisation through the so-called 'spin-off' method. The latter came in two variants, i.e. simple and special spin-off. The difference between these two rested on the commitments taken by the new owners for a certain period of time, usually between 2 and 5 years. While simple spin-off does not place any commitments on the new owner, the special spin-off method may require the new owner to maintain the old SOE activity, commit certain level of investment, retain employment, and so on. In any case, through the spin-off process, the Agency bundles all or part of the viable SOE assets into a new limited liability company that inherits the rights and interests of the old SOE's assets, but is not liable for its debts or claims. The liabilities remain with the old SOE, which continue to legally exist. The Agency then sells the shares of the new company in an open tender to private investors. The proceeds are transferred in the trust fund to address Agency commitments (e.g. claims) as stipulated in the legislation.

While the assets of viable SOEs undergo a spin-off process, SOEs without any prospect of survival undergo voluntary liquidation. The Agency initiates the liquidation process whenever it deems that the latter is in the interests of preserving the remaining value of a defunct SOE and protecting the creditor interest in the SOE.

---

international mechanisms governing Kosovo and the local representatives, with the former having the right to veto any board decision. Moreover, a number of judges in the Special Chamber of the Supreme Court are still 'internationals'. All this was done to preserve the credibility of the process.

[17]The Department of Trade and Industry (DTI) was established based on the UNMIK Regulation no. 2000/63. DTI was responsible for managing the overall issues related to the trade and industry in Kosovo.

The Current State of Affairs

Altogether, around 520 SOEs with over 3000 assets have entered the privatisation process. They cover a large spectrum of industrial sectors, mostly in manufacturing. Around 460 SOEs are under liquidation, a process that has been finalised for only 12 SOEs. So far, less than 50% of assets have been sold either through the spin-off procedure or through voluntary liquidation of SOEs. Over 750 new companies have been established and sold through the spin-off method, out of which 26 were established through special spin-off (some of these are still being monitored by the Agency). The rest, i.e. around 530 assets, have been sold through the liquidation process. Over 1700 assets are still held by the PAK and remain to be sold. However, over the last decade and a half, the most viable assets of the former SOEs have been sold, mainly to domestic and diaspora investors. A significant chunk of the land of the agricultural cooperatives has not yet been privatised (around 23,000 hectares), and there are still some significant mining and other capacities that await privatisation.

The proceeds from privatisation have amounted to over €650 million, while the total cost of the process has been around €114 million, mostly financed by donors, government transfers, and a 5% fee collected by the Agency for each transaction. Over €120 million have been paid to satisfy creditor claims. Around €110 million have been distributed to former employees of SOEs, while the transfer to the government budget has exceeded €90 million. A further €30 million was to be distributed in 2016.

One of the major bottlenecks in the process has been the lack of urgency with which the courts deal with submissions related to privatisation, of which there have been around 29,000 so far (lawsuits, claims, requests for preliminary injunctions). At the time of writing, the largest backlog was with the Special Chamber of the Supreme Court, where some 23,000 claims are pending a decision.

The Performance

The evidence on the success or failure of the privatisation process is anecdotal at best. The popular belief is that the privatisation process has brought the economy to its knees, particularly the industrial sector. A summary by one observer resonates with this widely held view:

> 'Although no comprehensive evaluation has so far been undertaken of the economic impact of privatisation in Kosovo, the available evidence indicates that the process has contributed to limiting Kosovo's socio-economic potential, by restricting the operational possibilities of enterprises and transforming them into cash at a time of low value—and by blocking employees from work while awaiting privatisation, and not assisting with post-privatisation employment or social protection' and '. . .privatisation has led to a loss of jobs in Kosovo. . .', while '[t]he process has been marred by allegations of incompetence and mismanagement, and accusations of corruption abound.' (Knudsen 2010: 89)

It is debatable whether privatisation has restricted the operational possibilities of SOEs since many of them ceased their activities following years of mismanagement, neglect, and looting. In addition, unemployment predates the privatisation process; it was already high in the late 1980s and was exacerbated by the mass dismissal of Albanian employees in the early 1990s. Furthermore, it would be highly questionable to channel donor or government investments into the social sector. Djankov & Murrel (2002) argued that the hardening of budget constraints (i.e. placing limits on subsidies to enterprises) has had a positive effect on the restructuring of SOEs. The critique related to post-privatisation aftercare activities, together with the poor governance of the privatisation process, is better substantiated.

Beyond anecdotal evidence, the literature on privatisation in transition economies in Eastern Europe and the former Soviet Union provides some insights into the factors that are critical to the success of the privatisation process. First, it is generally believed that the method of direct sales, such as that adopted in Kosovo, delivered better results compared to the mass privatisation programmes adopted in some other transition countries (Zinnes et al. 2001; Djankov & Murrel 2002; Estrin et al. 2009). Generally, privatisation methods that enabled concentrated ownership rather than dispersed ownership led to more restructuring of privatised companies. In addition, privatisation to outside owners proved more successful compared to sales to insiders (e.g. management buyout). Although the privatisation methods used in Kosovo did not restrict the potential buyers, privatisation by insiders has been rare. Furthermore, foreign investors have generally favoured the direct sale method of privatisation (Goldberg & Nellis 2008). By bringing know-how and capital, foreign direct investment (FDI) has been vital for the regeneration of former state-owned enterprises in most transition countries. However, foreign firms have not participated much in the privatisation process. The largest share of FDI has come from Kosovo's diaspora, who provided about €57 million or 9% of total sales revenues from privatisation.

A further argument is that the success of privatisation is conditional on the policy and institutional development of the country. For instance, Estrin et al. (2009) found that when privatisation was accompanied by complementary reforms, it had a positive effect on the level of aggregate output. Similarly, using panel data from 25 transition countries, Zinnes et al. (2001) found a positive relationship between privatisation and GDP growth, so long as it is accompanied by hard budget constraints and in-depth institutional reforms. According to them, the transfer of ownership alone is not enough to improve economic performance, suggesting that improvements in institutions such as those related to prudential, regulatory, and budgetary authorities are also needed. Goldberg and Nellis were even more specific on the types of institutions needed for successful privatisation:

> ...developed property rights; enforceable contracts, or, more generally, court decisions that are timely and based on the law, not payments or social precedence; regulatory agencies that deliver timely, law-based decisions that are reasonable and credible for both investors and consumers; and a public administration that meets modicum standards of predictability, competence, and probity. (Goldberg & Nellis 2008: 349)

In Kosovo, privatisation was carried out in a weak regulatory and institutional environment. The post-war institutional mechanisms had been built from scratch, and there was a systematic lack of human and technical capacities. Coordination was almost non-existent. In such circumstances corruption flourished, while property rights were not effectively enforced. To this day, the poor enforcement of contracts is a grave concern.[18] Furthermore, the sluggish performance of the Special Chamber of the Supreme Court—as discussed earlier—is characteristic of the entire judiciary. Furthermore, although a central bank had been established in the early days of the international administration, developing a sound financial market took longer, and a functioning capital market did not exist until after 2010. On a final note, from the entire social sector, only Trepça benefited from government subsidies due to its economic, social, and political importance.

In summary, it is clear that extensive research is required to evaluate the impact of the privatisation process in Kosovo, especially its effects on industrialisation. The above discussion indicates that privatisation has not been much of a success mainly due to systemic shortcomings in the institutional and policy environment. However, the poor quality of institutions makes other alternatives to privatisation even less feasible. This discussion remains highly relevant for Kosovo because, as pointed out earlier, over 50% of SOE assets still await privatisation. It is even more discouraging that the value of the remaining socially owned assets is gradually diminishing, either due to mismanagement or theft. Taking these factors into account, I would echo Kaufmann and Siegelbaum's observation that 'privatisation—with all its inadequacies—is preferable to its absence' (1996, 456). In any case, even though privatisation may have no alternative, a careful weighing of options is needed over some key mining and agricultural assets that have not yet been privatised so as to ensure increased production capacities for the wider development of the country.

Conclusion

In the last 15 years, Kosovo has faced some serious economic challenges. Among the most pressing has been the position of the external sector. Particularly, the persistent and huge negative trade balance in goods has proven to be a daunting problem for policymakers. Governing bodies—both local and international—believed that trade liberalisation would remedy the situation. Trade with neighbouring countries were liberalised first, followed by the liberalisation of trade with the EU. The belief in the benefits of liberalisation is still widely held, and the government has negotiated an FTA with Turkey. In addition, it is planning to begin negotiations with EFTA countries and is weighing up the advantages of membership in the WTO. However, trade liberalisation has not produced the expected results, as it did not enhance the competitiveness of domestic industries. It did, however,

[18] According to the World Bank Doing Business report 2017.

exacerbate the consumption bias of an already heavily consumption-dependent country.

The benefits from trade liberalisation were limited due to supply-side constraints. As with other countries, research on Kosovo has established that liberalisation is a necessary but not a sufficient mechanism to boost exports. Greater emphasis should be placed on domestic measures to enhance production capacities. The recent literature argues that policymakers should consider industrial policy mechanisms to boost the country's productive capacities. The above discussion has shown that although Kosovo has adopted some industrial policy measures, they are limited and rather fragmentary.

The most important industrial policy reform has been the privatisation of the SOEs. During the Yugoslav era, Kosovo built a significant industrial base, but it suffered greatly from political developments in the 1990s. It was believed that privatisation might be able to regenerate the former social sector after years of underinvestment, mismanagement, and looting, by transferring ownership rights to the private sector. A privatisation programme was designed to address the economic, social, and political requirements of the time, using specific methods to transform the property. However, the success of the process is questionable. Although the evidence is scarce, it seems that privatisation fell short of success largely due to systemic shortcomings in the institutional and policy environment supporting the process.

The discussion of the privatisation process in the context of industrial growth in Kosovo is still highly relevant, as over 50% of the assets of the former SOEs have not yet been sold or liquidated. With informed policymaking, the transformation of some of these remaining assets could contribute to increasing the production capacity of the country and contribute to a wider economic development. This would extend the production base, which is already being gradually expanded by new private initiatives. Only once a critical mass has been achieved are the effects of trade liberalisation likely to become more visible.

References

Bartlett, W. (2003). An integrated export policy for Kosova. In Riinvest (Ed.), *Trade policies and export promotion in Kosova*. Prishtina: Riinvest.

CBK. (2015). *Annual report 2015*. Prishtina: Central Bank of Kosovo.

Djankov, S., & Murrel, P. (2002). Enterprise restructuring in transition: A quantitative survey. *Journal of Economic Literature, XL*, 739–792.

Enti Krahinor i Statistikës. (n.d.). *Vjetari Statistikor i Kosovës*. Prishtina: Progres – Svetozar Gjorgjeviq.

Estrin, S., Hanousek, J., Kočenda, E., & Svejnar, J. (2009). The effects of privatization and ownership in transition economies. *Journal of Economic Literature, 47*(3), 1–30.

Gashi, P. (2014). Human capital and export decisions: The case of small and medium enterprises in Kosovo. *Croatian Economic Survey, 16*(2), 91–120.

Gashi, P., Hisarciklilar, M., & Pugh, P. (2016). Kosovo – EU trade relations: A dynamic panel poisson approach. *Applied Economics*. https://doi.org/10.1080/00036846.2016.1245836.

Gashi, P., Pugh, G., & Hashi, I. (2014). Export behaviour of smes in transition countries. *Small Business Economics, 42*, 407–435.
Goldberg, I., & Nellis, J. (2008). Methods and institutions – How do they matter?: Lessons from privatization and restructuring in the post-socialist transition. In I. Lieberman & D. Kopf (Eds.), *Privatization in transition economies: The ongoing story*. Amsterdam: Elsevier.
IMF. (2016). *Republic of Kosovo IMF country report No. 16/22*. Washington DC: International Monetary Fund.
Kaufmann, D., & Siegelbaum, P. (1996). Privatization and corruption in transition economies. *Journal of International Affairs, 50*(2), 419–458.
Knudsen, R. A. (2010). Privatization in Kosovo: The International Project 1999–2008. NUPI report. Oslo: Norwegian Institute of International Affairs
Lydall, H. (1989). *Yugoslavia in crisis*. Oxford: Clarendon Press.
MTI. (2015). *15 years of transition in Kosovo: Implication for trade*. Prishtina: Ministry of Trade and Industry.
OECD/WTO/World Bank (2014). *Global value chains: Challenges, opportunities, and implications for policy*. Report Prepared for Submission to the G20 Trade Ministers Meeting, Sydney, Australia.
Palairet, M. (2002). *Trepča, 1965–2000*. Berlin: European Stability Initiative.
Savezni Zavod za Statistiku. (1989). *Jugoslavija 1918–1988 – Statistički Godišnjak*. Beograd: IŠKRO Savremena Administracija.
Sawyer, M. (2005). *The UK economy*. Oxford: Oxford University Press.
Stiglitz, J., Lin, J., Monga, C., Patel, E. (2013). *Industrial policy in the African context* (World Bank Policy Research Working Paper 6633).
Uvalić, M. (2010). *Serbia's transition: Towards a better future*. London: Palgrave Macmillan.
Zinnes, C., Eliat, Y., Sachs, J. (2001). *The gains from privatization in transition economies: Is "change of ownership" enough?* (IMF Staff Papers No. 48).

Social Policy During a Decade of Centre-Right Governance in Macedonia

Maja Gerovska Mitev

Introduction

The analysis in this chapter shows that during the 10-year period of the VMRO-DPMNE rule, social protection has been reshaped in order to serve clients that are less vulnerable than in the past. Active labour market policies (ALMPs) have been designed in a way that excludes "hard to serve" clients and have targeted those more easily activated among the unemployed. The introduction of arbitrary increases in welfare entitlements has become a new norm. The creation of social policy throughout the period has slowly dissolved into a monolithic and top-down policy process, excluding any possibility for reflection, for the use of critical approaches or for the utilisation of prior knowledge and experience.

Ideological preferences for, and political influences on, the creation of social policy have been a constant source of interest among researchers and analysts. Theoretical and empirical findings have shown that traditional conservative ideology implemented through decommodification and stratification favours a form of social policy that privileges and preserves the family and is unwilling to alter status and class structures (Esping-Anderson 1990). Assessing the impact of political parties on the dynamics of social expenditure, Kittel and Obinger (2002) found that the share of conservative parties in a government restrains the growth of social expenditure. However, political and partisan forces, ideologies and institutions are only some of the key elements in the social policy process (Schneider and Ingraham 1984). Other important variables that relate to social policy outcomes include the level of economic development, as well as the maturity of the social security system.

M. Gerovska Mitev (✉)
Faculty of Philosophy, Institute of Social Work and Social Policy, University Ss. Cyril and Methodius, Skopje, Macedonia
e-mail: gerovska@fzf.ukim.edu.mk

R. Osbild, W. Bartlett (eds.), *Western Balkan Economies in Transition*, Societies and Political Orders in Transition, https://doi.org/10.1007/978-3-319-93665-9_9

Social policy in Macedonia has always evolved through an indirect process, depending on economic and political conditions and priorities. In addition, the trajectory of social policy during the post-independence phase (1991–2000) followed the reform requirements of the international financial institutions (IFIs), which undermined the legacies of the previous social policy (e.g. generational solidarity in the pension system and universality of the social protection system). The outcome of such a subordinated and detached social policymaking process was a weakened social protection scheme, providing minimal protection to an increasingly narrow group of vulnerable people.

The entry into power in 2006 of VMRO-DPMNE, a centre-right political party with demo-Christian and conservative values, initially made little difference to the existing patterns of social policy. Although the main priorities within their electoral programme (2006–2010) were economic reform and the reduction of unemployment, these were not immediately implemented through specific social policy programmes or reform proposals.[1] In fact, they did not aim to achieve their main priorities through the social protection system. The party lacked a thorough knowledge of the social protection system, and it may have been this factor that led to a fragmentation of the system and a decrease in the use of redistribution as a means of equalising resources and opportunities for more vulnerable people. Prominent among the social policy instruments that have dominated their policy agenda at a later stage were active employment and self-employment programmes and measures. An analysis of their initial social policy programmes and their current approaches to social protection shows a huge discrepancy between them. Differences can be seen in relation to the principles, scope and targeting of social policy, all of which are analysed in more detail in the following sections.

Socio-economic and Political Context of Social Policy Creation in the Last Decade

The economic conditions in Macedonia have never been advantageous for a more comprehensive approach to the design of social policy. However, since 2004 the country has experienced a positive trend in GDP growth, peaking in 2007 when real GDP increased by 6.5%. This rapid growth came to an end in 2009, when real GDP fell by 0.4%, and since then, up to 2016, it never increased by more than 4% per annum. However, even during the 5 years of rapid economic growth at above 4% from 2004 to 2008, living standards did not improve much, and the unemployment rate declined by only 3.4% points. Although the unemployment rate has continued to decline since then, it is still exceptionally high standing at 26.1% in 2015. The Bretton Woods Institutions have acknowledged that economic growth in Macedonia

[1] Programme of VMRO-DPMNE for Rebirth 2008–2012, "Rebirth in 100 Steps: Upgraded and Expanded", Skopje: VMRO-DPMNE.

has not benefitted all segments of society. The VMRO-DPMNE government strictly followed the recommendations of the World Bank and the IMF to accelerate structural reforms by improving the investment climate, decreasing the informal economy through a reduction of social security contribution rates and introducing a flat tax rate on personal income (and abolishing the previously progressive tax system). Unfortunately, this economic determinism was not accompanied by comprehensive social policies. On the contrary, the main motto of the conservative VMRO-DPMNE government, in all their political platforms, emphasised that "the best social policy is a sound economic policy". Such an approach clearly signalled that social policy was not seen as a productive factor, but rather as an expense that should be limited and only provided to those who had earned the right to benefit from it.

The social outcomes of the economic reforms were slow and often not very successful. Since 2006 the employment rate has been improving, albeit with modest progress, from 35 to 42% over the 10-year period. Unemployment, although significantly reduced, remains among the highest in the region and in Europe with particularly worrisome trends among young people (in 2015 the unemployment rate was 47% among 15–24 years old and 39% among 25–29 years old). Poverty too is very high, at a rate of 22% in 2015, with highest rate among children aged 0–17 (29%) and households with three and more children (52%). The unequal income distribution has only started to improve since 2014, while the Gini index for 2015 at 34% indicates high disparities.

While the initial years of the VMRO-DPMNE-led government (2006–2009) can be associated with more dynamic economic reforms and progress, as well as a more open and transparent policymaking process, this has changed more recently. Since 2009, there have been serious and constant criticisms related to the independence of part of the judiciary (European Commission 2009), the growing dependency of the media on the state (OSCE 2009), the high level of politicisation (Atanasova and Bache 2010) and corruption in the public sector (UNODC 2011). In addition, the process of adopting laws without any public debate or consultation culminated in changes to the Law on Higher Education which introduced a controversial new school-leaving exam and in amendments to a number of laws related to the introduction of social contributions for "honorary workers". This type of sudden and isolated policymaking led to large demonstrations by students, temporary workers and various civil society organisations.

Other political and societal actors, such as the political parties in the opposition block, civil society organisations and trade unions, were not included in the policy process as constructive partners. Only voices that affirmed the government's actions were acclaimed and supported. Hence, a, monolithic approach to the creation of social policy emerged that led towards policies and measures that were not based on the needs of the population for social protection (as evidenced by the trends of low incomes, high poverty, extremely high unemployment among youth and so on), but were rather either hand-picked from different international policy menus in a process of policy transfer that lacked any strategic coherence with the existing social protection system and which were instantly adopted to serve the short-term goals of the ruling party.

Family Benefits Through the Conservative Lens

Macedonia's family and child protection system was formed during the socialist period before 1990 and comprised benefits targeted at parents and their children. The main mechanisms of support were contribution-based paid maternity leave and different forms of child benefits such as financial support for the first-born child, a child allowance for school children, a special child allowance for disabled children and cost-sharing assistance for preschool education. The principles of family and child support were less universal than in the past consisting only of financial support for the first-born and were largely based on employment. However, the general characteristic of most tax-financed social benefits, including child benefits, was their low absolute amount. Hence, they could not significantly contribute much to poverty reduction, but nevertheless represented an important monthly supplement for low-income parents.

The introduction of a parental allowance for the third child in 2010 denoted a different pattern of child benefits. Its particularity was in the fact that it was almost four and half times higher than the child benefit, twice as much as the special child allowance, and its explicit target was not low-income households. Rather, it was a universal flat rate transfer with no income threshold or condition. The introduction of universal social transfers could be welcomed in a context in which targeted and means tested benefits have occupied much of the social policy agenda. However, as indicated by Bradshaw and Finch (2002), policies towards families and children are typically much influenced by the particular national labour market and demographic context. In Macedonia, the demographic argument for introducing the parental allowance for a third child can be justified. According to the data from the State Statistical Office and Eurostat, the natural rate of population growth fell from 2.7 per thousand in 2004 to 2.3 in 2009, and the fertility rate fell from 1.80 live birth per thousand women in 2002 to 1.5 throughout 2005–2009.[2] Yet, other national trends, such as the high poverty rate among households with three and more children, the low labour market participation of women, accompanied by a continual decrease in the number of beneficiaries of social transfers targeted at low-income families (i.e. social financial assistance and child allowance), signify that the introduction of the parental allowance for the third child did not correspond to the socio-economic context and the priorities of the social protection system. Instead, all households with three or more children, not only the poorest, received those benefits. According to an analysis by UNICEF, "it is the costliest scheme within the social protection portfolio and estimates indicate that in less than 10 years' time its annual budget will be close

[2]*State Statistical Office Makstat database (2005–2009) and Eurostat online data.*

Table 1 Beneficiaries of parental allowance for the third child, 2010–2015

Year	Parental allowance for third child			
		Beneficiaries		
	Number of children	Mother	Father	Guardian/other
2010	5256	5250	1	–
2011	8249	8236	8	1
2012	11,216	11,196	15	1
2013	13,799	13,773	20	2
2014	17,117	17,078	30	4
2015	20,930	20,877	45	4

Source: SSO (2016)

to 51.7 million Euros, which represents 0.75 per cent of current GDP" (UNICEF 2013: 64).

Apart from the economic argument that this benefit could place a serious financial burden on the budget (see Table 1), the demographic data also show that it has not achieved its primary goal of stimulating population growth. Since its introduction, the fertility rate remained stable at 1.5 throughout 2010–2015. Meanwhile, the natural increase in population fell from 2.5 in 2010 to 1.3 in 2015.

The introduction of these untargeted social transfers by the ruling VMRO-DPMNE party goes hand in hand with the main priorities of their ideology, namely, the preservation of the traditional family. When comparing with other countries, we find similar policy approaches in societies led by conservative parties. For example, in Hungary, family policy is focused on "expansion of the income of better-off families and the shrinking protection of poor families" (Szikra 2014). However, she also confirms that this approach did not lead to higher birth rates (2014). The conservative Law and Justice party in Poland introduced the Family 500+ programme in February 2016, which provides universal child-raising benefit of 500 zloty (€114) per month for a second child under 18. Sowa (2016) worries that the Polish law could decrease the employability of low-qualified women of reproductive age, create overlapping benefits, diminish the administrative capacity to process applications and lead to the abuse of benefits. According to a Polish parent, 500 zlotys per month will not encourage more children; what is needed are "cheaper housing loans, the opportunity to return to work after pregnancy and more well-financed kindergartens" (Berardi 2016). Indeed, Luci and Thevenon (2011) show that while cash benefits can have an effect on the timing of births, their effect on the final fertility choices of individuals is doubtful and that "a coherent mix of family policies, supporting a combination of family and work in a comprehensive way, encourages fertility" (Luci and Thevenon 2011: 11). Hence, in the Macedonian case, due to high unemployment rate as well as absence of steady economic growth that would make households feel more confident about expanding their family size, it may be expected that parental allocation for the third child will not bring about a positive effect on population growth. However, if this benefit were to be reoriented towards low-income households with children, it could have beneficial effects in reducing the high rates of child poverty and poverty among households with three and more children. A similar policy proposal has already been put forward by UNICEF, which advocates a "merging of Parental and Child Allowances to develop a new model that improves targeting, raises coverage of the poorest families from 18 to 54 per cent, and increases impact and cost-efficiency" (Carraro and Beazley 2013).

Three other new social transfers have been introduced targeted towards (1) single parents with disabled children, (2) children without parents or parental care and (3) mothers who give birth to a fourth child. These measures also demonstrate the lack of a coherent strategy within the social protection system and its atomisation into separate unconnected policy programmes. Although all the targeted groups deserve attention and support from the social protection system, the timing of the introduction of these measures and their anticipated use, their lack of targeting and the absence of any linkage with similar measures brings them all into question. The absence of a coherent approach to targeting social transfers can also be seen through the introduction of financial assistance for single parents with disabled children. This benefit is targeted only towards the registered unemployed and persons not receiving pension after their retirement age (62 for women and 64 for men). Why these groups have been chosen and why other single parents with disabled children are excluded are neither clear nor publicly discussed. The introduction of financial assistance to mothers of a fourth child is even more peculiar. This right is guaranteed to those mothers who have had a fourth child since 2009; it can only be used after they reach pensionable age of 62 and cannot be accessed in the years after giving birth when it is needed most. Finally, the provision of separate rights for children without parents and parental care openly stigmatises them. The timing of advocating and of introducing these new social transfers coincided with pre-election periods, suggesting that they have more of a clientelistic logic than one related to real social need.

As a result, it may be argued that the policy approaches that the ruling party have adopted concerning the social and child protection systems consist of unsystematic and disconnected social programmes, without any coherent priorities or goals. Thus, while population growth is a clear aim, it has not been achieved by social transfers. At the same time, a reduction of poverty either in general or among specific groups, although an important social problem, has not been a priority aim of the government as the budget for social transfers to low-income households is much lower than the budget for other types of social transfers to households irrespective of their income.

Reforms Related to Active Labour Market Programmes

Since the VMRO-DPMNE came to power in 2006, the issue of unemployment has constantly been placed high on the government agenda. Attracting foreign direct investment has been the main policy instrument in the fight against unemployment. This indeed proved to be an important tool, which in the early years of the VMRO-DPMNE government increased due to privatisation, while later on special economic zones and fiscal incentives for investors such as a 10-year profit tax holiday were

Table 2 Numbers of unemployed people registered at the Agency for Employment (2007–2016, December)

	Actively looking for work	Other unemployed	Total
2007	354,661		354,661
2008	342,227		342,227
2009	340,931		340,931
2010	321,341		321,341
2011	281,144		281,144
2012	243,403	419	243,822
2013	96,200	121,658	217,858
2014	123,661	100,147	223,808
2015	114,979	95,758	210,737
2016	104,523	96,251	200,774

Source: Agency for Employment, Skopje

offered to foreign investors.[3] Active labour market policies were quite modest in the period from 2008 to 2011. They received only a low level of fiscal support, ranging from 0.07% of GDP in 2008 to 0.11% of GDP in 2011, and covered only 2% of the unemployed during this period (Mojsoska-Blazevski 2011).

Fostering active labour market policy, particularly its effective take-up, is not easy in the Macedonian context, as the profile of the registered unemployed is very unfavourable. Due to some inherited rights from the previous socialist system, many of the unemployed register at the Employment Agency only to gain access to free health insurance granted to all unemployed. Hence, many of them are not interested in finding a job or participating in the labour market. So, in 2010, the government introduced changes within the Employment Agency and transferred those registering only for free health insurance and not actively looking for work to the Health Insurance Fund. This has reduced the numbers of registered unemployed by almost 80,000 people. Despite this, many of the registered unemployed lack primary education and are long-term unemployed. So the law was amended to differentiate between unemployed persons that actively look for job and who must report at the Agency every month, other unemployed persons looking for job who must register every 6 months and persons who have twice rejected an employment offer from the Agency.[4] This has halved the number of registered unemployed, as those not actively seeking work are not counted in the overall number of registered unemployed (see Table 2). Worryingly, they are excluded from access to measures for labour market activation. Despite the fact that the status of "passive" unemployed can be changed to "active" unemployed at the request of the unemployed person, participation in the active labour market policies (ALMPs) is not automatically granted, as the ALMP measures require claimants to be registered as actively

[3]This is the "Invest in Macedonia" project. See Agency for Foreign Investments and Export Promotion, http://www.investinmacedonia.com

[4]The Law for Employment and Unemployment Insurance Official Gazette of RM, 153/2012.

employed for a minimum of 6 months. This arbitrary modification has been detrimental to many people, particularly to the most disadvantaged communities, such as Roma.

Operational plans for active employment programmes and measures published in 2014, 2015 and 2016 do not envisage any activation measures for those registered as "other unemployed".[5] This is especially problematic, as this group is quite large (48% of the registered unemployed) and is composed of the most vulnerable. Hence, they will continue to be counted among the unemployed, unless some long-term measures are introduced to improve their literacy, education and employability.

The most recent ALMP measure was carried out as a separate project outside the formal system for employment protection. The policy approach involves avoiding existing measures and programmes and substituting them with project-type short-term programmes. The project "Employing Macedonia" was solemnly announced and initiated in March 2015 (Gerovska Mitev 2015). Its main goal was to speed up the reduction of unemployment from 27% in the first quarter of 2015. The project targeted five categories of registered unemployed persons, incentivising employers with tax or social contribution exemptions. The project succeeded in reaching its goal, creating 19,000 jobs in 10,140 companies (MLSP 2016), and a second phase "Employing Macedonia 2" has been implemented.

At first glance, the project succeeded in achieving its goals and targets. However, detailed inspection of its elements identifies critical issues. While contrasting with other government strategies and goals, it fails to activate the vulnerable unemployed. In this respect, one could argue that the exclusive focus on tax and social contribution exemptions may jeopardise the solvency of social insurance funds and discriminate against employers who are regular tax and social contribution payers. Moreover, it is inconsistent with other reforms that have been undertaken such as the introduction of mandatory fully funded pension insurance and the reduction of social contribution rates, which are based on regular payments of social contributions. Also, requiring employers to guarantee the created jobs for a period of 5 years (3 years for small- and medium-sized enterprises—SMEs) in a context in which most SMEs face liquidity problems speaks volumes about the short-term goals of this project in which the take-up of the measures is more important than their sustainability. Maybe the most problematic aspect is that most measures fail to focus on the provision of training or the enhancement of skills. Since on-the-job training enhances skills, those that do not benefit from state job subsidies should be provided with other options to improve their employability.

In addition, despite the fact that one of the five targeted categories includes vulnerable unemployed people, in order to be able to benefit from the measure, they must have been registered for at least 3 months before the start of the project. In this way the "other unemployed" are not in a position to benefit from the "Employing Macedonia" project. Finally, anecdotal evidence suggests that many

[5]Ministry of Labour and Social Policy, Operational Plans for Active Employment Programmes and Measures.

of the unemployed who were included in the project have been removed from the Agency's unemployment statistics of the Agency, without actually initiating their employment contracts.

The fragmentation of employment policy instruments into short-term projects without incorporating them into the overall employment and social protection schemes does not support the transitions from social protection to the labour market nor the workfare of those who are long-term dependents on the social protection system.

Adequacy of Social Benefits: Social Financial Assistance and Pensions

An additional line of policy undertaken since 2014 by VMRO-DPMNE relates to increases in the amounts of social protection and social insurance. In particular, instead of indexing and adjusting pensions and social assistance according to changes in the cost of living or the average wage, the government began to increase them in nominal terms (e.g. a fixed increase of 5%). As indicated by IEG "the replacement of the indexation mechanism for pensions by ad-hoc increases and discretionary policy decisions has increased the risks to the stability of the pension system, has reduced the predictability of public financial management and has heightened the risks to fiscal sustainability" (IEG 2016: 8).

This discretionary approach is particularly problematic for social financial assistance (SFA), whose amount is extremely low. For example, the SFA is defined in nominal terms, and in 2016 it was 2451 denars (about €40) for a household with one member. For every additional household member, the base increases by a coefficient of 0.37, up to five family members. The amount is paid in full during the first 3 years, but only 50% is paid from year four onwards. For example, for a couple with two children aged 5 and 10 with both parents unemployed, the amount of the monthly SFA would be 5173 denars (about €84) less the total income of the family.

Up until 2014, the amount of SFA was adjusted on an annual basis according to the cost of living for the previous year. However, as mentioned above over the last 3 years it has been increased at a fixed rate of 5%, although if compared with the increase in the cost of living this did not make a huge difference. Nor was the scope of eligible households increased. The World Bank noted: "freeing of resources from improved targeting has not been used to relax eligibility criteria for financial assistance to cover more vulnerable groups marginally above the threshold. This could have been a step forward for the social protection agenda given that one-fourth of the country's population, or around 150,000 households, is below the poverty line" (IEG 2016: 14). Taking into consideration the timing of these increases, it could be argued that they served electoral purposes rather than anything else.

Despite the nominal increases in the SFA, spending on social transfers remains low. The only sources of information are World Bank estimates and government

Table 3 Central government expenditures on social assistance and pensions (% GDP)

	2011	2012	2013	2014	2015	2016
Social assistance (all types)	4.9	5.0	4.7	4.5	4.4	4.4
Pensions	8.5	8.8	9.0	9.2	9.3	9.5

Source: World Bank (2015)

administrative sources. Despite nominal increases of SFA, its share in GDP has actually been declining (see Table 3).

On the other hand, the share of pension expenditure in GDP has increased. This presents a serious challenge. Its growth is not due to the 5% nominal increase in pensions in recent years, but is a combined effect of cuts in social insurance contribution rates and the transition costs for the introduction of a second mandatory private pension pillar based on individual accounts. According to the Public Expenditure Report "the increase of the pensions share in total expenditures has not only elevated the risks to fiscal sustainability, but also negatively affected the effectiveness of public expenditures and the equity of public resource use" (IEG 2016: 11).

The use of discretionary power to set the amount of social welfare benefits represents a new welfare approach introduced by the VMRO-DPMNE government. It is a form of clientelism, similar to that in the Mediterranean welfare states, that has been identified as "patron–client relations that entail the provision of tangible resources in return for political support" (Eisenstadt and Roniger 1984). This approach has been expanded by introducing new measures, such as the arbitrary setting of the level of social welfare entitlements.

Discussion

The last 10 years of political leadership under the VMRO-DPMNE government has brought new approaches to the creation and distribution of social welfare rights. The new policies and rights are not path-dependent, i.e. they do not correspond to the legacies of the previous social protection system that existed under the socialist system prior to 1991. Although these new measures are not definitive, they nevertheless signify a change in the scope and principles of the social protection system. Several dimensions of change are noticeable in the policies related to employment, social and child welfare and social insurance.

First, vulnerability is no longer a leading principle in assessing rights in the social protection system. Following the introduction of new social welfare benefits with no upper income threshold, whose total amount is above the "traditional" social rights targeted towards low-income households and disabled people, the bulk of social transfers have shifted towards the "less vulnerable". In a context of low economic growth and a high rate of poverty and unemployment, this seems unjust and unsustainable.

Second, the atomisation of separate social rights and the "projectisation" of social programmes have placed additional burdens on the social protection system and employment schemes. The introduction of new rights only demonstrated the lack of a coherent and strategic approach towards the creation of social policy. The introduction of at least eight new rights turned the social assistance scheme into a highly categorical system, with preferential treatment and arbitrary amounts of certain entitlements. The projectisation of the active labour market policies and their targeting towards more active beneficiaries has further distorted the goals and purpose of policies for vulnerable people.

Third, the discretionary setting of the amounts of social transfers has decreased the stability of the social protection and social insurance systems and has eroded the democratic principles on which they are based. The electoral tuning of welfare spending according to political preferences "is ideal for binding poor voters to a long-term relationship based on material dependence" (Diaz-Cayeros et al. 2016: 103).

Consequently, instead of moving the trajectory of the welfare state towards new forms of provision according to demographic, economic and social realities, the new social policy developments in Macedonia have provided strong arguments for going "back to the roots" and re-establishing and renewing the basic elements necessary for the functioning of the welfare state, namely, the democratisation of its processes and procedures, which ought to form the basis of a modern social protection system.

References

Atanasova, G., & Bache, I. (2010). Europeanization and F.Y.R. Macedonia: Towards a compound polity? *Southeast European and Black Sea Studies, 10*(1), 85–96.

Berardi, L. (2016). *The Family 500+: Poland's new child benefit programme*. New Eastern Europe. http://neweasterneurope.eu/2016/03/03/family-500-polands-new-child-benefit-programme/

Bradshaw, J., & Finch, N. (2002). *A comparison of child benefit packages in 22 countries* (Research Report No. 17). London: Department for Work and Pensions.

Carraro, L., & Beazley, R. (2013). *Strengthening social protection for children: Analysis and recommendations for a more equitable and efficient child benefit system*. Skopje: UNICEF. https://childhub.org/en/child-protection-online-library/strengthening-social-protection-children-macedonia

Diaz-Cayeros, A., Estévez, F., & Magaloni, B. (2016). *The political logic of poverty relief: Electoral strategies and social policy in Mexico*. Cambridge: Cambridge University Press.

Eisenstadt, S., & Roniger, L. (1984). *Patrons, clients and friends: Interpersonal relations and the structure of trust in society*. Cambridge: Cambridge University Press.

Esping-Anderson, G. (1990). *The three worlds of welfare capitalism*. Cambridge: Polity.

European Commission. (2009, October 14). *The former Yugoslav Republic of Macedonia 2009 progress report* (SEC(2009) 1335). Brussels: European Commission.

Gerovska Mitev, M. (2015). *'Employing Macedonia': Assessing strengths and weaknesses of the new governmental project* (ESPN Flash Report 2015/40). Brussels: European Commission, Directorate-General for Employment, Social Affairs and Inclusion.

IEG. (2016). *The former Yugoslav Republic of Macedonia: Public expenditure policy-based guarantee* (Project Performance Assessment Report No. 106281). Washington: Independent Evaluation Group, World Bank.

Kittel, B., & Obinger, H. (2002). *Political parties, institutions, and the dynamics of social expenditure in times of austerity* (MPIfG Discussion Paper 02/1). Köln: Max-Plank-Institut für Gesellschaftforschung.

Luci, A., & Thevenon, O. (2011). *Do fertility trends respond to family policies in OECD countries?* ftp://ftp.dondena.unibocconi.it/AlpPop2011/LuciThevenon.pdf

MLSP. (2016). *National action plan for employment 2016*. Skopje: Ministry of Labor and Social Policy.

Mojsoska-Blazevski, N. (2011). *Supporting strategies to recover from the crisis in South Eastern Europe country assessment report: The former Yugoslav Republic of Macedonia*. Budapest: International Labour Organisation.

OSCE. (2009). *The former Yugoslav Republic of Macedonia: Presidential and municipal elections, 22 March und 5 April 2009* (OSCE/ODIHR Election Observation Mission Final Report). Warsaw: OSCE Office for Democratic Institutions and Human Rights.

Schneider, S., & Ingraham, P. (1984). The impact of political participation and social policy adoption and expansion. *Comparative Politics, 17*, 107–121.

Sowa, A. (2016). *'Family 500+': A new family income-supporting benefit in Poland* (ESPN Flash Report 2016/45). Brussels: European Social Policy Network.

SSO. (2016). *Social welfare for children, juveniles and adults, 2015*. Skopje: State Statistical Office.

Szikra, D. (2014). Democracy and welfare in hard times: The social policy of the Orbán government in Hungary between 2010 and 2014. *Journal of European Social Policy, 24*(5), 486–500.

UNICEF. (2013). *Leave no child behind: Building equity for children*. Skopje: UNICEF.

UNODC. (2011). *Corruption in the former Yugoslav Republic of Macedonia: Bribery as experienced by the population*. Vienna: United Nations Office on Drugs and Crime.

World Bank. (2015). *FYR Macedonia public expenditure review: Fiscal policy for growth* (Report No. 93913-MK). Brussels: World Bank Group.

The Global Financial Crisis and Fiscal Policy in Montenegro

Nikola Fabris

Introduction

Fiscal policy in Montenegro has a long history of vulnerabilities. During the 1990s, Montenegro was first a part of the Socialist Federal Republic of Yugoslavia and then, after the country's disintegration, a part of the Federal Republic of Yugoslavia (FRY). During that period, fiscal policy was predominantly pursued at the federal level with fewer possibilities for Montenegro to influence fiscal policy. These years were also burdened by UN economic sanctions, the war in the region, a large influx of refugees, as well as growing social problems due to the bankruptcy of numerous companies. The fiscal deficit was on an upward trend. A decline in economic activity brought reduced the tax base and tax revenues, which was a major cause of the rising fiscal deficit. Thus, the level of tax revenue in 1993 fell to just one sixth of its value in 1991 (Fabris et al. 2004).

The budget deficit was persistently covered by the issuing of currency, spurring inflation. As a result of this policy, one of the highest and longest hyperinflations in the world occurred in 1993 and the beginning of 1994 (Dimitrijević 1996). The hyperinflation itself contributed to a decline in tax revenues—it devalued them in the period between their calculation and the moment of their collection (the Olivera–Tanzi effect). The hyperinflation was brought to an end by a stabilisation programme adopted in early 1994, but the problem of the budget deficit was not curbed and so the stabilisation programme soon failed.

As a result of bad policies at the federal level, during the NATO bombing of FRY in 1999, the Government of Montenegro decided to take authority over a significant part of economic policy. Starting from the longstanding custom of both citizens and corporations in Montenegro to save and transact business in Deutsche Marks, the

N. Fabris (✉)
Faculty of Economics, University of Belgrade, Belgrade, Serbia
e-mail: fnikola@ekof.bg.ac.rs

R. Osbild, W. Bartlett (eds.), *Western Balkan Economies in Transition*, Societies and Political Orders in Transition, https://doi.org/10.1007/978-3-319-93665-9_10

Government opted for the "dollarisation" model with the Deutsche Mark as a local national currency. Instead of the Dinar, the world's worst currency at the time, as estimated by Hanke (2000), Montenegro introduced a parallel currency system on 2 November 1999, in which the Deutsche Mark was made legal tender and allowed to freely float alongside Montenegro's other legal currency, the Dinar. The entire process was conducted swiftly and without the support or guidance of the International Monetary Fund. At the time when the Deutsche Mark was introduced as the means of payment, the fiscal deficit was around 20% of GDP (Žugić and Fabris 2013). In January 2001 the Deutsche Mark became the only legal tender, and from June 2002, the official means of payment became the Euro. Thus, although it remained in a federation with Serbia, Montenegro introduced its own monetary system and took over significant powers in pursuing its own fiscal policy.

Euroisation contributed to improved budgetary discipline. The government became aware that the primary issue of money was no longer an option to cover the fiscal deficit and began to pursue a low budget deficit or a balanced budget policy. It also facilitated the introduction of a hard budget constraint due to the limited possibilities of subsidising "failed" state enterprises and illiquid banks. Tornell and Velasco (1995) represent the viewpoint that a priori Euroisation does not provide strict fiscal limitations, arguing that "[f]ull [Euroisation] contributes to a greater fiscal discipline in comparison to a flexible exchange regime only if the fiscal authorities are sufficiently aware and worried about the future" (Tornell and Velasco 1995). Montenegro's experience fully confirms these assumptions.

With the introduction of Euroisation, the situation in the monetary and fiscal system of Montenegro started to show some signs of recovery. After one of the highest hyperinflations in the world, single-digit inflation rate was achieved in 2002. Having reached 20% GDP when Euroisation was introduced, the budget deficit was first reduced to single-digit levels and turned into a budget surplus in 2006.

In this way, fiscal policy gained great importance in the economic system of Montenegro, because it is the basic instrument of macroeconomic policy and an important tool for financial stability in Euroised economies where monetary policy instruments are no longer available (Žugić and Fabris 2014).

Fiscal Policy and Fiscal Reforms on the Eve of the Global Financial Crisis

Several years prior to the global financial crisis, the macroeconomic situation in Montenegro was quite favourable. Gross domestic product rose over the years and achieved real growth of 8.6% in 2006 and 10.7% in 2007 (CBCG 2008). The combination of private and public investments caused a rapid growth of the economy, which at the time represented a great challenge for Montenegro, having regained its independence in 2006. At the same time, annual inflation significantly decreased, falling to around 3% in 2005 and 2006. The budget attained surpluses in both 2006 and 2007, which significantly reflected the improvement of the fiscal position and led to a reduction of the public debt.

Intensive fiscal reforms were carried out in this period. The most significant measures that were implemented in the period 2007–2008 involved the reduction of corporate income tax to 9%, personal income tax to 9% and the establishment of the cumulative rate of social insurance of 30%, a reduction of withholding tax (from 15 to 9%) with a view to creating a more enabling environment for the development of entrepreneurship and foreign investments. Also, tax incentives were introduced for investments in property, plant and equipment for electric power production (solar, wind power and the like), which provided a tax relief for 50% of the relevant investment. The reform changed the treatment of capital gains as it taxes 50% of revenues from capital gains in the year in which they are earned, while 50% is relieved of tax, which is much more favourable compared to the earlier solution under which income from capital gains was fully taxed. Also, the law on social security contributions was enacted in 2007 (with the effective date as of the beginning of 2008) introducing a phased reduction of these contributions to 30% by 2010. In addition, amendments to the law on value-added tax prescribed a reduction of the tax rate from 17 to 7% for certain products that are essential for people's living standard (such as bread, milk and the like). The only increase in taxes referred to real property transfer tax that rose from 2 to 3%. This has established in Montenegro one of the most competitive tax systems in Europe.

With the amendments to the 2007 Organic Budget Law, the former extra-budgetary funds were given the status of state funds, and from 2008 to 2010, all funds have become an integral part of the budget of Montenegro. Consequently, there has been an improvement in transparency of the budget and the control of budget spending.

Legislative amendments brought about by an increase in the expenditure side of the budget included the law on salaries of civil servants and state employees, which affected a substantial increase in public sector wages. Table 1 shows the recorded fiscal parameters in the period 2006–2008.

Regardless of the impressive fiscal performance in this period, the root of most problems that emerged during the global financial crisis originated during this period. Namely, in this period the country had significantly reduced tax rates on one hand and significantly increased public sector wages on the other. The above reform would be viable only if Montenegro had continued its economic expansion for many years that followed. This was the main mistake of the fiscal reform, which had not anticipated that the near future could bring about a significant deterioration in economic performance.

During this period there was also a clearly noticeable increase in public expenditure, which exceeded 50% of GDP, up from 45.6% of GDP in 2006 (Table 1). In sum, Montenegro welcomed the global financial crisis with lower tax rates and significantly increased public expenditure.

Table 1 Fiscal parameters in the period 2006–2008

Public spending						
	Public revenues		Public expenditure		Public spending surplus/deficit	
	€ millions	% GDP	€ millions	% GDP	€ millions	% GDP
2006	978.7	45.6	910.2	42.4	68.5	3.2
2007	1329.1	49.6	1159.3	43.3	169.8	6.3
2008	1548.7	50.2	1556.5	50.4	−7.8	−0.2
Budget						
	Budget revenues		Budget expenditure		Budget surplus/deficit	
	€ millions	% GDP	€ millions	% GDP	€ millions	% GDP
2006	861.4	40.1	788.1	36.7	73.4	3.4
2007	1128.4	42.1	951.3	35.5	177.1	6.6
2008	1289.4	41.8	1272.0	41.2	17.4	0.6

Source: Ministry of Finance of Montenegro. Note: Public spending includes budget (central government), public funds and municipalities

Table 2 Budget and public spending deficits in the period 2009–2015

	2009	2010	2011	2012	2013	2014	2015
€ millions							
Public spending deficit	−159.5	−142.9	−167.9	−185.5	−78.2	−107.6	−302.7
Budget deficit	−126.1	−107.1	−185.7	−207.8	−215.8	−107.1	−291.3
% GDP							
Public spending deficit	−5.4	−4.6	−5.1	−5.8	−2.3	−3.1	−8.4
Budget deficit	−4.2	−3.4	−5.7	−6.5	−6.4	−3.1	−8.1

Source: Ministry of Finance of Montenegro and the author's calculations

The Impact of the Global Financial Crisis on Fiscal Performance

A Euroised and highly open economy such as Montenegro is largely susceptible to the transmission of external shocks. The emergence of the global crisis and the creation of a negative external shock significantly slowed down economic growth and jeopardised the execution of planned budget revenues. As soon as the last quarter of 2008, and later on throughout 2009, the public finances deteriorated significantly, primarily due to a decline on the side of the current public and budget revenues, but also owing to growing expenditure, resulting in a budget deficit. The decline in public revenues was mostly due to a decline in economic activity and a significant reduction in imports and exports and real estate demand and sales and a drop in foreign direct investments. The fiscal performance over the period from 2009 to 2015 is summarised in Table 2.

Given that the crisis seriously affected Montenegro's economy in the last quarter of 2008, in February 2009 the Government initiated austerity measures to reduce public spending. These measures included, among other things, the suspension of employment growth in the public sector, rationalisation of all expenditure categories and, in particular, discretionary spending. Some of the most important measures were a decrease in unproductive current budget spending (a reduction of the expenses for material and services of 10%) in the first half of 2009, and the curbing of the informal economy with a significant involvement of the tax and customs authorities.

However, measures aimed at stimulating the economy and boosting aggregate demand were carried out in parallel in order to mitigate the effects of the crisis. The most important measures included a reduction of the tax burden on individuals and businesses, the lowering of pension and health insurance contributions, the abolition of the tax for construction land and highway fees, a reduction of business electricity prices in parallel with subsidising the most vulnerable population groups, credit support to the development of SMEs by providing guarantees for the provision of long-term credit lines to the banking sector by the international financial organisations and an increase in investments in infrastructure through increased capital budget expenditure.

Nonetheless, the crisis severely hit the Montenegrin economy in 2009, bringing a large fall in real GDP of 5.7%, which significantly reduced tax revenues and resulted in a budget deficit of 4.2% of GDP after 3 years of budget surplus. The severity of the crisis can best be confirmed by the number of frozen accounts of companies and entrepreneurs in default. The number of blocked accounts increased from 9729 at the end of 2008 to 12,254 at the end of 2009, while the value of frozen accounts increased from 92.7 million euros to 177.2 million euros.[1]

Therefore, the fiscal policy reforms continued in 2010. The key reform measures that were implemented included the introduction of a mandatory opinion of the Ministry of Finance on the budgets of local governments, obligations of all spending units to obtain approval from the Ministry of Finance before signing procurement contracts and amendments to the law on salaries of civil servants and state employees enabling the Ministry of Finance to take a full control over recruitment and the total salary bill. A restrictive employment policy was adopted and the government passed a decision allowing the employment of one officer for every three public sector retirees or two redundant civil servants. Excise duties on mineral oils and tobacco and tobacco products were increased. At the same time, in order to encourage new hiring, the government reduced the personal income tax rate, while the amendments to the law on contributions for compulsory social insurance further alleviated the tax burden for employers.

As can be seen from the measures presented above, the rationalisation measures were introduced in 2010 in order to reduce fiscal expenditure, while also trying to revive the ailing economy with stimulating measures through fiscal incentives for new employment and attracting foreign investments. The combination of these measures yielded some positive results, because the fiscal deficit was reduced from

[1]Central Bank of Montenegro's database.

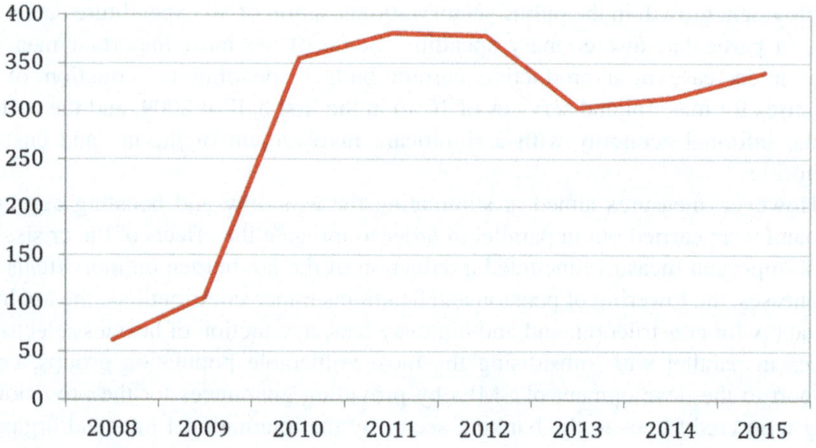

Fig. 1 Total issued guarantees for withdrawn funds in the period 2008–2015, euro million. Source: Ministry of Finance of Montenegro

126 million euros to 107 million euros, i.e. from 4.2% to 3.4% of GDP. Also, after the recession in 2009, GDP growth reached 2.5% in 2010.

However, the effects of the crisis did not recede and were visible in the increase of illiquidity, i.e. the growing number of companies with frozen accounts and the continued growth of non-performing loans in the banking system, which led to a decline in lending activity. Therefore, a similar policy was continued in 2011 that involved a combination of fiscal consolidation measures and incentives to stimulate economic activity.

The key measures of fiscal consolidation were an increase in excise duties on beer, cigarettes and other tobacco products, an increase of the maximum contribution base for pension and disability insurance and an expansion of the tax base for real estate taxation. At the same time, a wide range of measures was adopted to encourage economic recovery including introducing additional tax benefits for underdeveloped municipalities, raising the base for compulsory social insurance contributions, creating incentives for the payment of tax arrears, allowing the deferred payment of customs debt and cancelling some of the fees charged by the customs authorities. One of the problems that emerged in 2011 was the calling of government guarantees from 2009 to 2011 that the government had issued to foster economic activity. It turned out that the risk assessment for these guarantees had not unrealistic, with adverse consequences for the budget deficit and the growth of public debt. The following graph shows the trend of issued guarantees (Fig. 1).

The measures that were implemented from 2009 to 2011 in response to the crisis aimed to reduce public expenditure, particularly discretionary spending and the wage bill. Public spending declined from 50.4% at the end of 2008 to 44.8% of GDP at the end of 2011 (CBCG 2012). However, current budget expenditure was still 4.4% higher than in the comparative period of 2008 (prior to the implementation of rationalisation measures). Regardless of the control over hiring aimed at reducing the public sector wage bill, expenditure on wages increased in 2011 by 35.2% compared to 2008 and 30.9% in relation to 2010. Therefore, the objective was not achieved, and it was one of the reasons for the growth of the budget deficit, which by the end of 2011 had risen to 5.7% of GDP. However, it should be noted that the stimulative measures were reflected in GDP growth of 3.2%.

The process of fiscal consolidation and the implementation of measures to mitigate the crisis impact continued in 2012. However, revenues continued to decline and expenditures to increase due to unfavourable weather conditions which paralysed much economic activity.[2] New measures were introduced including the introduction of additional duties on a number of products and services, an increase in the level of excise duties and intensified activities to combat the informal economy.[3] The wage bill continued to grow in 2012. However, despite the measures taken in 2012, once again budget revenues declined while expenditure rose, resulting in a high budget deficit of 6.5% at the end of the year.

All this necessitated the new government measures in 2013 in the form of a serious programme of fiscal consolidation. On the expenditure side, the measures aimed at a continuing attempt to limit and reduce public sector wages; to limit the expenditure of public enterprises, regulatory agencies and local governments; and to freeze pensions. A broader set of measures was applied on the revenue side including an increase in VAT, imposing additional taxes on high salaries, intensified measures to combat the informal economy, a further increase of specific excise duties, a series of measures to reduce tax arrears and the introduction of an obligation on regulatory agencies to transfer all profit to the budget.

The effects of the fiscal consolidation measures were significant. In 2013, there was a year-on-year increase in budget revenues of 10.4%. However, expenditure also increased due to the repayment of called guarantees in the amount of 107.2 million euros (over 3% of GDP) and significant expenditure for litigation. At the end of 2013, the budget deficit was 6.4% of GDP, (it would have been less than 3% of GDP in the absence of the called guarantees). The fiscal consolidation measures were welcomed by the international financial institutions, particularly the IMF and the World Bank, and created the basis for a significant reduction of the budget deficit in the following years.

The consolidation of public finance was the first priority of the 2014 fiscal policy. In addition, significant actions were taken to curb the informal economy, which contributed to the strengthening of tax discipline and an increased in budget revenues by 8.9% (i.e. by 110 million euros). This result would have been even better had all the planned investment projects been implemented. The application of the crisis income tax rate of 15% and the increased VAT rate of 19%, coupled with continuous activities to curb the informal economy, led to an increase in revenues.

[2]This was one of the reasons why Montenegro fell back into recession in 2012, with a negative rate of GDP growth of −2.7%.

[3]The government set up the coordination team for the follow-up of measures for curbing informal economy that defined the operational plan for curbing informal economy.

Coupled with the restrictive expenditure policy that reduced discretionary spending, the suspension of the pension adjustment contributed to halving the fiscal deficit from 6.4% in 2013 to 3.1% of GDP in 2014.

A major novelty in the manner of pursuing fiscal policy came with the law on budget and fiscal responsibility in April 2014, which, inter alia, regulated budget planning and execution, borrowing and guarantees. The law also introduced fiscal rules, following the example of the EU Maastricht Treaty, which prescribes a budget deficit of 3% of GDP and a public debt of 60% of GDP.

In 2015, the construction commenced of the Bar/Boljare highway (Smokovac–Mateševo section), which was partly funded from the budget. Some 85% of the funds were provided by a favourable credit arrangement with Exim bank, while the state is contributing 15% of the project value. In addition, contrary to the government's opinion, the Parliament passed social legislation that induced an increase in public expenditure by about 3% of GDP. The implementation of these measures contributed to a 10% increase in public expenditure, and in combination with a slight decline in budget revenues, the fiscal deficit reached 8.1% of GDP, and public debt increased to more than 60% of GDP.

Montenegro's fiscal policy was in the following dilemma: should the country adopt a policy of saving in an effort to stabilise public finances or should it use policy of consumption to encourage economic growth and additional employment (Fabris and Galić 2015)? On the one hand, an increase in consumption is needed to stimulate a sluggish economy, while on the other hand, an increase in public spending leads to an increase in public debt and may deepen the crisis.

The Impact of the Global Financial Crisis on Public Debt

High economic growth rates over the period 2006–2008 induced an increase in budget revenues and budget surpluses, and a consequent prepayment of obligation towards creditors and a reduction of the public debt that stood at 27.5% of GDP (737.2 million euros) in 2007 (CBCG 2008). However, the crisis necessitated a whole set of measures aimed at boosting the economy that contributed to a persisting budget deficit and accelerated public debt growth. Table 3 shows the movement of the public debt over recent years.[4]

As can be seen from Table 3 the public debt in 2015 was two and a half times higher than that in 2007. The growth of the public debt from 2015 has been significantly affected by the highway construction, with an estimated share of around 23% of GDP. Given that the main rates for the public debt repayment will become due in the period 2016–2018, a further growth of the public debt is expected and the IMF projected that it could reach 85% of GDP at the end 2018 (IMF 2016).

[4]Net public debt of Montenegro amounted to some 65% of GDP at the end of 2015, when considering the value of the country's reserves at the time.

Table 3 Public debt of Montenegro

	External debt		Internal debt		Local self-government debt		Total public debt	
	€ millions	% of GDP	€ millions	% of GDP	€ millions	% of GDP	€ millions	% of GDP
2007	462.1	17.2	275.1	10.3			737.2	27.5
2008	481.7	15.6	413.0	13.4			894.7	29.0
2009	699.9	23.5	440.3	14.8			1140.2	38.2
2010	912.4	29.2	358.3	11.5			1270.7	40.7
2011	1063.7	32.6	419.8	12.9			1483.5	45.4
2012	1295.0	40.7	404.5	12.7			1699.5	53.4
2013	1433.0	42.6	500.7	14.9			1933.7	57.5
2014*	1561.7	45.2	381.2	11.0	128.8	3.7	2071.7	59.9
2015*	1956.4	54.4	320.3	8.9	142.2	4.0	2418.8	67.3

Source: Ministry of Finance of Montenegro. *Local self-government debt has been calculated separately

When we are talking about the public debt, we must take into consideration issued guarantees as well since they represent a potential debt. At the end of 2015, issued guarantees totalled 340 million euros. In the period 2011–2014, some 182 million euros worth of guarantees were repaid.

The main task for the following period must be must be to develop a credible fiscal consolidation programme, which would return fiscal policy on a sustainable path. Initial efforts have already been made, which involve requesting technical assistance from the IMF. The priority should be fiscal policy that will not allow additional burden and that will generate a surplus in the structural budget (Dimitrijević et al. 2016). Significant economic growth and inflow of foreign investments will be particularly important here, as will the implementation of large projects that will ensure a dynamic development necessary to mitigate the high level of debt and deficit. The guidelines for the pursuit of macroeconomic policy for the period 2015–2018 prioritises a responsible fiscal policy based on the principles of competitiveness, predictability and consistency (Ministry of Finance 2015).

Concluding Remarks

Before the outbreak of the crisis, Montenegro was a low indebted country with a budget surplus and high rates of GDP growth. However, being a small and highly open economy, it was severely hit by the crisis. This brought about recession, an increase in company insolvency (the value of frozen accounts increased from 92.7 million euros at the end of 2008 to 548 million euros at the end 2105), a deepening of social problems, difficulties in the functioning of the banking system and a decline in lending activity.

This resulted in a significant drop in public revenues, while at the same time, there was an increased need for fiscal support due to the aggravated social problems. In the first years of the crisis, there was a fiscal space for these needs to be met. However, the reform implemented on the eve of the crisis further reduced tax revenues while increasing public expenditure on wages, which only worsened the situation and proved to be unsustainable in the recessionary environment. Another significant burden was the calling of a large number of guarantees that had been issued by the state to stimulate economic activity. Also, a key problem has been that the government did not implement an effective control of public sector wages until 2013.

The government reacted by combining both stimulative measures and fiscal consolidation measures. The result of such a policy was the budget deficit that persisted until 2009 and an increasing public debt ratio. The fiscal consolidation measures remained in effect until 2013 and were strongly welcomed by the international financial institutions; they yielded positive results and led to a decrease in the budget deficit. However, the highway construction project that commenced in 2015, as well as a set of social legislation that was not supported by the government have again widened the budget deficit and led to a growth in public debt.

At the end of 2015, net public debt reached 65% of GDP, and the highway project is expected to induce its further growth until 2018. However, it should be taken into account that the project funding was provided from the loan from a Chinese bank under very favourable conditions, so no additional funds will be necessary.

Since the public debt exceeded the ceiling of 60% of GDP, the law on budget and fiscal responsibility requires the passing of a public finance consolidation plan to bring the public debt back to the prescribed level. Development of a credible consolidation programme and its consistent application must be the fiscal policy priorities in the upcoming period.

References

CBCG. (2008). *Chief economist's annual report for 2007*. Podgorica: Central Bank of Montenegro.

CBCG. (2012). *Macroeconomic report of Central Bank of Montenegro*. Podgorica: Central Bank of Montenegro.

Dimitrijević, B. (1996). *Hiperinflacija*. Belgrade: Svetlokomerc.

Dimitrijević, B., et al. (2016). *Ekonomska politika – regionalni aspekti* [Economic policy – regional aspects]. Belgrade: Faculty of Economics.

Fabris, N., & Galić, J. (2015). Essay on saving and consumption. *Journal of Central Banking Theory and Practice, 4*(3), 123–136.

Fabris, N., et al. (2004). *Economic policy in dollarized economies with a special review of Montenegro* (Working Paper No. 1). Podgorica: Central Bank of Montenegro, Podgorica.

Hanke, S. (2000). *The beauty of a parallel currency*. http://www.independent.org/newsroom/article.asp?id=372

IMF. (2016). *World economic outlook*. Washington, DC: International Monetary Fund.

Ministry of Finance. (2015). *Guidelines for macroeconomic and fiscal policy for the period 2015–2018*. Podgorica: Ministry of Finance.

Tornell, A., & Velasco, A. (1995). Fiscal discipline and choice of exchange rate regime. *European Economic Review, 39*(3–4), 759–770.

Žugić, R., & Fabris, N. (2013). Koordinacija monetarne i fiskalne politike u Crnoj Gori [Coordination of monetary and fiscal policy in Montenegro]. *Ekonomske ideje i praksa, 8*, 53–64.

Žugić, R., & Fabris, N. (2014). Framework for preserving financial stability in Montenegro. *Journal of Central Banking Theory and Practice, 3*(1), 27–41.

Economic Reforms in Serbia and Prospects for Economic Recovery and Growth

Will Bartlett

Introduction

The economic transition began in Serbia with the overthrow of the Milošević government in 2000 and entry into power of the DOS coalition government (Uvalić 2010). The 2000s saw a period of strong economic growth, with GDP increasing at a rate of 5.4% per annum from 2001 to 2008. Industrial production began to recover, increasing from a volume index of 96 in 2003 to 113 in 2008.[1]

However, the economic recovery came to a shuddering halt in 2009 as the spillover effects of the global financial and Eurozone crises began to be felt. These effects were surprisingly persistent with an average annual fall of GDP of −0.1% from 2009 to 2014. The period since the onset of the economic crisis has been a roller coaster of hesitant recovery followed by renewed recession. As growth faltered, the ratio of gross investment to GDP fell from precrisis peak of 25% in 2008 to just 18% by 2016.[2] More than half a million jobs were lost between 2009 and 2012, mainly in the private sector (Prica 2013). Unemployment peaked at 24% in 2012, before apparently falling back to 17.9% in the fourth quarter of 2015.[3] Real

[1]The index of industrial production is based on 2010=100 (Statistical Office of the Republic of Serbia, online data).

[2]Eurostat online data, variable code [nama_10_gdp].

[3]The validity of the unemployment data has been disputed by the Fiscal Council, which has argued that "it is not very likely that such favourable trends have actually occurred, i.e. that the fast growth of employment and drop of unemployment, registered from the end of 2012, are most likely the consequence of unreliable data of the SORS describing the labour market and not the true improvements in economy" (Petrović et al. 2016, p. 5). This was met with a furious response from the Statistical Office which issued a rebuttal of the claim on its website (see SORS 2016, 2017).

W. Bartlett (✉)
LSEE, European Institute, London School of Economics and Political Science (LSE), London, UK
e-mail: w.j.bartlett@lse.ac.uk

R. Osbild, W. Bartlett (eds.), *Western Balkan Economies in Transition*, Societies and Political Orders in Transition, https://doi.org/10.1007/978-3-319-93665-9_11

wages also fell and have remained in the doldrums. Expressed in Euros, average wages have fallen since 2008 when they were 401 € per month, to 374 € per month in 2016.[4] The downward trend in poverty that had characterised the boom period was reversed, and by 2016 a quarter (25.5%) of the population was at risk of poverty, and almost two fifth (39%) of the population were in a situation of social exclusion taking into account both material and relative deprivation (SORS 2017).

Since 2015 there have been some signs of economic recovery. Real GDP growth has been positive, and industrial production has picked up. Politicians and promoters of the reforms in the international agencies have lost little time in announcing a turnaround in economic fortunes, and that this demonstrated the effectiveness of the reforms that had been adopted in recent years. Of course, the return to growth may equally have been due to the normal upturn of the business cycle.

The political scene has also changed as a result of the crisis. At the height of the boom, parliamentary elections in 2008 brought the Democratic Party (DS) to power under the electoral coalition "Serbia for Europe", governing in coalition with the Serbian Socialist Party (SPS), and with DS leader Boris Tadić as President. For the first time since the assassination of Prime Minister Djindjic, Serbia returned to its EU path (Obradović-Wochnik and Wochnik 2012). Soon afterwards, the Serbian Radical Party split over the question of EU accession, and the pro-EU wing led by Alexander Vučić and Tomislav Nikolić set up the Serbian Progressive Party (SNS) with EU accession as a main objective. An important achievement of the DS-led coalition government was the signing of a Stabilisation and Association Agreement (SAA) with the EU in 2010. Following the unexpected blow to the economy from the effects of the economic crisis in 2009, the government turned to the IMF for support and in September 2011 signed up to a US$1.5 billion Stand-By Arrangement. In March 2012, Serbia was granted EU candidate status, and Tadić called parliamentary and presidential elections for May in the expectation of an easy victory. However, the election produced a surprise win for Nikolić in the presidential elections, while the SNS won enough votes to form a coalition government with the SPS whose leader, Ivica Dačić, became prime minister.

In April 2013, the prime ministers of Serbia and Kosovo initialled an agreement on normalisation of relations between the two countries, opening up the stalled EU accession process (Pond 2013). This was somewhat surprising, as the previous government under the moderate DS leadership had resisted this move. Perhaps it took a more hard line government to make a deal that offended nationalist sentiment in Serbia.

Following the successful normalisation negotiations, the SAA entered into force in September 2013, firmly situating Serbia on the EU path. Soon after, in October 2013, perhaps with an eye to managing expectations in advance of the forthcoming election in early 2014, Alexander Vučić dramatically declared "[w]e are virtually on

[4]National Bank of Serbia online data, "Osnovi makroekonomski indikatori" (Basic macroeconomic indicators).

the verge of bankruptcy".[5] Accession negotiations with the EU were formally begun in January 2014. On 6 March 2014, Serbia received a US$1 billion loan from the United Arab Emirates (UAE) with an interest rate of 2% and a grace period of 10 years; it was used to cover the current account deficit and compensate for mounting capital flight.[6] With this success, and promises to turn the economy around, the SNS improved its vote in the 16 March 2014 elections sufficiently to enable Vučić to become prime minister.

Since 2014, the government has worked assiduously to consolidate its power domestically by strengthening control over the press[7] and the judiciary[8] while at the same time presenting an image of reform progress to the international organisations and the EU bureaucracy. This effort was rewarded with the signing of a further 36-month 1.2 billion euros precautionary Stand-By Arrangement with the IMF in February 2015, followed by the opening of the first negotiation chapters in December of the same year (Chapter 32 on financial control and Chapter 35 on the normalisation of relations with Kosovo). Prime Minister Vučić announced early elections to be held on 24 April 2016, widely seen as an attempt to consolidate power, while the SNS was still riding high in the polls. This step was taken in advance of new measures of structural reform that were likely to be deeply unpopular.

The Economic Reform Programme

The efforts to reassure Serbia's international partners that the country was committed to normalisation of relations with Kosovo and to a path of pro-market reforms paid off in the form of the new deal with the IMF mentioned in the previous section. The importance of this agreement was that it provided an aura of respectability to the government's economic programme under the IMF imprimatur, raising expectations and stimulating investment. The aims of the programme were to achieve fiscal consolidation, financial sector resilience and structural reforms to stimulate private investment, employment and growth (IMF 2015a). This section reviews progress with this reform agenda.

[5]Interview on Prva TV, reported by Gordana Filipović and Misha Savić, Bloomberg, 7 October 2013. Actually, 2013 was a rather good year for the balance of payments, which allowed a build-up of foreign reserves—quite the opposite of going "bankrupt".

[6]"UAE signs $1 billion loan pact with Serbia", *Gulf News*, 6 March 2014.

[7]See "Serbia's independent media faces ongoing smear campaigns", International Press Institute, 22 April 2016.

[8]See Ilić, M. (2015) "Serbian judges removal 'threatens judicial independence'", Belgrade: BIRN. http://www.balkaninsight.com/en/article/serbian-judge-s-removal-threatens-judicial-indepen dence--12-21-2015

The Government Sector and Fiscal Consolidation

Due to postcrisis borrowing to finance the government budget deficit, public debt increased steadily from 26% of GDP in 2008 to 76% of GDP in 2015.[9] Three fifths of this was external debt that was vulnerable to exchange rate risk. Budget deficit reduction was a policy priority because it was considered that high levels of public expenditure would lead to an oversized state sector that would crowd out private investment (World Bank 2015). As noted above, by 2016 gross investment had fallen to relatively low levels, and most would probably agree that in order to achieve a sustainable economic recovery, investment would need to return to the much higher levels of the precrisis period.

Fiscal policy reforms aimed to reduce the general government budget deficit that had reached as high as 6.7% of GDP in 2014 (up from 1.9% of GDP in 2007) by controlling mandatory spending. A sharp fiscal consolidation achieved a reduction in the deficit to 3.7% of GDP in 2015, well below the planned deficit of 5.9% (IMF 2016). This was achieved through severe cuts to public sector wages and to pensions. A solidarity tax was imposed on public sector wages above 60,000 dinars per month (520 €). In October 2014, a supplementary budget replaced the solidarity tax with an across-the-board 10% nominal wage cut for all public sector employees whose wages were above 25,000 dinars (210 €). In addition, pensions between 25,000 and 40,000 dinars were reduced by 22% and higher pensions by 25%, while the minimum retirement age and the statutory retirement age for women were increased. The indexation of public sector wages and pensions was suspended (IMF 2015b). However, according to the Fiscal Council the space for further budget reductions was used up, and in 2016 there was pressure to reverse these cuts.[10] The favourable outcome on the budget deficit was partly due to lower than forecast inflation and to an unexpected increase in tax revenues (from increased tobacco duties). But this was a one-off gain that was unlikely to be repeated.

A further measure to reduce public expenditure was a quantitative restriction on the number of employees in the public sector to reduce employment in the general government by 5% each year through the application of a 5:1 attrition rule. Each public institution, including universities, was given an employment ceiling that they were forbidden to exceed. In 2015, the targeted reduction of 6000 employees was achieved along with an additional 5000 early retirements brought forward in advance of the penalty for early retirement that had been introduced in the Labour Law, so achieving the planned 5% reduction in public employment (IMF 2015b). A comprehensive reform of the public sector wage structure was also planned to align base wages and unify pay grades across comparable jobs. The health, local governments, police, judiciary and compulsory social insurance organisations were identified as

[9]Eurostat online data variable code [cpc_ecgov].

[10]Interview by the author with Fiscal Council, March 2016. The 2017 budget envisaged targeted increases in public sector wages and in state pensions (see "IMF Staff Completes Review Mission to Serbia", Press Release No. 16/474, Washington: International Monetary Fund).

having the highest potential for efficiency gains and employment reduction. In-depth functional reviews were to achieve savings through restructuring the public sector, involving politically unpopular layoffs euphemistically known as "right-sizing"—no doubt one reason why the government decided to call early elections in April 2016 to strengthen their hand in advance.

Fiscal consolidation enabled a relaxation of monetary policy. Nominal interest rates began to fall, partly in response to the weakening of inflation due to falling oil prices. From a peak of almost 12% at the end of 2012, the NBS discount rate (the so-called policy rate) fell to 4.25% in February 2016. However, the reduction in interest rates was slower than the drop in inflation, and so real interest rates actually increased. High real interest rates may have contributed to falling investment, which reached a low of 16.7% in 2014 and only began to slowly pick up thereafter reaching 17.7% in 2016.[11] Whereas in previous years investment recoveries depended on large single projects such as the Italian investment in Fiat or the Russian investment in the NIS energy company,[12] this recovery took place across all sectors of the economy. The Fiscal Council has argued that this is the start of a sustainable increase in investment related to lower nominal interest rates, the fiscal consolidation programme and the stabilisation of the exchange rate.[13]

The Financial Sector and Financialisation

A large part of the domestic banking sector had come under foreign ownership through the privatisation process of the mid-2000s. In the space of 2 years, from 2004 to 2006 the share of bank assets under foreign ownership had increased from 38% to 79%.[14] Most of the foreign banks were based in the EU.[15] This opened up a massive process of credit expansion and euroisation of the economy (Chailloux et al. 2010). The credit boom underpinned the rapid growth that took place during this period and led to a process of financialisation based on consumer credit that fuelled the boom by giving consumer power to a wide spectrum of the population. Up to the end of 2008, composite credit growth increased at an average rate of 45% per annum. However, with the onset of the crisis, from mid-2009 credit growth came to a complete halt, and in 2013 and 2014, average credit growth turned negative as

[11] Eurostat online data, variable code [nama_10_gdp].

[12] The Russian company Gazprom owns 56% of the shares in NIS, and a further 30% are owned by the Serbian state. NIS is one of Serbia's largest companies with its own representative office in Brussels in support of Serbia's EU integration. See http://www.nis.eu/en/about-us/company-information

[13] Personal communication to the author by the Fiscal Council staff.

[14] EBRD structural change indicators, online database, 2016.

[15] In 2014, 21 out of the 29 banks active in Serbia were under foreign ownership. One quarter of bank assets are owned by affiliates of two Italian banks. There are also four Greek, three French and three Austrian banks.

foreign banks engaged in a sustained process of deleveraging to shore up their domestic capital base in response to new regulatory pressures in the Eurozone.[16] Total financial claims of foreign banks on their affiliates in Serbia fell from US$12.7 billion in the fourth quarter of 2009 to US$5.5 billion in the fourth quarter of 2015.[17] The draw-down of assets by the foreign banks put a stop to their new lending activities to the business sector in Serbia.

As credit dried up, many businesses were unable to keep up their loan repayments, and the proportion of non-performing loans (NPLs) held by the banks rapidly increased, creating a Serbian version of the sub-prime loan disaster. By the second quarter of 2015 the proportion of NPLs reached a staggering 22.8% of total loans (EIB 2015).[18] The share of NPLs in Serbia is the highest in region outside Albania. About three fifths of NPLs are held by private companies and one sixth by private households (mainly defaulted mortgages). Effective resolution of NPLs is held up by weaknesses in the enforcement of secured creditor rights and costly and lengthy enforcement and insolvency court proceedings (GoRS 2015). Although annual credit growth has picked up to 4.3% in the first quarter of 2015, corporate loans continued to decline (by 7% year-on-year). The high level of NPLs has contributed to the sclerosis in the financial system and further diminished the provision of new credit to the private business sector, undermining efforts to encourage the entry of entrepreneurial fast-growth SMEs. In response to the deteriorating credit conditions and the growth of NPLs, financial sector reforms have come to the top of the agenda in the economic reform programme. The NPL Resolution Strategy aims to strengthen the bank resolution framework, resolve the NPLs that have built up since the onset of the economic crisis and increase the dinarisation of the economy. In addressing the NPL issue, the National Bank of Serbia carried out a set of diagnostic studies and developed a strategy that aimed to remove obstacles to loan write-offs by banks, promote asset sales to private investors, strengthen the insolvency regime in the courts, introduce a personal insolvency framework and promote out-of-court voluntary debt restructuring (IMF 2015d).[19] Credit conditions began to ease in 2016 (EBCI 2016), and the ratio of NPLs to total loans began to ease, reaching 20.2% in mid-2016.[20]

[16]National Bank of Serbia, online data file "2014_II-1_bankarski_sektor_e.xls" Chart II.1.7. See also EBCI (2015).

[17]Bank for International Settlements online data: http://stats.bis.org/statx/srs/table/A6?c=RS&p=20154

[18]Almost 75% of NPLs are overdue for more than 360 days, while more than 50% are overdue for more than 2 years. Loan restructuring is exceedingly slow due to cumbersome insolvency proceedings and weaknesses in the enforcement of creditor rights (IMF 2015d).

[19]The NBS hosted a 2-day conference "Belgrade Initiative—Resolution of Non-Performing Loans in Serbia" held in April 2015 on this issue: http://www.nbs.rs/internet/english/15/mediji/vesti/20150429.html

[20]See the Vienna Initiative website on NPLs: http://npl.vienna-initiative.com/countries/serbia/

Structural Reforms

Structural reforms have been the third plank of the government's economic reform strategy designed to improve the responsiveness of the supply side of the economy. The aim has been to ensure that when economic growth took off there would be fewer constraints due to a lack of capacity or to rigidities that might hinder a reallocation of resources to the most productive uses. In other words, structural reforms were designed to create a liberal market economy by targeting the institutional framework, the labour market and the system of social protection. New laws on employment, pensions, privatisation and bankruptcy were passed in 2014, soon after the new government came to power. It is expected that markets will be further liberalised through the adoption of the EU *acquis*, which promotes competition and prohibits state aid. Capital markets have already been extensively liberalised through the process of financialisation as explained above.

The paradigm of the new institutional economics and its variant, public choice economics that has been adopted by the World Bank, emphasises the role of secure property rights and a supportive institutional framework for new business entry including an impartial judiciary capable of settling claims in a timely manner (Djankov et al. 2002, 2003). Structural reforms are expected to improve the business environment to encourage the entry of new entrepreneurial firms and incentivise investment, especially by foreign investors. In this respect, Serbia has recently introduced reforms to improve the processes for obtaining construction permits and for paying taxes. As a result, in 2016 Serbia moved up nine points the rankings of the World Bank "Ease of Doing Business" scorecard to 59th place out of 189 countries, up from 68th place in 2015.[21] The improvement would have been even greater were it not for a fall in the rank position for "ease of getting credit" by seven places.[22]

Judicial reforms have proved more challenging. Political interference in the recruitment and appointment of judges and prosecutors hinders judicial impartiality (EC 2015), and the administration of justice is slow with a significant backlog of cases (World Bank 2014a, b). The weak rule of law deters foreign investors from entering the market. Unlike in the Central European post-socialist states, Serbia lacks a strong "comprador" elite that represents the interests of multinationals and is able to pave the way for foreign direct investors (Drahokoupil 2008). Investors are usually discouraged from investing in businesses with weak legal safeguards, and so during the EU membership negotiations, Chapter 23 (judiciary and fundamental rights) and Chapter 24 (justice, freedom and security) will remain open until the end of the process, making the judicial system a key factor in the speed of Serbia's EU accession. The outcome will reveal whether political elites in Serbia are willing to

[21]The rank position for construction permits improved from 178th place to 139th place and paying taxes from 165th place to 143rd. See http://www.doingbusiness.org/data/exploreeconomies/serbia

[22]The rank position worsened from 52nd to 59th place.

open the economy to outside competition or wish to remain essentially protective of the domestic market.

Also high on the agenda was the privatisation of the public enterprises. Two categories of state-owned enterprises were identified. The first consisted of over 500 companies in the portfolio of the privatisation agency some of which have been protected under a moratorium on bankruptcy, which has now been removed. Of these, 188 were to go through a bankruptcy procedure, although the moratorium was extended by 1 year for 17 companies (IMF 2015c). However, no progress was made in implementing the plan, which would have involved large-scale layoffs and would have been politically unpopular. The second group consisted of large public utilities in electricity, gas, railways, roads and telecoms, most of which are loss-making enterprises.[23] A financial restructuring plan for the electricity company was set out in June 2015 introducing a 4.5% tariff increase, identifying cost cutting measures, and improving collection rates. The railway company was unbundled into separate passenger, freight and infrastructure companies in July 2015 (IMF 2015d). Yet, the IMF concluded in early 2016 that "[t]he restructuring of state-owned enterprises, including utilities, remain a difficult challenge" (IMF 2016). In a pre-election success for the government, an agreement was reached in April 2016 to sell the Zelezara Smederevo steel works to Hesteel, a Chinese company, for 46 million euros.[24]

The labour market has also been a focus of structural reforms. In July 2014, a new Labour Law was adopted that linked severance payments to the length of current employment rather than, as before, to the length of employment in all previous jobs, allegedly discouraging employers from taking on workers with a previous work history. In addition, the maximum duration of short-term contracts was raised from 1 to 2 years. Improved active labour market policies were introduced in the 2015 National Employment Action Plan.[25] The Law on Employment was amended in April 2015 to better align disbursement of social benefits for the unemployed with specific training programmes, and a new Law on Inspection Oversight was adopted in April to help fight corruption and the grey economy (IMF 2015b).

[23]These are among the largest employers in the country. The electricity company EPS employs 38,000 workers and the railway company Zeleznice Srbije employs 18,000 workers.

[24]The European Commission requires guarantees that Hesteel will only export products manufactured in Serbia to the EU. It also requires proof that the state has not subsidised the company since February 2015, when new EU rules on state aid to the industry took effect ("Sales contract for Zelezara Smederevo to be signed on April 18", In Serbia, 12 April 2016).

[25]It includes job matching services, career counselling and training for pre-redundancy and the unemployed, employer subsidies targeting disadvantaged job seekers, employee subsidies, self-employment support, public works, active measures for employees with disabilities and cofinancing of active labour market policies.

The External Sector and the Balance of Payments

A major aim of the government's economic programme has been to reduce Serbia's dependence on external loans and to prioritise export-led growth based on improved international competitiveness. As Prime Minister Vučić stated at the Davos international forum "[u]ntil 2008, Serbia's economic growth model was import and consumption driven, financed by privatisation revenues and borrowings. . ..In order to reverse the trends and put the country in a dynamic and sustainable growth path, led by investments and imports [sic], it was necessary to carry out economic reforms consisting of macroeconomic stabilisation and removing the barriers to doing business".[26] In part, the necessity to reverse the pattern of growth led by "foreign borrowings" is impelled by the need to halt the growth in external debt. In this section I take a look at the external sector to identify the main strengths and weaknesses of Serbia's external position and try to identify whether this approach to economic growth is feasible.

In 2008, the current account deficit reached a peak of 21% of GDP as economic growth sucked in imports, while exports failed to grow due to lack of competitiveness.[27] Yet by 2015 the current account deficit was just 5% of GDP (2 billion euros). Exports of goods had increased by 80% between 2009 and 2014 (compared to a 40% increase in imports) reducing the balance of trade deficit from 5 billion euros in 2009 to 3.6 billion euros in 2014 (partly covered by an inflow of remittances of 2.4 billion euros).[28] The improvement in the current account deficit was partly due to the surprisingly strong performance of exports of goods and services, which increased from 28% of GDP in 2007 before the crisis to 50% of GDP in 2016. This may have been related to the ratification of Serbia's Stabilisation and Association Agreement (SAA) with the EU in June 2010, which triggered the unilateral abolition of customs duties to the EU for most of Serbia's exports of goods.[29] Quantitative restrictions on all Serbia's goods exports to the EU were also abolished. On her part, Serbia was required to gradually reduce tariffs against EU goods over a 6-year period (i.e. up to 2016) and to immediately abolish customs duties on industrial products imported from the EU, as well as quantitative restrictions on both industrial and agricultural goods.

One notable feature of this outcome has been the rapid growth of exports in ICT services. Serbia has developed a comparative advantage in exports of ICT services, which account for 36% of service exports, by far the highest share in the Western Balkan region. According to a recent report, "Software designed in Serbia is mostly produced for western markets, where most of purchasers and customers are located.

[26]Alexander Vučić (2016) "The future of Serbia's economy", Davos: World Economic Forum.

[27]National Bank of Serbia online data.

[28]Remittances had fallen from a peak of 3.1 billion euros in 2009, from 10.1% of GDP to 7.3% of GDP (see Gligorić and Janković 2015).

[29]The Community Common Customs Tariff was applied from the date of signing the agreement, with the exception of some agricultural products.

The most important products include software for automatic remote meter reading, solutions for online betting and lottery, applications for communication, network equipment software, and services in the field of advanced web development" (Mortier 2015).

The other main negative item in the current account is primary income, i.e. factor income related to earnings from labour, capital and land held abroad, which includes prominently dividends from foreign investment. Foreign investment has generated an increasing outflow of funds since the onset of the crisis, as profits have been repatriated to investors' home countries rather than being reinvested in Serbia. These outflows reached 2.0 billion euros in 2016, mainly in the form of dividends and interest payments.[30] Within this, reinvested earnings were a net negative item indicating an outflow of funds amounting to 770 million euros in 2016.[31] Earnings on portfolio investments also contributed to the outflow from 2012, related to large portfolio investments made in 2012–2014.[32] All this gives a rather different perspective on the role of foreign investment in the Serbian economy than is usually presented. Most studies focus on the FDI inflows and their role in financing the current account deficit (World Bank 2015, p. 15). However, on the income side, there is a corresponding outflow in the form of repatriated profits, dividends and interest payments that is seldom taken into account. This is not to say that FDI does not have potential benefits in terms of employment, technology transfer and exports. Indeed, while foreign affiliates[33] comprise just 3% of enterprises in Serbia, they account for 20% of employees and produce 34% of value added of the economy.[34] The EU is a major source of this investment, providing over three quarters of all foreign affiliates, four fifths of foreign affiliates' employees and accounting for over two thirds of their value added. It can be seen that EU business interests have a strong stake in the successful reforms of the Serbian economy.

Compensating for the outflow of primary incomes in the form of dividends and net disinvestment, Serbia attracts a large inflow of remittances as "secondary income" within the balance of payments, i.e. monetary transfers that do not represent the direct earnings from capital, land and labour. In 2017, the net value of such remittances amounted to 2.7 billion euros, more than offsetting the outflow in the form of dividend payments on foreign investments in Serbia. Most of these flows,

---

[30]Data on net primary income from National Bank of Serbia online data "Balance of payments 2007–2016".

[31]Direct investment income is income earned on equity, dividends, reinvested earnings and interest on loans. Income from portfolio investment is mainly interest payments on company bonds. These earnings are classified as primary income within the current account of the balance of payments statistics.

[32]Portfolio investments differ from direct investments in that they do not involve control rights over an enterprise above 10% of total shares.

[33]Foreign affiliates are enterprises in which the share of foreign capital is 50% or more.

[34]SORS (2015) "Foreign affiliates in the Republic of Serbia in 2014 (inward FATS)", Belgrade: Statistical Office of the Republic of Serbia.

1.9 billion euros, represented the remittances sent home by Serbian migrant workers' abroad, many of whom work in Germany.[35]

Capital Account and Foreign Investment

As already mentioned, the current account deficit is partly covered by the inflow of foreign investment, both direct investment and portfolio investment. These flows tend to be fairly volatile and are easily affected by large one-off investments such as the 1 billion euros invested by Fiat in car production in Kragujevac in 2013. This has made a significant contribution to the recovery of Serbia's exports, through the production of the new Fiat 500L motor car, mainly exported to EU countries, principally Italy.

In 2016, the total net FDI inflow was 1.9 billion euros.[36] Although this represented an increase of over the 753 million euros in 2012, it was still below the precrisis peak of 2.5 billion euros in 2007 and 2008 (let alone the record 3.3 billion euros of 2011). The EU has been the major provider of net FDI, accounting for 69% of the total in 2016. Considering individual countries, the largest originators of FDI were the Netherlands (18.0%), Luxembourg (13.3%), Switzerland (12.4%), Austria (12.2%) and Germany (9.3%). It is notable that Russia provided only 1.1% of all inward investment to Serbia in 2016, whereas the United Arab Emirates provided 4.3% of such investment. The latter is of particular interest owing to its increasing presence in Serbia, not least as the developer of the controversial urban regeneration scheme "Belgrade Waterfront" which is intended to create a sort of Balkan Dubai on the river Sava (Bartlett et al. 2017).

It is perhaps inevitable that there has been a substantial inflow of investment from some dubious sources, especially investment channelled through tax havens around the world. Leading the pack in this respect is the Netherlands, from where the enormous sum of 342 million euros of FDI apparently originated in 2016 (alongside 252 million euros from Luxembourg). It is well known that multinational companies around the world use Dutch "conduit entities" as a tax avoidance mechanism and are actively involved in tax treaty shopping (Weyzig 2013; Haberly and Wojcik 2014). The Netherlands does not impose withholding tax on dividends, and so dividend payments made through Dutch conduits are free of tax. It is therefore a popular location for multinational companies to route their investment to host countries. Much of this investment may actually originate from Serbia in a process known as "round tripping", whereby host country investors establish a conduit entity in the Netherlands (or similar low-tax jurisdictions) through which to channel domestic investment before it is returned

[35]Three tenths (31%) of Serbian migrant workers abroad live in Germany and 23% in Austria (OECD online migrant database).

[36]Data on net direct investment from National Bank of Serbia online data "Balance of payments 2007–2016".

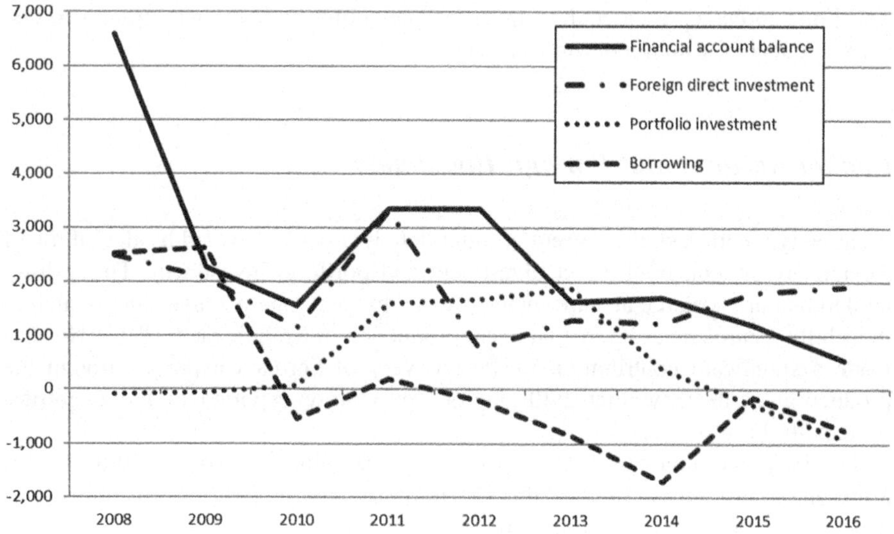

Fig. 1 Foreign direct investment and other investment (€ millions). Source: National Bank of Serbia, online balance of payments statistics. Note: The net balance of the four time series shown in the figure add to or subtract from the stock international reserves

to Serbia in the form of FDI.[37] Such investment may also potentially benefit from the generous tax breaks that Serbia offers to attract foreign investment. Since all such deals are non-transparent, the proportion of total FDI of this form cannot be estimated. However, the steady decline in the share of recorded nominal domestic investment in GDP in recent years suggests that it may not be insubstantial. Other investments that may be related to tax avoidance include the 55 million euros originating from Cyprus and the 21 million euros originating from the British Virgin Islands, not to mention the investments originating from Switzerland. In addition some outward investments go to offshore tax havens such as the net outward investment of 1.6 million euros to Panama and the 28.9 million euros to Liechtenstein. It may be said that the origin of FDI is of little concern if it brings much needed investment and creates jobs, especially if these are in competitive export sectors. While about three quarters of FDI that flowed into Serbia in the precrisis period was in non-tradable sectors (World Bank 2015), it is likely that the new influx of FDI is more oriented to exportable goods sectors, as in the case of the Fiat investment mentioned above.

In addition to direct FDI other important components of the financial account of the balance of payments are portfolio investment and "other" investment (see Fig. 1).[38] Portfolio investment was relatively insignificant until 2011 when some large portfolio investment began to be recorded (1.6 billion euros in 2011 rising to

[37]For a general outline of the phenomenon, see IMF (2003).

[38]Portfolio investments in the form of shares are distinguished from direct investments in that they account for less than 10% of ownership of an enterprise.

1.9 billion euros in 2013). However, this seems to have been a temporary inflow as it almost disappeared in 2014 and even went into reverse in 2016 indicating a capital outflow.

Alongside this, "other investment" in the form of "currency and loans" accounts for a relatively large component of the capital account. It reflects total foreign borrowing by the public and private sectors. In the precrisis period, this was large and significant, at 2.9 billion euros in 2009 (larger than FDI). However, in the postcrisis period, this went into reverse, and by 2014 the outflow of other investment was 1.7 billion euros. It represents an outflow of capital from Serbia or "capital flight" through large-scale deleveraging of asset positions by EU-based banks that has taken place in response to the Eurozone crisis and the need for EU banks to recapitalise their domestic positions. In 2014, capital flight of this type outweighed inward FDI by a substantial margin and required the NBS to cover the current account deficit by a large run-down of international reserve assets. As mentioned above, it was assisted in 2014 by an emergency loan from the UAE of US$1 billion. The combined effect of these outflows of portfolio and other capital is very large, and in 2016 they together offset inward FDI to such an extent that the overall net balance of the financial account approached zero.

External Debt

While the current account deficit has been partly financed by inflows of equity capital in the form of FDI, it has also been financed through foreign borrowing. From a stock of 12.5 billion euros in 2005, external debt had more than doubled to 26.4 billion euros in 2015, representing 80.1% of GDP.[39] Nevertheless, the cost of servicing on the debt has remained fairly moderate, both in absolute terms and in relation to GDP. The debt service ratio to export earning actually fell from a peak of 49% in 2009 to 24% in 2015.[40] While this is a large share of export revenues, it is on a downward trend making the debt burden sustainable. The reason is to be found in the improving export performance which has made the debt servicing more affordable, in the global reduction of interest rates on international debt and in the ability of the government to attract an increasing proportion of long-term debt at lower or concessional interest rates substituting for high-cost short-term debt.

[39]Eurostat online data variable code [cpc_ecmny].

[40]World Bank World Development Indicators.

Conclusions: Prospects for the Success of the Economic Reform Programme

Serbia was badly affected by the Eurozone crisis. The economy came to a standstill for 6 years from 2009 to 2015 and is only now showing signs of recovery. Before the crisis, economic growth depended on an inflow of external capital, which supported a large current account deficit and a consumer boom; but in the postcrisis period, inflows of foreign capital are much diminished. More significantly, the share of gross investment in GDP has fallen from 25 to 17%. In addressing these problems, several experts have promoted a "new growth model" that would develop a much more effective export sector that would finance growth without dependence on foreign capital (FREN 2010; Uvalić 2012). There is now convincing evidence that this has to some extent been realised, since the export sector performed quite strongly in the postcrisis period. In particular, the ICT services sector has become a strong performer in the export market. Other sectors such as the state-managed defence industry have also done well. The balance of trade deficit has diminished, as has the current account deficit. External balance is also supported by a strong and sustained inflow of foreign remittances.

In 2014 following the SNS gained an electoral victory, which gave the government a mandate to carry out unpopular economic reforms. The reforms have prioritised fiscal consolidation, financial sector resilience and structural reforms designed to boost productivity, employment and growth. The reform programme was supported by an IMF Stand-By Arrangement signed in February 2015 and by the opening of EU accession negotiations in December. Early elections in April 2016 were designed to further solidify the ruling party's majority in parliament in advance of the more unpopular stage of reforms. These are likely to see mass layoffs from the last batch of loss-making public enterprises undergoing privatisation and from the public sector in a drive to diminish the size of the state and rebalance the economy towards private sector development.

Yet, one could ask how far the decline in the share of investment in GDP really been due to an oversized public sector, a high level of employment in state bodies and over-regulated labour markets. As we have seen, other factors may have been involved in the declining investment rate. A first consideration is the role of international capital flows. High levels of deleveraging have seen an outflow of capital from the country as EU parent banks have withdrawn funds from their Serbian affiliates to shore up their capital base at home in a process known as deleveraging. Secondly, foreign investors have been more willing to return the profits of their investment to their home countries in the forms of dividends, insider loans and interest payments than to reinvest profits in the Serbian economy. Thirdly, much of the international investment inflow seems to have originated from conduit entities in the Netherlands, Luxembourg and Switzerland in a process of tax treaty shopping. How much of this is due to round tripping of domestic investment in pursuit of aggressive tax planning is unknown. In sum, given extensive capital flight and fictitious capital inflows, efforts to reverse the decline in domestic investment based on reductions in the purchasing power of public sector workers and pensioners seem unlikely to succeed.

An equally serious problem has been the collapse of the credit system following the onset of the economic crisis as non-performing loans have accumulated in the banks, reducing their willingness to provide new credit to the business sector. The problem is being addressed with the support of the European Bank Cooperation Initiative (the Vienna Initiative), but so far this has not prevented an increase of NPLs to the second highest level in the region.[41] This problem has put a strong break on the recovery of domestic investment and should receive appropriate priority in the future development of the economic reform programme.

Finally, fiscal consolidation appears to be a necessary condition for recovery given the rapid growth of the share of public sector debt in GDP in recent years and the large share of this debt that is denominated in foreign currencies. Fortunately, due to the low interest rate climate in the European and global economy, the debt service burden is rather low and appears to be falling. This might suggest that the apparent problem of the debt is not as great as many have suggested. In the EU, fiscal consolidation has become the mantra of economic policy, but so far does not seem to be having the desired effect of stimulating economic recovery. In Serbia, to the extent that fiscal consolidation underpins a low level of investment in GDP, it may even be counterproductive. What seems to be needed is a boost to public investment in support of the private sector, both to reduce the overhead costs of private production but also to stimulate demand and provide a market for private sector suppliers.[42] A focus on this, and on the success stories of the Serbian economy in the field of exports, seems to be the way to go for the future rather than a potentially futile effort to shift the costs of adjustment onto low-paid public sector workers and pensioners.

References

Bartlett, W., Ker-Lindsay, J., Alexander, K., & Prelec, T. (2017). The United Arab Emirates as an emerging actor in the Western Balkans: The case of investment in Serbia. *Journal of Arabian Studies, 7*(1), 94–112.

Chailloux, A., Ohnsorge, F., & Vavra, D. (2010). *Euroisation in Serbia* (Working Paper No. 120). London: European Bank for Reconstruction and Development.

Djankov, S., La Porta, R., Lopes-de-Silanes, F., & Schleifer, A. (2002). The regulation of entry. *Quarterly Journal of Economics, 117*(1), 1–37.

[41]The highest level is found in Albania.

[42]As the Fiscal Council has noted: "...the poor realization of public investments, which has become a chronic issue of Serbian public finances, is a cause for concern. In the first four months of 2015, according to Fiscal Council's estimates, the implementation of public investments is already about 10 billion dinars behind schedule—which, simultaneously, is one of the major contributors to such a low fiscal deficit at the beginning of the year" (Fiscal Council 2015, p. 3).

Djankov, S., La Porta, R., Lopes-de-Silanes, F., & Schleifer, A. (2003). Courts. *Quarterly Journal of Economics, 118*(2), 453–517.

Drahokoupil, J. (2008). The rise of the comprador service sector: The politics of state transformation in Central and Eastern Europe. *Polish Sociological Review, 162*(2), 1231–1413.

EBCI. (2015). *CESEE deleveraging and credit monitor*. European Bank Coordination Initiative (the Vienna Initiative).

EBCI. (2016). *CESEE deleveraging and credit monitor*. European Bank Coordination Initiative (the Vienna Initiative).

EC. (2015). *Serbia: 2015 report*. SWD(2015) 211 final, Brussels, 10.11.2015.

EIB. (2015). *CESEE bank lending survey – H2 2015*. Luxembourg: European investment Bank.

Fiscal Council. (2015). *Fiscal consolidation in 2015 and the main challenges for reforms*. Belgrade: Fiscal Council.

FREN. (2010). *Serbian post-crisis economic growth and development model 2011–2010*. Belgrade: Foundation for the Advancement of Economics.

Gligorić, M., & Janković, I. (2015). Highlight 1: Improvement possibilities of remittances' economic potential in Serbia. *Quarterly Monitor, 43*, 48–55.

GoRS. (2015). *NPL resolution strategy*. Belgrade: Government of the Republic of Serbia.

Haberly, D., & Wojcik, D. (2014). Tax havens and the production of offshore FDI: An empirical analysis. *Journal of Economic Geography, 15*(1), 75–101.

IMF. (2003). *Round tripping* (Issues Paper (DITEG) No. 13). Washington, DC: The International Monetary Fund.

IMF. (2015a). IMF Executive Board Approves €1.2 billion Stand-By Arrangement for Serbia. Press Release No. 15/67, February 23, 2015.

IMF. (2015b). *Republic of Serbia* (IMF Country Report No. 15/161). Washington, DC: The International Monetary Fund.

IMF. (2015c). *Republic of Serbia: Letter of intent, memorandum of economic and financial policies, and technical memorandum of understanding*. Washington, DC: The International Monetary Fund (June 11).

IMF. (2015d). *Republic of Serbia* (IMF Country Report No. 15/296). Washington, DC: The International Monetary Fund.

IMF. (2016). *IMF concludes visit to Serbia* (Press Release No. 16/78). Washington, DC: The International Monetary Fund.

Mortier, A. (2015). *ICT Sector in Serbia: May 2015*. Brussels: Brussels Invest & Export.

Obradović-Wochnik, J., & Wochnik, A. (2012). Europeanising the 'Kosovo Question': Serbia's policies in the context of EU integration. *West European Politics, 35*(5), 1158–1181.

Petrović, P., Brčerević, D., & Minić, S. (2016). *Economic recovery, employment and fiscal consolidation: Lessons from 2015 and prospects for 2016 and 2017* (FC Research Paper 16/01). Belgrade: Fiscal Council.

Pond, E. (2013). Serbia reinvents itself. *Survival, 55*(4), 7–30.

Prica, I. (2013). Effects of the global financial crisis and the Eurozone crisis on the social sector in Serbia. In W. Bartlett & M. Uvalić (Eds.), *The social consequences of the global financial crisis in South East Europe* (pp. 159–172). London: LSEE Research on South East Europe.

SORS. (2016). *Responding to the wrong interpretation of Labour Force Survey by the Fiscal Council*. Press Release, 9 March 2016.

SORS. (2017). *Poverty and social inequality in the Republic of Serbia in 2016* (Statistical Release Number 087 – Year LXVII, 03/04/2017). Belgrade: Statistical Office of the Republic of Serbia.

Uvalić, M. (2010). *Serbia's transition: Towards a better future*. Basingstoke: Palgrave Macmillan.

Uvalić, M. (2012). Serbia's transition to a market economy: Why has the model not delivered? *Montenegrin Journal of Economics, 8*(2), 87–98.

Weyzig, F. (2013). Tax treaty shopping: Structural determinants of foreign direct investment routed through the Netherlands. *International Tax and Public Finance, 20*(6), 910–937.

World Bank. (2014a). *Serbia judicial functional review*. Belgrade: Multi-Donor Trust Fund for Justice sector Support in Serbia.
World Bank. (2014b). *Perceptions of the judiciary's importance in Serbia: Results of the survey with the general public, enterprises, lawyers, judges, prosecutors and court administrative staff*. Belgrade: Multi-Donor Trust Fund for Justice sector Support in Serbia.
World Bank. (2015). *Serbia systematic country diagnostic*. Washington, DC: The World Bank Group, Europe and Central Asia Region.

Conclusions: Achieving Sustainable Growth Through Outward Looking Policies and Regional Integration

Will Bartlett and Reiner Osbild

Introduction

The book has investigated the current problems of economic and social development in the Western Balkans. As noted in the introductory chapter, these countries have emerged from a serious economic recession and are in search of a new growth path on their way to eventual EU membership. However they are beset by numerous economic and social problems that hinder their progress, and this book has set out some of the main policy issues that need to be addressed. The economic policies include promoting export-led growth by developing trade in services, promoting regional trade liberalisation and developing supply capacity by completing privatisation and improving competitiveness of the private sector. For their successful implementation, these policies require a resolution of the public and private debt crises and improvements to the practices of macroeconomic governance. On the side of social policies, the book has discussed the need to reduce unemployment, poverty and inequality and to raise the quality of human capital through reforms of the education systems.

In recent years, the prospective EU accession of the region has received renewed attention and urgency but is beset by many obstacles, some of which are discussed in this book. The latest policy initiative to support the Western Balkan countries on their road to the EU has been the plan for an integrated regional economic area promoted under the auspices of the Berlin Process, under which annual summits of Western Balkan leaders have been held to promote this perspective (Marciacq 2017).

W. Bartlett (✉)
LSEE, European Institute, London School of Economics and Political Science, London, UK
e-mail: w.j.bartlett@lse.ac.uk

R. Osbild
University of Applied Sciences, Emden, Germany
e-mail: reiner.osbild@hs-emden-leer.de

R. Osbild, W. Bartlett (eds.), *Western Balkan Economies in Transition*, Societies and Political Orders in Transition, https://doi.org/10.1007/978-3-319-93665-9_12

A consolidated multi-annual action plan (MAP) to create a regional economic area in the Western Balkans was adopted in July 2017 covering the problem areas of trade, investment, mobility of skilled professionals, and digital integration. Although the MAP identified some of the critical issues facing the region, the plan is ‘relatively silent’ about other problems facing the region including the weak governance of public administration, the difficulties facing SMEs in accessing finance and the widespread corruption and informality in the region (Sanfey and Milatović 2018a). This book identifies other issues on which the plan is silent, including the serious debt crisis in the region, the lack of supply capacity to respond to trade liberalisation, and the worsening indicators of unemployment, poverty, and inequality.

The Debt Crisis

The impact of eurozone crisis has weighed heavily on the region, which suffered a deep recession from which some of the countries are only beginning to emerge. The recession brought about increasing levels of unemployment, poverty and inequality. The need for new growth model has been widely acknowledged, and differing views have been advanced on the right polices to adopt in response to this and the type of new growth model that should be pursued to enable countries to catch up with the EU (Snoy 2011; World Bank 2017; Sanfey and Milatović 2018b). Should fiscal consolidation be backed by structural reform? If so, which reforms should be prioritised? Fiscal adjustment in the region has been postponed leading to a depending burden of public debt, while the economic crisis and bank deleveraging have worsened the problem of non-performing loans and exacerbated private sector indebtedness. Do these problems have their roots in the behaviour of the globalised financial sector or the unreformed clientelistic practices of the public sector?

Unlike the peripheral countries of the eurozone, the debt burden worsened in the Western Balkans following the onset of the crisis in 2009 rather in anticipation of it (Bartlett and Prica 2018). The analyses in this book have systematically addressed the private sector debt burden, the problem of non-performing loans and the problems facing the banking system in the region. But public debt is also clearly a problem, and in the Western Balkan countries, it has been allowed to run up to its limits as ruling parties have sought to maintain popular support in the wake of the economic crisis through the informal institutions of clientelism.[1] However, governments have eventually been forced to implement the austerity policies to address this problem, as advised by the international institutions. This has brought changes to the political cultures through a reversion to authoritarian political practices in some countries. Clientelism has also affected social policy reforms, leading to the adoption of measures designed to protect the middle classes more than the truly vulnerable groups that ought to be the real beneficiaries of welfare state policies.

[1]On the concept of clientelism in the Western Balkans societies, see Cvejić (2016).

For example, Albania initially avoided the spillover from eurozone crisis through debt-fuelled public spending (Pere and Bartlett 2018). Now the chickens are coming home to roost as the country has been forced by rising debt levels to adopt the policies of fiscal consolidation, which has had the unfortunate consequence of undermining attempts to reduce inequality and poverty. To deal with these problems and achieve its EU integration aims, many institutional reforms still need to be completed, including an improvement in the quality of institutions, the rule of law being a prominent example. To reduce indebtedness, policies should focus on improving the competitiveness of the economy, encouraging a faster rate of technological development and moving towards a path of high value-added production in international trade.

In Bosnia and Herzegovina, a dysfunctional public administration has worsened the public debt burden. In conditions of stagnant public revenues, an uncompetitive economy and a poor business environment, the increase in public debt is holding back economic development (Poljašević and Trivić 2018). The stagnation of corporate lending activity has adversely affected economic growth, since the profitability of companies is low and a high share of loans is used to repay existing loans. Consumption loans have been increasing as households have fallen into debt through excessive borrowing to meet their basic needs.

Montenegro has also experienced a public debt crisis after a period of delayed fiscal consolidation. Before the outbreak of the global economic crisis, Montenegro had a relatively low level of debt, a budget surplus and high rates of GDP growth. However, the recession caused an increase in company insolvency, difficulties in the functioning of the banking system and a decline in lending activity (Fabris 2018). This has led to a reduction in public revenues and an increased need for fiscal transfers due to the worsening social problems. In the first years after the crisis, the government ran a budget deficit leading to an increase in the public debt ratio to 65% of GDP in 2015. Fabris argues that the development of a credible fiscal consolidation programme and its consistent application must be a policy priority in the next few years.

Serbia also ran into a debt crisis following the delayed adopting of fiscal consolidation measures following the onset of the economic crisis. The SNS government that came to power in 2014 launched new economic reforms, prioritising fiscal consolidation, financial sector resilience and structural reforms designed to boost productivity, employment and growth. The standard diagnosis of Serbia's economic ills has been that a poor investment and growth performance have been due to an oversized public sector, a high level of employment in state bodies and overregulated labour markets. However, Bartlett (2018) questions whether this diagnosis is the whole story and whether reductions in public sector pay and pensions will translate into higher levels of private sector investment. He argues that other factors may be involved, including the high level of banking sector deleveraging, capital flight as foreign investors have sought to repatriate profits rather than reinvest in the Serbian economy, and tax treaty shopping and round tripping in pursuit of aggressive tax planning. He concludes that a boost to public investment is needed in support of private sector growth, rather than the continuation of an effort to shift the costs of adjustment onto low-paid public sector workers and pensioners.

International Trade

The promotion of international trade both within the region and more generally through improving economic competitiveness is one of the main aims of the MAP plan for a regional economic area. Prominently, the need for the liberalisation of services trade is identified in the plan. Further liberalisation of trade in services among the Western Balkan countries is envisaged under the CEFTA agreement. Yet, while services trade is growing in the region, too little attention has been given to trade in high value-added services such as business services (Prica 2018). Compared to the non-Baltic new member states (NMS), the Western Balkan service sectors are dominated by low value-added traditional services sectors. However, the Western Balkan exports in services are growing faster than in the NMS and faster than their own GDP, indicating an improving export performance possibly supporting a process of gradual catchup with the more developed countries of the EU.

Trade liberalisation is a necessary, but not sufficient condition to initiate export-led growth. Supply constraints must be overcome through privatisation and increased inflows of foreign direct investment (FDI).[2] This problem has been especially severe in Kosovo, which has faced a persistent negative trade balance, which trade liberalisation has failed to address. Although liberalisation was expected to enhance the competitiveness of domestic industries, its main effect has been to deepen the consumption bias of an already heavily consumption-dependent economy (Gashi 2018). Supply-side constraints have prevented Kosovo from taking full advantage of liberalisation, and Gashi argues that in the future greater emphasis should be placed on domestic measures to enhance production capacities through the completion of the privatisation process.

Social Policies

The analyses presented in this book have shown that reforms to social protection have been distorted by pervasive practices of clientelism that tend to serve the middle classes rather than the most vulnerable groups in the Western Balkan societies. In the case of Macedonia, the ruling centre-right political party (VMRO–DPMNE) initiated many new social policy projects from 2008 to 2016 in the fields of social protection,

[2]Serbia has been one success story in promoting FDI in recent years, while Albania has been less so. Identifying the reasons for these differences may give an important insight into the FDI attraction policies that are most likely to work (Bartlett et al. 2017).

employment, child protection and social insurance (Gerovska Mitev 2018). During the 10-year period of the VMRO–DPMNE rule, social protection was reshaped to serve less vulnerable clients. Active labour market policies were designed to exclude 'hard to serve' clients and targeted those more easily activated among the unemployed. The introduction of arbitrary increases in welfare entitlements became a new norm. This approach to social policy underpinned popular dissatisfaction with the ruling party and was one of the factors leading to its eventual downfall in 2017.

Unemployment and inequality have been major problems of the transition process in the Western Balkan region along with emigration of skilled young people. The transition process has not significantly improved people's quality of life as privatisation, deindustrialisation and job cuts have increased the unemployment rate and reduced the overall standard of living (Ganić 2018). Other serious problems include the persistence of high unemployment rates, large-scale emigration, an outflow of educated and skilled workers and widespread poverty.

Increased mobility of skilled professionals within the Western Balkan region is an important element of the plan to create a regional economic area (MAP), but there are serious doubts about the type of skills being taught at universities, and there is a need for university reform to address this issue (Bartlett and Uvalić 2018). Many students drop out of their studies leading to a low completion rate; of those students who do graduate, many face the prospect of unemployment; of those who do find a job, many are in jobs that are not matched to their level of qualification, reducing their job prospects in relation to graduates in well-matched jobs. In order for the higher education systems to make a better contribution to building human capital and to the competitiveness and growth of the region's economies, significant reforms are needed, and better cooperation between employers and universities should be encouraged.

Conclusion

The key to reducing the high levels of public and private debt that have built up in Western Balkan economies in recent years is to promote export-led economic growth through the liberalisation of international trade, which should at the same time facilitate the reduction of unemployment, poverty and inequality. The virtuous circle implied by this remedy is based on the assumption that the root causes of indebtedness are to be found in trade deficits. Trade deficits can be cut by reducing demand for imports or increasing export revenues. The former approach leads to policies that emphasise austerity programmes, while the latter approach emphasises the need to boost export capacity. The latter is not assisted by austerity programmes but rather by an alternative approach that relies on higher public expenditure to support private sector competitiveness. Such policies should be carried out in growth-enhancing ways through greater expenditure on education to boost workforce skills and through effective active labour market policies to raise the extremely low level of labour force participation in the region (Oruč and Bartlett 2018). In supporting export-led growth, the MAP plan for a regional economic area aims to further liberalise regional trade in services, backed up by increased mobility of professional workers, greater digitalisation of the economies and improved attractiveness of the region for foreign direct investment.

Yet liberalisation may be ineffective if not also backed up by improvements to the supply capacity of the economy for both goods and services. This in turn requires completion of the privatisation processes, especially as regards the public enterprises that support the informal institutions of clientelism through their close connections to ruling parties and political elites. It also requires the enhanced digitalisation of the region to underpin the growth of high-tech start-ups in the creative industries. These are already beginning to emerge in Serbia and some of the other economies of the region. To succeed in this, the resistance from the incumbent state-owned telecommunication companies to enhanced competition and to new entry by disruptive rivals should be challenged. This can only be done by regulatory agencies that are politically independent and that genuinely seek to resist the monopolistic tendencies of the incumbents. In addition, regional cooperation in the design of investment incentives for foreign investors rather than a tax competition that drives a 'race to the bottom' is a necessity. In implementing such a policy, the state has an important role of play in providing appropriate conditions for attracting foreign investment in the form of a level playing field and linking the region into the global value chains that structure the world economy (OECD 2017).

Finally, success with export-led growth based on greater competitiveness, improved labour force skills and openness to the introduction of the latest technologies should not ignore the deep social divisions within the Western Balkan region. The adoption of social policies that assist the poorest in society and aim to rescue poverty and inequality should be at the top of the agenda, not as a by-product but as essential component of building competitiveness of the economies. Social policies have in some cases been co-opted to the interests of the middle classes through discretionary spending and policies driven more by the interests of clientelistic political cultures rather than a concern for fairness and justice. Yet, in order to make the greatest impact on the engagement and expansion of supply capacities, it will be essential to engage all sections of society, drawing in greater numbers of people from disadvantaged groups into the labour force in order to take full advantage of the opportunities for growth afforded by trade liberalisation. In boosting the capacity of the labour force to contribute to future growth, it will also be necessary to carry out some deep reforms to education systems, not least to systems of higher education, to ensure that the future skills of the labour force are adequate to meet the needs of the labour market and emerging technologies.

References

Bartlett, W. (2018). Economic reforms in Serbia and prospects for economic recovery and growth. In R. Osbild & W. Bartlett (Eds.), *Western Balkan economies in transition: In search of a sustainable growth path*. Berlin: Springer.

Bartlett, W., & Prica, I. (2018). Debt in the super-periphery: The case of the Western Balkans. *Third World Thematics*. https://doi.org/10.1080/23802014.2017.1438850

Bartlett, W., & Uvalić, M. (2018). Higher education and the graduate labour market in the Western Balkans. In R. Osbild & W. Bartlett (Eds.), *Western Balkan economies in transition: In search of a sustainable growth path*. Berlin: Springer.

Bartlett, W., Krasniqi, B., & Ahmetbasić, J. (2017). Study of special economic zones (SEZs) in the Western Balkans. Brussels: European Commission DG NEAR. https://www.researchgate.net/publication/321156818_Study_on_Special_Economic_Zones_SEZs_in_the_Western_Balkans

Cvejić, S. (2016). On inevitability of political clientelism in contemporary Serbia. *Sociologija, LVIII*(2), 239–252.

Fabris, N. (2018). The global financial crisis and fiscal policy in Montenegro. In R. Osbild & W. Bartlett (Eds.), *Western Balkan economies in transition: In search of a sustainable growth path*. Berlin: Springer.

Ganić, M. (2018). The labour market, social inequality, and the role of emigration: The case of the Western Balkan economies. In R. Osbild & W. Bartlett (Eds.), *Western Balkan economies in transition: In search of a sustainable growth path*. Berlin: Springer.

Gashi, P. (2018). Trade and industrial development in Kosovo. In R. Osbild & W. Bartlett (Eds.), *Western Balkan economies in transition: In search of a sustainable growth path*. Berlin: Springer.

Gerovska Mitev, M. (2018). Social policy during a decade of centre-right governance in Macedonia. In R. Osbild & W. Bartlett (Eds.), *Western Balkan economies in transition: In search of a sustainable growth path*. Berlin: Springer.

Marciacq, F. (2017). *The European Union and the Western Balkans after the Berlin process: Reflecting on the EU enlargement in times of uncertainty*. Sarajevo: Friedrich Ebert Stiftung.

OECD. (2017). *Tracking the special economic zones in the Western Balkans: Objectives, features and key challenges*. Paris: Organisation for Economic Cooperation and Development.

Oruč, N., & Bartlett, W. (2018). *Labour markets in the Western Balkans: Performance, causes and policy options*. Sarajevo: Regional Cooperation Council.

Pere, E., & Bartlett, W. (2018). On the way to Europe: Economic and social developments in Albania. In R. Osbild & W. Bartlett (Eds.), *Western Balkan economies in transition: In search of a sustainable growth path*. Berlin: Springer.

Poljašević, J., & Trivić, J. (2018). Public and private debt: Recent developments in Bosnia and Herzegovina. In R. Osbild & W. Bartlett (Eds.), *Western Balkan economies in transition: In search of a sustainable growth path*. Berlin: Springer.

Prica, I. (2018). Trade in services in the Western Balkans. In R. Osbild & W. Bartlett (Eds.), *Western Balkan economies in transition: In search of a sustainable growth path*. Berlin: Springer.

Sanfey, P., & Milatović, J. (2018a). The Western Balkans regional economic area: From economic cooperation to economic integration. In R. Osbild & W. Bartlett (Eds.), *Western Balkan economies in transition: In search of a sustainable growth path*. Berlin: Springer.

Sanfey, P., & Milatović, J. (2018b). *The Western Balkans in transition: Diagnosing the constraints on the path to a sustainable market economy*. London: EBRD.

Snoy, B. (2011). *Synopsis of findings on the need for new growth initiatives in the Western Balkans*. Brussels: IFI Coordination Office.

World Bank. (2017). *The Western Balkans: Revving up the engines of growth and prosperity*. Washington, DC: The World Bank.

The manufacturer's authorised representative in the EU is Springer Nature Customer Service Centre GmbH, Europaplatz 3, 69115 Heidelberg, Germany. If you have any concerns regarding our products, please contact ProductSafety@springernature.com

Printed and bound by CPI Group (UK) Ltd, Croydon, CR0 4YY

30/09/2026

02225655-0018